CW01394512

West Africa and the U.S. W

Since the terrorist attacks on the American homeland on September 11, 2001, fighting the menace has become the frontier issue on the U.S.' national security agenda. In the case of the African continent, the United States has and continues to accord major attention to the West African sub-region.

This book:

- evaluates where we can place West Africa within the broader crucible of the U.S. war on terrorism;
- establishes the key elements of the U.S.' counter-terrorism policy in West Africa;
- examines the U.S. counter-terrorism strategies in West Africa, and evaluates if they are being pursued both at the bilateral and multilateral levels in the region;
- interrogates the relationship between stability in the sub-region and the waging of the U.S.' war on terrorism.

Specifically, the book examines the crises of underdevelopment—cultural, economic, environmental, political, security and social—in the sub-region, especially their impact on shaping the conditions that provide the taproots of terrorism. Clearly, addressing these multidimensional crises of underdevelopment is pivotal to the success of the U.S. war on terrorism in the sub-region.

This book will be of great interest to students and scholars of terrorism, homeland security, African Studies, conflict management, and political violence.

Kelechi Kalu is Director at the Center for African Studies and Professor of African and African American Studies at Ohio State University, U.S.

George Klay Kieh is Professor of Political Science at the University of West Georgia, U.S.

Routledge Studies in US Foreign Policy

Edited by:
Inderjeet Parmar, University of Manchester and John Dumbrell, University of Durham

This new series sets out to publish high quality works by leading and emerging scholars critically engaging with United States Foreign Policy. The series welcomes a variety of approaches to the subject and draws on scholarship from international relations, security studies, international political economy, foreign policy analysis and contemporary international history.

Subjects covered include the role of administrations and institutions, the media, think tanks, ideologues and intellectuals, elites, transnational corporations, public opinion, and pressure groups in shaping foreign policy, US relations with individual nations, with global regions and global institutions and America's evolving strategic and military policies.

The series aims to provide a range of books – from individual research monographs and edited collections to textbooks and supplemental reading for scholars, researchers, policy analysts, and students.

West Africa and the U.S. War on Terror

Edited by
George Klay Kieh and Kelechi Kalu

Routledge
Taylor & Francis Group

LONDON AND NEW YORK

First published 2013
by Routledge
2 Park Square, Milton Park, Abingdon, Oxfordshire OX14 4RN

Simultaneously published in the USA and Canada
by Routledge
711 Third Avenue, New York, NY 10017

First issued in paperback 2014

Routledge is an imprint of the Taylor and Francis Group, an informa business

British Library Cataloguing in Publication Data
A catalogue record for this book is available from the British Library

Library of Congress Cataloging in Publication Data
West Africa and the US war on terror / edited by George Klay Kieh & Kelechi Kalu.
       p. cm. – (Routledge studies in US foreign policy)
    Includes bibliographical references and index.
    1. Terrorism–Africa, West–Prevention. 2. Terrorism–United States–Prevention. 3. War on Terrorism, 2001-2009. 4. United States–Foreign relations–Africa, West. 5. Africa, West–Foreign relations–United States. I. Kieh, George Klay, 1956- II. Kalu, Kelechi Amihe.
    HV6433.A358W47 2011
    363.325'170973–dc23
                      2012004153

ISBN 978-0-415-53942-5 (hbk)
ISBN 978-1-138-85143-6 (pbk)
ISBN 978-0-203-10482-8 (ebk)

Typeset in Times New Roman
by Taylor & Francis Books

Contents

Figures

Contributors

Pita Ogaba Agbese is Professor of Political Science at the University of Northern Iowa. He previously served as Acting Chair of the Department of Political Science and Director of the Center for International Peace and Security Studies at the University of Northern Iowa. Professor Agbese received his Ph.D. from Northwestern University in 1984. He has published extensively on issues such as civil–military relations in Africa, democratization in Africa, civil society in Africa, the environment in Africa, and civil conflicts in Africa. His most recent book is a co-edited volume with George Klay Kieh, Jr., *The State in Africa: Issues and Perspectives*, 2008.

Idowu Okheren Ejere is the CAADP Technical Assistant at the Forum for Agricultural Research in Africa (FARA). She holds a Bachelor of Science degree in International Relations from Igbinedion University, Nigeria, and a Masters of Arts degree in Globalization and Development from the Institute of Development Studies (IDS), University of Sussex, United Kingdom. She is currently studying for a PhD at the Natural Resources Institute (NRI), University of Greenwhich, United Kingdom. Her current research is focusing on how policies and resource management impact on food security in resource endowed nations of Africa. Ms. Ejere was a Nigerian youth representative to the Commonwealth Heads of State and Government Meeting (CHOGM) 2005, and is a member of the Commonwealth Youth Forum (CYF), Development Studies Association (DSA), and Chatham House.

Russell D. Howard is a retired Brigadier-General in the U.S. Army. Presently, he is the President of Howard's Global Solutions and Senior Fellow at Joint Special Operations University. He is also Director of the Monterey Institute of International Terrorism Research and Education Program (MonTREP). He served at every level of command in the U.S. Army Special Forces from Detachment through Group Command and finished his military career as Head of the Department of Social Sciences at the United States Military Academy at West Point. Howard earned an M.A. in International Management from the Monterey Institute of International Studies, and a Masters of Public Administration degree from Harvard University. He is the Founding Director of both the Combating Terrorism

Center at West Point and the Jebsen Center for Counter-Terrorism Studies at the Fletcher School. Some of his previous positions include Army Chief of Staff Fellow at the Center for International Affairs at Harvard University and Assistant to the Special Representative to the Secretary General during UNOSOM II in Somalia, and Commander, 1st Special Forces Group, Airborne.

Kelechi Kalu is the current Director of the Center for African Studies at OSU. His publications include articles in the *International Journal of Politics, Culture and Society, Africa Today, Journal of Nigerian Affairs, Journal of Asian and African Studies, Journal of Third World Studies, Journal of African Policy Studies, West Africa Review, The Constitution: A Journal of Constitutional Development*, and several book chapters on African and Third World issues. He is editor of and contributor to *Agenda Setting and Public Policy in Africa* (2004). Dr. Kalu has served as Consultant to the World Bank on Public Sector Governance. His current book project is on Political Restructuring in Post-Conflict States in Africa, which is part of a larger project funded by the Ford Foundation. Professor Kalu serves on the editorial board of several journals and currently is the Book Review Editor (Africa) for the *Journal of Asian and African Studies.*

George Klay Kieh, Jr. is Professor of Political Science at the University of West Georgia. He has served as Dean of the College of Arts and Sciences at the University of West Georgia, Dean of International Affairs at Grand Valley State University, Michigan, and Chair of the Department of Political Science at Morehouse College, Georgia. He received his Ph.D. in Political Science from Northwestern University, Evanston, Illinois. His research interests are in the areas of peace and conflict studies, security studies, American Foreign Policy, the state, democratization, international political economy and international organizations. Recent books include: *Liberia's State Failure, Collapse and Reconstitution*, 2012, *Assessing the Bush Administration's Policy Toward Africa* (co-authored), 2009, *The First, Liberian Civil War: The Crises of Underdevelopment*, 2008, *Africa and the New Globalization* (edited), 2008, and *The State in Africa: Issues and Perspectives* (co-edited with Pita Ogaba Agbese), 2008.

Dean A. Minix is the Dean of the College of Liberal and Fine Arts at Tarleton State University in Stephenville, Texas. He also teaches in the Department of Political Science at Northern Kentucky University. He received his Ph.D. from the University of Cincinnati with emphasis in international politics, American and comparative foreign policy, and American political behavior. Minix is President of the International Studies Association-Southwest. On August 2, 1990, the date of the Iraqi invasion of Kuwait, Dr. Minix concluded a tour of the Middle East where he participated in briefings with Iraqi and American Embassy officials. Minix continues to instruct abroad, most recently in China and Israel. His current teaching areas are: Homeland security, international terrorism, war in the modern world, Hollywood's wars, introduction to world politics, and political methodology.

Boubacar N'Diaye is Associate Professor of Political Science and Pan-African Studies at The College of Wooster, Ohio. He holds a Ph.D. in Political Science from Northern Illinois University. He is a widely published author specializing in civil–military relations, democratization, security sector governance, and capacity building in Africa. His most recent works and practitioner activities pertain to military involvement in African politics, Pan-Africanism, the democratization efforts in Africa, and capacity building, especially in African parliaments and civil society organizations. Professor N'Diaye has been a consultant to African, U.S., and international agencies and organizations such as SIPRI, ACSS, ECOWAS, AU, UN, and a member of several academic journal editorial and NGO Institutional Advisory Boards. A founding member and member of the executive board of the African Security Sector Network (ASSN), Professor N'Diaye is also involved in various academic and advocacy endeavors designed to transform security establishments and institutionalize democratic governance in the security sector of African states.

Julius E. Nyang'oro is Professor and Chair of the Department of African and Afro-American Studies at the University of North Carolina, Chapel Hill. He holds a B.A. in Political Science from the University of Dar es Salaam, Tanzania; an M.A. and Ph.D. in Political Science from Miami University; and a J.D. from Duke University. His primary research interest has been on Africa's comparative political economy, particularly the role of the state in national development. He has consulted with USAID on a variety of projects involving NGOs, civil society, public policy, and development. Some of his recent publications include "The 2005 General Elections in Tanzania: Implications for Peace and Security in Southern Africa," Institute for Security Studies, Pretoria, South Africa, Occasional Paper no. 122 (2006); "Terrorism Threats and Responses in the Southern African Development Community Region", in Andre Le Sage (ed.), *African Counterterrorism Cooperation: Assessing Regional and Subregional Initiatives*, Dulles, VA, Potomac Books, 2007.

Sylvester Odion-Akhaine obtained his Ph.D. in Politics from the University of London in 2004. He has served as General Secretary to United Action Democracy, and has been the Executive Director of the Centre for Constitutionalism and Demilitarization from 1998 to date. He was a Stanford University Fellow on Democracy, Development, and the Rule of Law in 2005. His current research topics are Democracy and Human Rights Diplomacy, Political Economy, Global Governance, and Demilitarization.

Zakaria Ousman is currently the Honorary Consul for the nation of Pakistan. His professional experience includes work as Senior Advisor (humanitarian affairs), Office of the Chadian Special Representative to the UN

Peacekeeping forces in Chad/CAR and as Director of the Centre for Peace, Security, and Sustainable Development. He has worked for the World Food Program throughout Africa, including the Democratic Republic of the Congo, Rwanda, Burundi, Uganda, Burkina Faso, Equatorial Guineau, Sudan, and Somalia. He has been a Program Officer for UNICEF in Chad and for the International Labor Organization in Senegal. He has consulted with the World Bank, UNDP, the Lake Chad Basin Commission, African Development Bank, Coopération Francaise, and Development Alternatives, Inc. He holds a degree in engineering from C.N.R.A. Bambey, Senegal. He has taught at the University of Khartoum, the University of Mogadischu, the University of Nouakchott, and the University of Ndjamena. His specializations include extremist religious movements, natural resource management, and economic development.

Vinton Prince is Professor of History at Wilmington College, Ohio. He received his Ph.D. in history from the University of Virginia in 1969.

Andrea M. Walther is Program Manager of DAI's Civil–Military Operations/Relations Training program, the Trans-Sahara Security Symposium (TSS). The TSS program attempts to build the capacity of African military officers and key civilian stakeholders to improve civil–military coordination, implement effective pre- and post-conflict stabilization operations, and counter the emergence of extremism across the TSCTP region of West Africa. Her research and writing focuses on the expanding role of the Department of Defense in Sub-Saharan Africa and the U.S. government's "3D" work in the region. During the summer of 2008, Andrea conducted her Masters thesis research at EUCOM and AFRICOM in Stuttgart, Germany, on JSOTF-TS operations in West Africa and worked at the Kofi Annan International Peacekeeping and Training Center (KAIPTC) in Accra, Ghana. Prior to her time focusing on Africa, Andrea worked for Mayor Cory Booker and the City of Newark, NJ's Office of Homeland Security, the Council on Foreign Relations, and the United Nations Security Council. Andrea received a B.A. in International Relations from Tufts University and a Masters MALD in International Security Studies from the Fletcher School of Law and Diplomacy.

Preface

Since the 9/11 attacks on the American homeland, the study of terrorism has experienced a meteorite rise in the security studies sub-field. This is evidenced by the various books, monographs, book chapters and journal articles that have been written about the various dimensions of the phenomenon. Some of the studies have focused on the regional and sub-regional dimensions of terrorism. However, within the context of the United States' "Global War on Terrorism"and in the specific case of the African region, the scholarly literature has accorded primacy to the northern and eastern sub-regions of the continent. Consequently, the literature on the other sub-regions, including West Africa, is inchoate. Clearly, that gap in the literature needs to be addressed.

This research project on "West Africa and the U.S. War on Terrorism"was proposed against the backdrop of contributing to and addressing that gap in the literature. The rationale for the project's focus on West Africa is threefold. First, West Africa is important to the discussion about terrorism because with its high human security deficit, it is a sub-region that is ripe for the resort to terroristic acts by aggrieved parties. Significantly, given the fact that the United States is aligned with various regimes in the sub-region that have failed to address the human security tragedy, aggrieved parties may use terrorism as an instrument for attacking American interests in the area. As well, such aggrieved parties may form alliances with other groups such as Al-Qaeda in attacking American interests in the sub-region.

Secondly, as a result of the failure of the majority of the states in the sub-region to address the human security concerns of their citizens West Africa has a high incidence of state fragility. Hence, these fragile states are vulnerable to terrorist attacks by domestic groups. Also, transnational terrorist groups like Al-Qaeda may take advantage of the vulnerability of such fragile states and establish bridgeheads in them. These could, in turn, be used as launching pads to attack American interests in both the sub-region and globally. Thirdly, since the West African section of the Gulf of Guinea has an abundance of oil, it has become increasingly important to the U.S.' energy security needs. Thus, should terrorists and terrorist organizations undertake actions that disrupt the supply of oil and allied products; there would be serious economic reverberations within the United States.

Clearly, the project would not have been possible without the financial, material and moral support and encouragement of various entities and individuals. The Mershon Center for International Security Studies at The Ohio State University was pivotal to the success of the project. The Center provided the research grant that funded the project, including the conference which was held at The Ohio State University in October 2009. The Mershon Center also provided the venue and the associated logistics for the conference. We would like to express our thanks and appreciation to the Director of the Mershon Center, Rick Herrmann, for his unflinching support and encouragement throughout the project. As well, we would like to thank the staff of the Mershon Center for their many contributions to the success of the project; especially, Ann Powers, Cathy Becker, Kyle McCray, and Cheryl Walter for logistical support throughout the conference.

We are also grateful for the support provided by the Office of International Affairs at the Ohio State University for the conference. Special thanks to Associate Provost Dieter Wanner, and Maureen Miller and Victor Van Buchem. The staff at the Center for African Studies at Ohio State University worked tirelessly to make the conference successful; and for that, we thank Darby O'Donnell and Laura Joseph whose organizational skills made the work less challenging. Lastly, we thank everyone, including the student assistants, for the many contributions they made to the success of the conference that resulted in this book project. Also, we are grateful to Laura and the staff for assisting us in the preparation of this volume.

Without the work done by the contributors to this volume, there would be nothing to show for the conference. We thank all contributors for participating in the entire project. We thank them for contributing to the various lively discussions and exchanges at the conference and for completing all necessary work on their papers that resulted in this volume. Also, we appreciate the keynote address given by former Assistant Secretary of State for African Affairs, Professor Jendayi Frazier. Her active participation in the conference added much value to the proceedings. Finally, we appreciate the time and effort that everyone who was associated with the conference and this volume invested toward the success of this project.

George Klay Kieh, Jr., University of West Georgia
Kelechi A. Kalu, Ohio State University

Part I
Background

1   Introduction

The travails of the U.S. war on terrorism

George Klay Kieh, Jr. and Kelechi Kalu

Introduction

On September 11, 2001, the foundation of the United States was jolted, as a result of the terrorist attacks launched against the homeland by Al-Qaeda. As John Owens and John Dumbrell observe, "The attacks constituted the first significant enemy assault upon the United States mainland since the war of 1812."[1] The attacks were both brazen and horrific. The terrorists used planes belonging to various American airlines to launch the attacks on the towers of the World Trade Center and the Pentagon. Given that the United States is perceived as the world's most formidable military force replete with a plethora of weapon systems and types, the prevalent view was that no actor in the international system would have the gumption to attack the American homeland. The reason was the certainty of the devastating response of the United States against the attacker.

The horrific nature of the attacks was reflected in the death and destruction visited on the United States, as well as the locations targeted by the terrorists. For example, 2,752 persons were killed in the World Trade Center,[2] 125 persons were killed[3] at the Pentagon, and 45 persons died when United Airlines Flight 93 crashed in rural southwest Pennsylvania, after the planned attacks by the terrorists, who commandeered the plane, were aborted by some of the passengers.[4]

The aftermath of the attacks witnessed a shift in the locus of American national security policy: Terrorism was immediately catapulted to the forefront of the national security agenda. One of the resultant significant manifestations was the declaration of a "Global War on Terrorism" by the then incumbent Bush administration. In his address to a Joint Session of the United States Congress, President Bush outlined the parameters of the "war" thus:

> On September the 11th, enemies of freedom committed an act of war against our country … Americans have many questions tonight. Americans are asking, "Who attacked our country?" The evidence we have gathered all points to a collection of loosely affiliated terrorist organizations known as Al Qaeda … Al Qaeda is to terror what the Mafia is to

crime ... Our war on terror begins with Al Qaeda, but it does not end there. It will not end until every terrorist group of global reach has been found, stopped and defeated.[5]

Importantly, in order to wage the "long war" against terrorism, the United States embarked on a global campaign ostensibly designed to recruit allies, especially in the various regions and sub-regions of the world. In this vein, Africa, which had hitherto been considered as peripheral to the United States' emergent post-Cold War national security interests, experienced a meteorite rise. As John Davis notes, "The war on terror ... distinguished Africa's strategic relevance and brings many of its states to the 'fore.' In this realm, the states within the Horn of Africa and those in the Sahel have emerged as critical 'frontline states' in this new global conflagration."[6]

This chapter examines several major issues. First, the U.S. war on terrorism will be framed by deciphering its scope and identifying obvious enemies. Second, the chapter maps out the contours of the U.S. counterterrorism policy, which provides the *terra firma* for the counterterrorism strategies. Next, West Africa is examined within the context of the U.S. war on terrorism. This is then followed by the discussion of the focus of the book. Lastly, the chapter lays out the organization of the book by summarizing the constituent chapters.

Framing the U.S. war on terrorism

Who are the enemies in the U.S. war on terrorism? According to the U.S. State Department, the principal enemy is Al-Qaeda, a group defined as a "globalized insurgency that employs subversion, sabotage, open warfare and, of course terrorism."[7] The U. S. government further asserts that the group has two major interlocking objectives. The group seeks to acquire weapons of mass destruction or other means to inflict massive damage on the United States and its allies and interests and the broader international system.[8] As well, the U.S. government posits that Al-Qaeda seeks to "overthrow the existing world order and replace it with a reactionary, authoritarian, transnational entity."[9]

In addition, the U.S. war on terrorism is directed at extant enemies: Global actors that provide leadership, resources, inspiration, and guidance to extremists.[10] Among these are states that sponsor international terrorism.[11] The list includes Cuba, Iran, Sudan, and Syria.[12] In sum, the enemies against whom the U.S. war on terrorism is directed are Al-Qaeda, other terrorist groups around the world that seek to attack the United States and its interests, and states and other actors that support terrorist groups. In short, the war on terrorism is global in scope with multiple enemies, and it has an indefinite life span – it is "a super long war." As President George W. Bush noted in the aftermath of the 9/11 attacks, "[O]ur war on terror begins with Al-Qaeda, but it does not end there. It will not end until every terrorist group of global reach has been found, stopped and defeated".[13]

The question is: Why is the United States the focus of Al-Qaeda's terrorist attacks? According to American officialdom, the central cause of the 9/11 terrorist attacks on the United States and the subsequent ones against American interests around the world is the fact that the terrorists hate the American way of life. In articulating this view, President George W. Bush argued:

> Americans are asking "Why do they hate us?" They hate what they see right here in this chamber: a democratically elected government. Their leaders are self-appointed. They hate our freedoms: our freedom of religion, our freedom of speech, our freedom to vote and assemble and disagree with each other. They want to overthrow existing governments in many Muslim countries such as Egypt, Saudi Arabia and Jordan. They want to drive Israel out of the Middle East. They want to drive Christians and Jews out of vast regions of Asia and Africa.[14]

Similarly, in his Inaugural Address, President Barrack Obama declared:

> We will not apologize for our way of life, nor will we waiver in its defense. And for those who seek to advance their aims by inducing terror and slaughtering innocents, we say to you now that our spirit is stronger and cannot be broken—you cannot outlast us, and we will defeat you.[15]

Undoubtedly, terrorist attacks are reprehensible. However, in framing its war on terrorism using the above statements, the U.S. government fails to take cognizance of the roots of terrorism. Generally, terrorism is a method that is used to respond to perceived cultural, economic, political, and social injustices. In the specific case of the United States, American officialdom misses the point in portraying the "hatred for the American way of life" as the *causa moven* for terrorist attacks against the United States and its expansive global interests. On the contrary, the United States is the major target of terrorism because over the years it has provided the leadership for the construction of an unjust international order that is based on the exploitation and marginalization of the states and peoples of the Third World. For example, American and other metropolitan-based multinational corporations have and continue to exploit the peoples of the Third World. For example, in Nigeria, Shell is making huge profits from the country's oil. Also, the "structural adjustment programs" (SAPs) of the International Monetary Fund (IMF) have devastated the economies of various peripheral states, and banished their peoples to continuing and abject poverty. In the area of trade, under the unjust "system of unequal exchange," Third World countries continue to receive less for their primary products, while they are forced to pay more for manufactured goods from the United States and other core states.

Furthermore, the United States continues to support various authoritarian regimes that are asphyxiating political rights and freedoms, and failing to address basic human needs—jobs, education, health care, food security, etc.—

of their respective peoples in the Third World. For example, the U.S. government supports the authoritarian regimes in Bahrain, Kuwait, Saudi Arabia, Ethiopia, Uganda and Yemen. Until his removal through a mass-based popular revolt, the U.S. government provided the economic and military "oxygen" that kept the repressive Mubarak regime well and alive in Egypt for 30 years, amid the violation of political human rights and the neglect of the social and economic needs of the majority of the Egyptian people. Even when it had the opportunity to match its pro-democracy rhetoric with praxis, the U.S. government was more concerned about the protection of its "security interests" than in the promotion of democratization in Egypt. Eventually, the Obama administration was forced by the mass uprising in Egypt to abandon its client regime.

The U.S. counterterrorism policy

The centerpiece of the U.S. counterterrorism policy is to "disrupt, dismantle and defeat Al-Qaeda and its affiliates."[16] The significant derivatives include the following:

1   the protection of the American homeland;
2   securing the world's most dangerous weapons and materials;
3   the denial of safe havens to Al-Qaeda; and
4   the building of positive partnerships with Muslim communities around the world.[17]

The U.S. counterterrorism strategies

Based on its counterterrorism policy, the U.S. has developed various strategies that are designed to wage the "war" against terrorism. At the vortex of the U.S. counterterrorism strategy is the preponderant reliance on the use of military means as the *deus ex machina* for "defeating terrorism." As President Obama insists, " ... as the [United States] face[s] multiple threats—from nations, non-state actors, and failed states—the [United States] will maintain the military superiority that has secured our country, and underpinned global security, for decades."[18] So, like its predecessor, the Obama administration has continued the militarization of the U.S. counterterrorism strategies.

Accordingly, two major clusters of agencies serve as the vehicles: The U.S. military and security apparatus, and various states and inter-governmental organizations around the globe. The former involves direct U.S. military actions against Al-Qaeda and its affiliates. The latter entails using various states and organizations as "foot soldiers." In the case of the direct use of military force, for example, in 2009, the Obama administration deployed 68,000 additional troops in Afghanistan.[19] This brought the total number of American troops in the theater to 98,000.[20] Also, the Obama administration has continued the strategy of using drone aircraft to unleash missile attacks in the border area between Pakistan and Afghanistan.[21] While these attacks are targeted against the Taliban forces, they have nonetheless occasioned the deaths of civilians.[22]

In the case of states and international organizations, the U.S. has developed various bilateral and multilateral relationships. In Africa, for example, the U.S. has forged security relationships with various African states including Egypt, Morocco, Mauritania, Niger, Nigeria and Senegal. One of the key pillars of these emergent bilateral relationships is the training of the armed forces and security forces of these states in various counterterrorism methods, including border protection, as well as the provision of weapons and equipment to enable them to help wage the U.S. war on terrorism.

At the multilateral level, the U.S. has developed various counterterrorism initiatives involving the African Union (AU) and sub-regional organizations and clusters of selected states. Two major ones are the Trans-Sahara Counterterrorism Partnership (TSCP), the successor to the Pan-Sahel Initiative, and the Gulf of Guinea Guard Initiative. Among the participating states are five West African countries—Mali, Mauritania, Niger, Nigeria, and Senegal. Under the initiative, thousands of troops from West African states as well as other African countries have been trained in various dimensions of counterterrorism. In Chapter 6, Julius Nyan'goro and Andrea Walter discuss the details of the TSCP. The Gulf of Guinea Guard Initiative (GGGI) is designed to aid various African states by improving their maritime security of the western coast of Africa.[23] Specifically, the initiative is intended to help ten African states, including four in West Africa—Benin, Ghana, Nigeria, and Togo—over the course of the next ten years to either develop or improve their maritime security.[24] The foci of the initiative are port security, and the protection of coastal regions inside these countries' territorial waters.[25] The rationale is that since most of the vessels that terrorists use need shore-based support, it is therefore useful to concentrate on the coastal regions.[26]

In terms of the non-military aspects of the counterterrorism strategies, public diplomacy is used as one of the major instruments. The centerpiece is to convey American values to others overseas so as to win their "hearts and minds."[27] The dimensions of the public diplomacy strategy include cultural exchanges, the establishment of a regional media hub to deal with the Arab media, and a 24-hour rapid-reaction team that monitors news accounts overseas and recommends messages to counter damaging stories about the United States.[28]

Since the U.S. launched its war on terrorism, it has had some military successes. One of the notable ones was the destruction of Al-Qaeda's sanctuary in Afghanistan.[29] The cumulative effects of the military assaults have led to the dislodging of the group. The resultant effect has been the group's fervent search for alternative sanctuaries both in the region and elsewhere in the world.

Another success has been the arrest and detention of several Al-Qaeda leaders and operatives. By 2010, about six top leaders of the group had been arrested and detained.[30] Also, several operatives in Afghanistan, Iraq, and Pakistan, among others, have been arrested and detained at Guantanamo and prisons in various countries around the world. Moreover, some of the group's top leaders have been killed. For example, about ten key leaders were killed between October 2002 and June 2010.[31] These leaders were pivotal to the group's operations in various countries, including Afghanistan, Iraq, and Pakistan. Clearly, the biggest success was the killing of Osama Bin Linden, the leader of Al-Qaeda, on May 1, 2011, after a gun battle with U.S. Navy SEALs and CIA paramilitary forces at a palatial compound in the Pakistani city of Abbottabad.[32] However, these successes, especially the killing of bin Laden, should not suggest that Al-Qaeda and its allies are on the verge of defeat. On the contrary, the "war on terrorism" is far from being over. Two major cases in the aftermath of bin Laden's death are instructive. On June 1, 2011, Al-Qaeda carried out a revenge attack, when its fighters attacked a Pakistani security check post and killed several policemen.[33] Similarly, on May 12, 2011, Pakistan's Taliban, an ally of Al-Qaeda, carried out a suicide attack that killed more than 80 people in Shabqadar in northwestern Pakistan.[34]

On the other hand, there have been some failures. The counter-terrorism strategy has been increasingly militarized, as evidenced by the continual preponderant reliance on the use of military means. As Nick Ottens asserts, "The stealth war begun during the Bush Administration has expanded considerably under President Barrack Obama."[35] As has been discussed, for example, the Obama administration has increased the number of American troops in Afghanistan. This action reflects the U.S. government's belief that Al-Qaeda and other terrorist groups can be defeated militarily. Clearly, this orientation fails to take cognizance of the political and socio-economic root causes of terrorism, and the imperative of addressing them. In other words, the U.S. increasing reliance on the use of military means is not sufficient to defeat terrorism. Instead, the use of military means must be one aspect of a multi-dimensional counterterrorism strategy that places premium on the taproots of terrorism, and formulates and implements steps to address them.

Another lacuna in its strategy is that the U.S. is undermining its war on terrorism by enlisting some of the autocratic regimes around the world as partners. As Robert Tynes observes in the case of Africa, "The current U.S. terrorism policies appear to be counter-productive, facilitating and/or maintaining autocratic styles of governance."[36] For example, the U.S. government is collaborating with the authoritarian regimes in Bahrain, Djibouti, Ethiopia, Kuwait, Saudi Arabia, Uganda and Yemen. Also, until their removal through "people's power," the autocratic regimes in Tunisia and Egypt were major "foot soldiers" in the prosecution of the U.S.' war on terrorism. By collaborating with authoritarian regimes, the U.S. is undercutting both the moral basis and legitimacy of its war on terrorism. This is because these authoritarian regimes lack the moral standing and the legitimacy required to galvanize their respective citizenries in helping to wage the campaign against terrorism. In fact, these authoritarian regimes are themselves guilty of the use of terrorist tactics against their respective populations as the linchpin of their autocratic rule.

Similarly, the implementation of the counterterrorism strategy has at times led to the violation of political human rights by the U.S. and some of its collaborating regimes. In the case of the U.S., as Joanne Mariner charges, "Since September 2001, the U.S. government has been directly responsible for a broad array of serious human rights violations in fighting terrorism, including torture, enforced disappearance, arbitrary detention, and unfair trails."[37] As well, some of the various collaborating regimes in Afghanistan, Egypt, Jordan, Poland, Romania, Syria and Thailand have and continue to abuse the political human rights of terrorist suspects.[38] The abuse has ranged from the "disappearance" of terrorist suspects to torture.[39] As a *quid pro quo*, these collaborating regimes have received billions of dollars in U.S. military and counterterrorism assistance.[40] In addition, as a result of U.S. pressure, some of the collaborating regimes have adopted abusive practices as the kernels of their emerging domestic counterterrorism regimes.[41] Most notably, the U.S. has encouraged them to pass draconian laws, often laws that expand police powers, reduce due process guarantees, and set out vague and overboard definitions of terrorism.[42] In the specific case of Africa, as Robert Tynes laments, "Civil liberties and political rights are being compromised. African liberty is being constricted, and democracy is being squashed."[43]

In the area of public diplomacy, the effort has been undermined by the discrepancy between the U.S. government's democracy promotion rhetoric and its support for authoritarian regimes. Against that background, the effort to "win hearts and minds" is not having the desired effect, because as John Brown argues, "Even the best public diplomacy cannot overcome policies that the rest of the world does not like ... It is that American public diplomacy— at its best, an effort by the U.S. to show respect to the opinions of mankind and engage in global dialogue—has become perceived worldwide as the basest form of propaganda."[44] For example, Romi Khouri identifies some of the major impediments to the success of American public diplomacy in the Muslim World as follows: "[The U.S.] pro-Israel, pro-Arab autocrats foreign policy ... has devastated [Muslim] lands and cultures for nearly half a century."[45]

Locating West Africa in the U.S. war on terrorism

Why is West Africa important to the waging of the U.S. war on terrorism? The population of some of the countries in the region is made up predominantly of Muslims. For example, Muslims account for 99.9 percent of the Mauritanian population; 94 percent of the Senegalese population; 90 percent each of the population of the Gambia, Mali, and Niger; and 85 percent of the Guinean population.[46] In addition, Muslims account for 60 percent of the Sierra Leonean population, 55 percent of the Burkinabe population, and 50 percent of the Nigerian population. In total, there are about 134 million Muslims in West Africa, with Nigeria accounting for 64 million of them. This represents about half of the population of the sub-region (there are about 280 million people in the sub-region). Since the U.S. war on terrorism is focused on "radical

Islamic groups," these countries are critical to the effort of helping the U.S. prevent and minimize the spread of "radical Islam" among their respective populace, especially the development of support and empathy and the recruitment of fighters for Al-Qaeda and other terrorist groups.

Another major reason is the state fragility conundrum. In the view of American policy makers, West Africa has several fragile, weak or failed states. And this makes them vulnerable to terrorist capture. As Trygve Trosper argues, "Many West African governments are characterized by corrupt neo-patrimonial and/or military regimes. As weak governments increase in West Africa, the potential for terrorist safe havens to flourish there also increases."[47] In a similar vein, Nick Ottens notes, "Particularly, as terrorists retreat from Afghanistan and Iraq, they are seeking fresh safe havens from where to launch attacks against the United States and its allies."[48]

Preventing Al-Qaeda and other terrorist organizations from establishing footholds in West Africa constitutes a cardinal objective of the U.S.' war on terrorism. This is against the backdrop of Al-Qaeda's determination to establish its presence and influence in the sub-region. For example, in 2001, one of the leaders of Al-Qaeda, Ayman al Zawahiri, predicted that Nigeria would soon become a critical next front in the terror war against the West.[49] Toward this end, Al-Qaeda is reported to already be active in Nigeria.[50] Similarly, Al-Qaeda in the Islamic Maghreb (AQIM) is already operating in Mali's far northern desert area.[51] AQIM is also active in Mauritania and Niger.[52] Central to the concern about Al-Qaeda's presence in the sub-region is the issue of the establishment of commercial and financial networks by the group. According to a report issued by Global Witness, since the 1990s, Al-Qaeda has been involved in the rough diamonds trade in Sierra Leone and Liberia.[53] Al-Qaeda has used rough diamonds for several purposes: (1) as a means of raising funds for its cells; (2) to hide money targeted by financial sanctions; (3) to lauder the profits of criminal activity; and, (4) to convert cash into commodity that holds its value and is easily transportable.[54] Also, there is concern about domestic terrorist groups, especially the possibility of them collaborating with Al-Qaeda. In the case of Nigeria, for instance, there are growing concerns about the activities of Boko Haram and Al Sunna Wal Jamma.

Furthermore, the fact that the states in the sub-region have porous borders makes West Africa an important frontier. This is because the porosity of borders makes it easier for terrorist groups to move freely by land and sea, and to move weapons as well. For example, Nigeria has porous borders on both its land and sea edges.[55] Specifically, the country's land borders, especially in the northern part, has serious security implications given the activities of transnational terrorist groups such as Al-Qaeda in the Islamic Maghreb (AQIM) operating in the Sahel region of West Africa.[56] Similarly, Mali, Niger, and Senegal are situated in this region, and are also known to have porous borders.[57] Two major factors account for the porosity of borders in the sub-region. At the core is the constituent states' lack of capabilities to monitor their borders, including their coastlines. Prosper Addo refers to this overarching problem as "the lack of an appropriate mechanism for monitoring the movement of illegal activities across borders."[58]

There are also the twin problems of ungoverned and ungovernable territories in the sub-region. In the case of the former, there are vast areas in West Africa in which the state does not exercise control—what Joel Midgal calls "the lack of penetration by state institutions into the general society."[59] In addition, there is the lack of physical infrastructure to link these ungoverned areas to the political and economic heart of various West African states.[60] In the case of the latter, vast regions of West Africa are ungovernable, because the topography varies from the bone-dry desert of the Sahara to the semi-arid terrain of the Sahel, through the limited savannah and bush-reaching west and south, to the far more lush jungles and equatorial forests.[61] The absence of governability makes these areas conducive as safe havens for terrorist groups that can virtually establish their fiefdoms in them without being challenged by the state. In fact, Jason Motlagh refers to these ungovernable vast areas of the sub-region as "lawless swaths."[62]

Yet, West Africa is important to the U.S. war on terrorism because it is important to the U.S.' energy needs. West Africa's large crude oil and gas have been trumpeted as possible substitutes for America's growing dependence on crude exports from the unstable Middle East.[63] As former U.S. Vice President Dick Cheney observes, "West Africa is expected to be one of the fastest-growing sources of oil and gas for the American market. African oil tends to be of high quality and low in sulfur, making it suitable for stringent refined products requirement, and giving it a growing market share for refining centers on the east coast of the U.S."[64] Also, the West African oil province (the so-called ECOWAS region of the Gulf of Guinea) holds about 33.8 billion barrels of proven reserves, accounting for about 3.1 percent of the global total.[65] Taking into account unproven reserves increases West Africa's share to around 7 percent of the world's total.[66] In addition, currently, Nigeria is the fifth largest supplier of U.S. oil.[67] Against this backdrop, the U.S. wants to ensure that terrorist groups do not disrupt the supply of oil from the sub-region through various acts of sabotage, thereby adversely affecting the economies of the U.S. and its allies.

The focus of the book

The book seeks to explore several interrelated issues. First, it attempts to place West Africa within the broader crucible of the U.S. war on terrorism. Specifically, what are the U.S. threat perceptions in West Africa vis-à-vis its economic, political and security interests in the sub-region? Second, what are the elements of the U.S. counterterrorism policy in West Africa? In other words, what is the roadmap that the U.S. government has formulated to guide the prosecution of its war on terrorism in the West African sub-region? Third, what are the U.S. counterterrorism strategies in West Africa? How are they being pursued both at the bilateral and multilateral levels in the region? What are the emerging effects of these strategies? Fourth, the book interrogates the relationship between stability in the sub-region and the waging of the U.S. war on terrorism. Specifically, the book examines the crises of underdevelopment—cultural, economic, environmental, political, security, and social—in the sub-region, especially their impact on shaping the conditions that provide the taproots of terrorism. Clearly, addressing these multidimensional crises of underdevelopment is pivotal to the success of the U.S. war on terrorism in the sub-region.

The organization of the book

The book is divided into five parts consisting of 11 chapters. In Chapter 1, George Kieh and Kelechi Kalu set the parameters of the volume by addressing several major issues. The initial issue revolves around the framing of the U.S.' war on terrorism in terms of the "enemies," and the scope of the "war." In other words, Kieh and Kalu lay out the targets of the U.S. war on terrorism and the theater in which it is being waged. Next, they examine the contours of the U.S.' counterterrorism policy that provide the compass for navigating the terrain of terrorism. This is followed by a discussion of the nature and dynamics of the U.S.' counterterrorism strategies—both military and non-military. As well, they assess the successes and failures of these counterterrorism strategies. Finally, Kieh and Kalu locate West Africa within the crucible of the U.S. war on terrorism by examining issues such as the large Muslim populations in some of the states in the region; the state fragility conundrum; the vexing issue of porous borders; the twin problems of ungoverned and ungovernable territories in the sub-region; and the importance of the sub-region's oil resource to the U.S.

Dean Minix and Vinton Prince provide the regional context of the U.S.' war on terrorism by focusing on Sub-Saharan Africa in Chapter 2. They begin with an overview of U.S. policy toward Africa as a way of providing the historical background to the continent's evolving relationship with the United States in the latter's war on terrorism. Then, they examine four African states—Angola, Nigeria, South Africa, and Ethiopia—that are important to the security interests of the United States. They argue that although Angola is not a "foot soldier" in the U.S.' war on terrorism, that country is important to the United States because of its oil. Hence, the United States is interested in ensuring that terrorists do not pose threats to the flow of oil from Angola. They argue that Nigeria is important to the U.S. for two major reasons: It is pivotal to the U.S.' energy needs and it is an active "foot soldier" in the carrying out of the U.S.' war on terrorism. South Africa has assisted the United States' war on terrorism through intelligence sharing. And because Al-Qaeda has links with other terrorist groups in Somalia that are inimical to American interests, Ethiopia's major role in the U.S.' war on terrorism is to help police Somalia.

Part two of the book begins with Chapter 3. In this chapter, Pita Ogaba Agbese examines the factors and forces that the United States perceives as threats to its interests in West Africa against the backdrop of its war on terrorism. Agbese begins by historicizing West Africa's station in the broader tapestry of American security interests. He asserts that the September 11, 2001 attacks on the United States transformed the nature and dynamics of the latter's threat perception as evidenced by the fact that West Africa was catapulted from a marginal role to an important one in the U.S.' security policy. Agbese also identifies the major issues that shape and condition U.S. threat perception and terrorism in the West African sub-region: Failed states, radical Islam, illegal drug trafficking, mal-governed, under-governed, and ungoverned spaces, the proliferation of small arms, threats to oil supply to the U.S. and its allies, and porous borders.

In Chapter 4, Idowu Ejere examines Nigeria's Niger Delta region, one of the major areas in which the U.S. perceives terrorist threats to its interests. She postulates that the Niger Delta region is enveloped by a state of crisis as evidenced by a growing "human security deficit" that includes mass abject poverty, and the lack of basic social needs and infrastructure. To make matters worse, there is escalating environmental degradation caused by oil drilling by metropolitan-based multinational corporations like Shell. Idowu laments that the Nigerian state has failed to seriously address the crisis. Hence, exasperated by a state of neglect, some groups in the region, including disaffected youths, have turned to the use of violence against the Nigerian state and MNCs. The crisis has implications for the U.S.' war on terrorism for two major interrelated reasons. The region could become a hotbed for terrorist activities against the United States and its allies, because of the role of the MNCs in visiting deprivation on the masses of the people of the Niger Delta region. Within this context, the region potentially could provide "safe havens" for terrorist groups with whom home-grown terrorists in the area could forge an anti-American alliance.

Russell Howard's Chapter 5 sets the stage for Part III of the book. This chapter, which deciphers the U.S.' counterterrorism policy in West Africa, begins by examining the activities of various terrorist groups in the sub-region. In the particular case of Al-Qaeda, Howard argues that the group has expanded its influence globally, as evidenced by the forging of relationships with what he calls "like-minded Salafist-jihadist groups." In the specific case of West Africa, he posits that Al-Qaeda in the Islamic Maghreb (AQIM) has established a foothold in Mali as part of Al-Qaeda's broader goal of establishing its influence in the sub-region. He then suggests that the thrust of the U.S.' counterterrorism policy in West Africa is to limit the capacity of Al-Qaeda to establish its foothold in the sub-region. Howard asserts that in order to achieve this overarching objective, steps must be taken to address various pathologies including bad governance and mass poverty, which Al-Qaeda could use as the veneer for establishing its influence in the sub-region.

In Chapter 6, Julius Nyang'oro and Andrea Walthers probe the impact of the U.S.' Trans-Saharan Counterterrorism Partnership (TSCP), the centerpiece of American counterterrorism strategy in Africa, on the war on terrorism in the West African sub-region. They begin by examining the predecessors to TSCP—Pan-Sahel Initiative that included the West African states of Mali, Mauritania, and Niger—and the Trans-Saharan Counterterrorism Initiative (TSCI) that included Mali, Mauritania, Niger, Nigeria, and Senegal. In terms of an assessment, Nyang'oro and Walthers argue that the positive aspects of the TSCP have been: (1) The fact that it is proactive; (2) it reflects the lessons learned from the implementation of its predecessors; and (3) there have been increased military–security resources to various areas in West Africa. On the other hand, they assert that the strategy's overarching weakness is its emphasis on defense and security and less on diplomacy and development. The initiative likewise suffers from both programmatic and implementation challenges, as evidenced by the fact that the various U.S. government agencies that are involved in the implementation of the initiative lack comprehensive and integrated strategies for the various activities. As a solution, they suggest a pecking order that consists of development, diplomacy, and defense as the kernels of the initiative.

Boubacar N'Diaye examines the role of the Mauritanian military in the U.S.' counterterrorism strategy in Chapter 7. He begins by surveying the major features of the society, as well as those of the military, in an effort to provide the context for understanding the "war on terrorism" in Mauritania. Against this background, he contends that Mauritania was chosen to serve as a "foot soldier" in the U.S.' war on terrorism because of its predominantly Muslim population, its strategic location in the northwest portion of the West African sub-region, and its strong ties with the U.S., which began in 2001. One of the Mauritanian military's critical roles is to combat both domestic terrorists and Al-Qaeda in the Islamic Maghreb (AQIM).

George Klay Kieh, Jr. probes the utility of good governance and regional security in the sub-region as counterterrorism measures in the U.S. war on terrorism in Chapter 8. He examines the various efforts that are designed to promote good governance in the various states in the sub-region, especially the various good governance regimes that have been developed. As well, he deciphers the regional security architecture and its constituent elements. He concludes that while good governance and regional security are useful for addressing terrorism, they are not sufficient. Alternatively, he suggests a human-security-based approach that is comprehensive in scope and focuses on the security of individuals and groups in the constituent states in the sub-region. Additionally, he argues that changes need to be made in U.S. foreign policy toward the sub-region, especially the exigency of aligning U.S. pro-democracy rhetoric with praxis.

In Chapter 9, Sylvester Odion-Akhaine examines the impact of the U.S.' war on terrorism on civil–military relations in West Africa. His central conclusion is that the U.S.' war on terrorism will engender what he calls a "security dilemma" for civil–military relations in the sub-region. This could be made worse by the proliferation of arms; the overdependence of West African militaries on American weapons; the elevation of the military–industrial complex to a central command structure in Africa; and provides the opportunity for the U.S. to impose its national interests and concerns on its client regimes.

Zakaria Ousman tackles the issue of the West African stability architecture in Chapter 10. He commences with an overview of the cultural, economic, environmental, political, security, and social challenges facing the sub-region. He attributes the multidimensional crises of underdevelopment to the confluence of internal and external factors, including bad governance and imperialism. The resultant effect has been the creation of instability in the sub-region. He concludes that the U.S.' war on terrorism can only succeed if stability is established in the sub-region by addressing these multiple crises of underdevelopment. The rationale is that these crises provide the veneer that terrorists can use to mobilize support and to recruit fighters among the populace.

In Chapter 11, Kelechi Kalu weaves together the various chapters, and draws some major lessons from them. First, he argues that the U.S.' war on terrorism needs to transcend its emphasis on a military-centric counterterrorism strategy. While military capabilities are important, they should nonetheless be part of a multidimensional counterterrorism strategy that focuses on development and democracy in the sub-region. Second and related, he adds that care should be exercised to ensure that the U.S. war on terrorism does not bolster authoritarian regimes in the sub-region. Third, in addition to the broader U.S. counterterrorism strategy, respect for basic human rights needs to be the centerpiece of the evolving domestic counterterrorism regimes in the sub-region.

Conclusion

West Africa is a major theater in the U.S.' war on terrorism because several of its constituent states have large Muslim populations. Also, several of the states in the sub-region are fragile, and thus vulnerable to terrorist incursions. Moreover, the sub-region has some ungovernable and ungoverned territories. Furthermore, with the recent discovery of oil in the Gulf of Guinea, the sub-region has become important to the meeting of the energy needs of the United States and its allies.

The chapter has attempted to address these and other interlocking issues that frame the U.S.' global war on terrorism in the sub-region. These include the examination of the targets of the war, and the scope of the war. Al-Qaeda is the principal target of the war. Toward this end, the war seeks to identify and dismantle Al-Qaeda's global terrorism network. The war is also intended to take punitive actions against other non-state actors and state actors that provide support to Al-Qaeda and its allies. The war is framed by a counterterrorism policy that has the defense of the American homeland and interests as the foci. In order to implement that policy, counterterrorism strategies were developed. Although the strategies have both military and non-military dimensions, the former is ascendant. And, the non-military dimension includes public diplomacy with emphasis on the Islamic world.

Notes

1 John Owens and John Dumbrell, "Introduction: America's 'War on Terrorism:' New Dimensions in U.S. Government and National Security," in John Owens and John Dumbrell (eds.), *America's "War on Terrorism"* (Lanham, MD: Lexington Books, 2008), p. 1.
2 CNN-USA, "World Trade Center: New York Reduces 9/11 Death Toll by 40," October 29, 2003.
3 Tom Templeton and Tom Lumley, "9/11 in Numbers," *Guardian*, August 18, 2002.
4 Ibid.
5 President George W. Bush, Speech to Joint Session of Congress After the World Trade Center and Pentagon Bombings, September 20, 2001.
6 John Davis, "Introduction: Africa's Road to the War on Terror," in John Davis (ed), *Africa and the War on Terrorism* (Aldershot: Ashgate Publishing, 2007), p. 1.
7 Office of the Coordinator for Counterterrorism, *The Terrorist Enemy* (Washington, D.C.: U.S. State Department, 2011), p. 1.
8 Ibid.
9 Ibid.
10 Ibid.
11 Ibid.
12 Ibid.
13 President George W. Bush, Speech to Joint Session of Congress, op. cit.
14 Ibid.
15 President Barrack Obama, Inaugural Address, January 20, 2009.
16 National Security Strategy of the United States, 2010 (Washington, D.C.: The White House, 2010), p. 19.
17 Ibid.
18 National Security Strategy of the United States, 2010, op. cit., p. 5.
19 Ann Scott Tyson, "Support Troops Swelling U.S. Force in Afghanistan," *The Washington Post*, October 13, 2009.
20 Luiz Martinez, "For the First Time, More U.S. Troops in Afghanistan than Iraq," *ABC News*, May 24, 2010.
21 Rasool Dawar and Kimberly Dozier, "Record Level of U.S. Drone Attacks Hit Afghan Militants," *The Huffington Post*, September 15, 2010.
22 Ibid.
23 Andrew Koch, "U.S. Seeks Security in African Waters," *Jane's Defense Weekly*, February 16, 2005, p. 17.
24 Ibid.
25 Andrew Feickert, U.S. Military Operations in the Global War on Terrorism: Afghanistan, Africa, the Philippines, and Colombia, CRS Report for Congress (Washington, D.C.: Congressional Research Service, 2005), p. 17.
26 Ibid.
27 Amy Zalman, "Under Secretary of Public Diplomacy, Karen Hughes, Resigns," About.com, November 6, 2007.
28 Ibid.
29 The Rand Corporation, U.S. Counterterrorism Strategy Must Address Ideological and Political Factors at the Global and Local Levels, Research Brief (Santa Monica, CA: Rand Corporation, 2006), p. 1.
30 Ibid.
31 "Al-Qaeda Leaders Who Have Been Killed and Arrested," *Hindustantimes*, June 1, 2010.
32 See *MSNBC News*, "U.S. Forces Kill Osama bin Laden in Pakistan," May 2, 2011.
33 See SAMAA, "About 200 'Launch Cross-border Attack' on Pakistan Post," June 1, 2011.

34 See Ben Doherty, "80 Die As Pakistan Bombing Launches 'Wave' of bin Laden Revenge Strikes," *Reuters*, May 14, 2011.

35 Nick Ottens, "America's Shadow War on Terror," *Atlantic Sentinel*, August 17, 2010.

36 Robert Tynes, "U.S. Counter-terrorism Policies in Africa are Counter to Development," *African Security Review*, 15(3), 2006, p. 110.

37 Joanne Mariner, "The Global Impact of the U.S.' War on Terror Abuses," *FindLaw*, March 11, 2009, p. 1.

38 Ibid., p. 2.

39 Ibid.

40 Ibid.

41 Ibid.

42 Ibid.

43 Tynes, "U.S. Counter-terrorism Policies," op. cit., p. 111.

44 John Brown, "Out to Pasture," *Guardian*, November 2, 2007.

45 Rami Khouri, "Karen Hughes' Two-year Halloween," *The Daily Star*, November 3, 2007.

46 See U.S. State Department, International Religious Freedom Report, 2010, (Washington, D.C.: U.S. State Department), www.state/gldr/rls/irf/2007/90081.htm (accessed February 21, 2011).

47 Trygve Trosper, "West Africa's War on Terrorism: Time and Patience, Paper # A173994" (Carlisle Barracks, PA: Army War College, 2009), p. 1.

48 Ottens, "America's Shadow War on Terror," op. cit.

49 See Scott Johnson, "Money Talks: The Islamists' Rebellion in Nigeria Isn't the Latest Front in the Global War on Terror," *Newsweek*, August 3, 2009.

50 See Ronald Palmer, "Political Terrorism in West Africa," in John Davis (ed.), *Africa and the War on Terrorism* (Aldershot: Ashgate Publishing, 2007), p. 107.

51 See Ernest Harsch, "Africa Looks Beyond 'War on Terror,'" *Africa Renewal*, October 2009, p. 16.

52 Ibid.

53 Global Witness, *For a Few Dollars More: How Al-Qaeda Moved into the Diamond Trade, A Report* (London: Global Witness, 2003), pp. 11–21.

54 Ibid.

55 See N. Florquin and E. G. Berman (eds), *Armed and Aimless: Armed Groups and Human Security in the ECOWAS Region* (Geneva: Geneva Small Arms Survey, 2005).

56 See C. Nna-Emeke Okereke, "Al-Qaeda in the Islamic Maghreb (AQIM) and the Question of Security in West Africa," *African Journal for the Prevention and Combating of Terrorism*, 1(1), 2010, pp. 65–67.

57 Freedom Onuoha, "Nigeria's Vulnerability to Terrorism: The Imperative of Countering Religious Extremism and Terrorism (CONREST) Strategy," *Peace and Conflict Monitor*, February 2, 2011, p. 1.

58 Prosper Addo, *Cross-Border Criminal Activities in West Africa: Options for Effective Responses*, KAIPTC Paper No. 12 (Accra: Kofi Annan International Peacekeeping Training Center, 2006), p. 1.

59 Joel Midgal, "Mental Maps and Virtual Checkpoints: Struggles to Construct and Maintain State and Social Boundaries," in Joel Midgal (ed), *Boundaries and Belonging: States and Societies in the Struggle to Shape Identity* (Cambridge: Cambridge University Press, 2004), p. 23.

60 See Angel Rabasa and John Peters, "The Dimensions of Ungovernability," in Angela Rabasa et al. (eds), *Ungoverned Territories: Understanding and Reducing Terrorism Risks* (Santa Monica, CA: The Rand Corporation, 2007), p. 7.

61 Kevin O'Brien and Theodore Karasik, "Case Study: West Africa," in Rabasa et al. (eds), *Ungoverned Territories*, op. cit., p. 174.

62 Jason Motlagh, "U.S. Takes Terror Fight to Africa's 'Wild West:' Critics Say Saharan Plan Backs Despots, is Magnet for Trouble," Chronicle Foreign Service, December 27, 2005.
63 Cyril Widdershoven, "West African Oil: Hope or Hype?" Institute for the Analysis of Global Security Brief, www.lags.org/africa.html (accessed February 23, 2011).
64 Ibid.
65 Ibid.
66 Ibid.
67 See James J. Forest and Matthew Sousa, *Oil and Terrorism in the New Gulf: Framing U.S. Energy and Security Policies for the Gulf of Guinea* (Lanham, MD: Lexington Books, 2006), p. 14.

2 Sub-Saharan Africa as another front in the U.S. global war on terrorism

Dean A. Minix and Vinton Prince

Introduction

It is perhaps noteworthy that Stratfor.com, one of the leading open-source, web-based intelligence companies, devotes only a scant page to Sub-Saharan Africa's strategic concerns in its recent annual report.[1] This scintilla of data is important nonetheless because it demonstrates the low-level visibility that the Sub-Saharan African Regional War on Terror (RWOT) has on the analysts' radar as a part of the larger Global War on Terror (GWOT). In point of fact, the United States Africa Command, or AFRICOM, which is one of six of the Defense Department's regional military headquarters, was only recently declared a fully unified command on October 1, 2008. Therefore, it is fair to say that Sub-Saharan African regional security threats are not notoriously high on the American strategic agenda, and this will probably continue to be the case for the foreseeable future, i.e., mostly undetectable ground chatter on the sub-radar screens.

Despite the present inattention toward this region its importance to global strategies continues to be significant and cannot be ignored. This chapter will look at some of the geopolitical issue areas of this region of the continent and examine how they interact and interconnect within a regional context of the larger frame of reference in the Global War on Terror, or as some prefer, the "Long War." In short, our focus is a geostrategic one insofar as this RWOT fits into the larger context of the GWOT.

Geopolitics is the intersection of environment and people. As such, these two variables are interactive. The environment influences people's behavior, and nowhere does it do more than in the competition over scarce resources. Such is certainly the case in Sub-Saharan Africa where natural resources and geography are the main commodities of value.

In a global recession, however, natural resources are quick to lose market value initially, and they are the last commodities generally to regain it. Sub-Saharan Africa is dependent upon investment capital from the rest of the world, and its global integration is limited to its raw material production. Since the global system during the recession is awash in raw materials that are cheap and getting cheaper, investment into Sub-Saharan Africa is one of the first capital flows to be suspended, and one of the last to be restarted.

Consequently, all the major global players in African politics and economy will take at least a year off, and projects of all sizes will be downgraded, delayed, or abandoned outright. The only major outside player that will do more than dabble in the region in the foreseeable future is the United States. And its interest will be largely limited to small counterterrorism operations in the Horn of Africa, which is a sideshow in the much broader jihadist war. Although China's involvement in Africa is not insignificant, the global recession has made Beijing reconsider many of its continental super-projects. However, when the recession recedes, and the global economy rejuvenates, this region's importance will rise again. There are only three primary players in the region that can impact either the regional or global politics on a larger scale. They are Angola, South Africa, and Nigeria. To some degree, Ethiopia and its impact in Somalia must also be considered. That only leaves the United States as the major out-of-town player, but it too will delay most of its activity in the region for at least a year given the recession.[2]

Some history

For almost two centuries of its 230 year lifespan, the U.S. has had virtually no foreign policy toward Sub-Saharan Africa. U.S. merchants dealt with local regimes on a private basis or went through the several colonial powers when they had claims, as in Senegal or Sierra Leone. The Navy did maintain anti-slavery patrols in West African waters in cooperation with Great Britain beginning in 1842, but those hardly constituted an "Africa Policy."[3]

From the 1820s onward, however, the United States did have to consider Liberia. Established by the American Colonization Society between 1822 and 1824, Liberia was a quasi-colony in its early years. Washington disavowed this reality, but the United States' flag flew over Monrovia for the first years. This colony amounted to an odd kind of Western imperialism at the expense of the indigenous populations. Liberia's immigrants, totaling about 15,000 between 1822 and 1865, were largely African American. The rest were primarily Anglophonic Afro-Caribbean or Afro-Brazilian. Each group brought New World sensitivities, values, and prejudices with them as they "returned" to an Africa they had never known.[4]

Between 1822 and the late 1840s, Liberia became an ever-increasing "problem" for Europeans operating in West Africa. It was neither fish nor fowl. The United States steadfastly refused to accept responsibility for its offspring in any meaningful manner. Both the French and the British challenged the validity of Liberia's laws and revenue acts. After all, Liberia was a ward of the private American Colonization Society, itself much troubled, not a "real country." In 1847 the Society cut its ties with Liberia, which declared itself an independent country. By the mid-1850s, all the European powers who mattered had accepted Liberia's new status. The United States withheld recognition until 1862, when the balance in Congress made this less controversial and easier to accomplish.[5]

Despite the recognition, the European powers continued to view Liberia as an American protectorate despite Washington's protests to the contrary. The United States did admit to having a "special interest" in the frequently troubled state, and that was good enough for London, Paris, and later Berlin. As the United States entered its second century, however, the "Age of the New Imperialism" made its lack of an African policy more problematic.[6]

The United States government sought neither colonies nor concessions in Sub-Saharan Africa in the late nineteenth century. Starry-eyed American imperialists tended to look toward the Caribbean Basin, Hawaii, other Pacific islands, and the ever-elusive opportunities in China. As the European interest in Africa increased, its issues were increasingly considered and acted upon by the capitals of Europe.

Because of its awkward Liberian "stepchild," the United States was invited to participate in the Berlin Conference on Africa in 1884. This was one of its few opportunities to sit at the "Big Boys Table," prior to the 1919 Paris Peace Conference after the First World War. Because of domestic considerations, Washington could not afford to show too much interest in Sub-Saharan Africa and no one holding an important office cared to do so at the time. Given the realities of American politics following Reconstruction, any sort of forward policy in Africa would have been extremely unpopular and doomed.

For most of its second century, the United States' policy toward Sub-Saharan Africa remained both consistent and disinterested. Liberia continued to receive occasional handouts plus occasional and often unfavorable loans, such as Harvey Firestone's 1926 $5 million loan in return for massive rubber concessions.[7] During the Second World War, a (black) division was stationed in Liberia to protect American rubber interests.[8] The United States also used the "war years" to put pressure on the British and French about their colonial holdings in Africa and elsewhere. One cannot give that pressure much, if any, credit for the later decolonization.

If one examines college offerings and commonly used books on U.S. foreign policy in the 1950s and 1960s, it becomes immediately obvious that most said little or nothing about Sub-Saharan Africa. As the winds of independence, however, swept across the continent both bureaucrats and schoolboys scrambled to catch up. Some obviously benefited from the situation, but for most massive confusion was closer to the norm. Index citations for "Africa" were rare, and frequently nonexistent. Half of the citations often just covered North Africa. Libya in some cases had more references than Liberia.[9]

The Kennedy administration paid far more attention to the "Alliance for Progress" than to all of Sub-Saharan Africa. The same can be said for South Vietnam, where the number of U.S. advisors expanded from 800 to 16,000. Kennedy had two main initiatives in Sub-Saharan Africa: The *ersatz* Korea-style intervention in the Congo and the Peace Corps. The latter, of course, was by no means limited to or primarily designed for Africa.[10]

Once Vietnam got out of hand, Sub-Saharan Africa slipped off the U.S.'s symbolic radar screen almost completely until the advent of *détente*. During the Cold War, Sub-Saharan Africa became a factor from the late 1950s until the late 1960s, but both the U.S. and the U.S.S.R. had limited success. Then Nixon and Brezhnev became "friends," and the Soviets interpreted this new arrangement to mean they were free to make inroads in places the United States had no immediate presence. The U.S., however, felt both powers ought to avoid those countries, a kind of "Self-Denying Ordinance." This was a certain recipe for misunderstandings and led to "Great Power" support for this or that side, usually through proxies, in northeastern and southern Africa. Many scars from those years still remain.[11]

Until relatively recently, therefore, one can say the United States has had little in the way of a consistent, let alone coherent, policy toward Sub-Saharan Africa. Apart from Cold War orthodoxy, what has there been beyond platitudes and occasional bits of action or, more commonly, reaction? Oil, for example, has been a factor in relation with Nigeria and Angola, but that is part of a normal "global petroleum foreign policy," not in a specific Africa policy tradition.

Sub-Saharan Africa's constraints on foreign direct investment

Given the geopolitical focus of this chapter, it is important to review the impact of this region's environment upon its politics. Industrialization is quite difficult given the topography of the area, thus foreign direct investment (FDI) is limited generally to resource extraction. And, most of this extraction is offshore.

FDI into Africa has grown in the twenty-first century—albeit irregularly—nearly doubling from 2002 to reach $36 billion in 2007, primarily because of the international search for natural resources at a time of high commodity prices. At the same time, Africa's share of global FDI fell from 5 percent in the 1970s, to about 2 percent today as capital flow elsewhere outpaced Africa's.[12]

This is an economically bleak perspective considering the political turmoil and the unyielding landscape of the region. A quick survey of the landscape reveals that most of Sub-Saharan Africa's (SSA) rivers are unnavigatable commercially, and that high land escarpments deny the needed dense penetration into the interior for industrial development. Given the geography, infrastructural development is meager, and African governments are often unwilling to reinvest in European colonial remnants. South Africa, Nigeria, and Angola account for 55 percent of FDI in the SSA region. If Sudan and Equatorial Guinea are added to this group, these five nation states account for 75 percent of the FDI in SSA.[13] The true implication of the data becomes clear when one considers that there are 47 countries in SSA.

FDI in Sub-Saharan Africa falls into three categories: (1) investment in infrastructure for basic commodity and manufactured goods distribution; (2) investment in infrastructure for the extraction of resources, such as mineral and metals; and (3) offshore oil and natural gas production.[14]

Country synopses

Angola

Geographically and economically, Angola is the sixth-largest country in Africa. Its gross domestic product (GDP) in 2007, at $44 billion, places its economy at just over one-third of the size of Nigeria's (which measured $115 billion in 2007) and at less than one-fifth the size of Africa's largest economy, South Africa ($255 billion in 2007). Angola's resource wealth is fairly well concentrated: The majority of its oil assets are located in the country's northwest corner in Cabinda province (and offshore from it) as well as offshore between Luanda and the northern town of Soyo. Its diamond centers are located in the central and north-central provinces, with newer fields being opened in the northeast and southeast.[15]

Following the civil war in 2002, the leadership of the Popular Movement for the Liberation of Angola (MPLA) has sought to make Angola a regional hegemon in part to lessen the chances of further inter-party warfare—especially from the rural parts of the country. The conclusion of the war allowed the MPLA-controlled government to consolidate its power and to concentrate on its two primary natural resources, oil and diamond production. Angola's proven reserves have grown from 5.4 billion barrells in 1997 to 9 billion barrells in 2008. Its oil production has grown more than tenfold in the years since independence, from 165,000 barrels per day (bpd) in 1975 to 1,870,000 bpd by the end of 2007, with roughly half of that growth occurring after 2002. Output is expected to grow by at least 500,000 bpd in the coming years, with at least three ultra deep oil fields to come online between 2009 and 2011. Angolan light sweet crude is in high demand globally, and it does not face the same guerrilla threats as Nigeria's. Luanda's location in the southern Gulf of Guinea has no chokepoints, and therefore the crude is easily transported to European and American markets.

Similarly, diamond production has almost doubled since 2002. Production at the end of the civil war was estimated at just over five million carats, itself a dramatic rise from the 750,000 carats produced in 1975. By 2007, output was approximately 9.7 million carats – and was under the undivided control of the government. Production is expected to expand further, with deals involving South African interests (including those of the African National Congress power broker Tokyo Sexwale) being negotiated to open fields in northeastern and southeastern Angola. The country is also expected to benefit from redirected investment as a result of the ongoing political crisis in mineral-rich Zimbabwe.[16]

Angola and the United States have a strengthened relationship since 2008, when the Angolan foreign minister visited Washington. During this visit, a Trade and Investment Framework Agreement was signed that will assist U.S. businesses to invest more robustly in Angola.[17] The U.S. State Department reports that Angola's borders remained porous and vulnerable to movement of small arms, diamonds, and other possible sources of terrorist financing. Angola's high rate of dollar cash flow made its financial system an attractive site for money laundering, and the government's capacity to detect financial crimes remained limited. The government's limited law enforcement resources were directed towards border control and stemming the flow of illegal immigrants into the country, which increased exponentially since the 2002 peace treaty ending Angola's protracted civil war. Corruption, lack of infrastructure, and insufficient capacity continue to hinder Angola's border control and law enforcement capabilities. Angola recently reached out to the U.S. government to support improving its maritime and airspace security.[18]

Given Luanda's economically plush condition relative to its neighbors, the government can concentrate on securing its borders, and playing the Chinese off against the Americans, when it is convenient to do so. Angola is therefore in a strong position in Sub-Saharan Africa. Its Achilles heel is the fact that it must import all foodstuffs and consumer goods. Insofar as a regional player in the war on terror, Angola is not a likely participant—yet.

Nigeria

Prior to the formal promulgation of AFRICOM, Nigeria announced that it would drop its opposition to the American "forward basing strategy," thus easing the way for other regional players to accede to its assimilation. AFRICOM will not operate from a fixed-base system, but instead will adopt a light footprint by using a lily-pad facilities approach. Both Nigeria and the U.S. have shared interests in maritime security in the oil-rich Gulf of Guinea—a region that supplies the U.S. with two million bpd, and Nigeria is the fifth largest supplier of the United States.[19] Nigeria's relinquished opposition will not go unnoticed in other African capitals as well. As Stratfor analyzes, "given the confluence of interests, the Obama administration will likely support Abuja's backroom moves to maintain a sphere of influence through West Africa, as well as an initiative to, in effect, buy the temporary loyalty of the Niger Delta region's Ijaw ethnic group with a power-sharing agreement."[20]

The government of Nigeria took steps regarding counterterrorism legislation. The National Focal Point on Terrorism, an interagency task force formed in February, 2007, composed of the State Security Service (SSS), the Nigerian Customs Service, the Ministry of Foreign Affairs, Immigration, and other relevant authorities, met periodically throughout the year. In October 2007, in an effort to improve coordination and communication between the legislative and executive branches, the UN Office on Drugs and Crime sponsored a workshop on counterterrorism legislation for Focal Point participants and members of relevant committees in the National Assembly. Also, a Senate bill based on the Commonwealth Secretariat's Model Legislative Provisions on Measures to Combat Terrorism passed its second reading on September 17, 2007, and was referred to the Senate Committees on National Security and Intelligence and the Judiciary for further review.

The Nigerian government approved the installation of U.S.-funded body scanners in all four international airports to detect explosives and drugs on passengers. The scanners were installed in March, May, and June, 2008. The Nigerian and U.S. governments also co-sponsored a conference on aviation security in Abuja from November 17–18, 2008. Despite repeated requests from the U.S. government, however, the Nigerian government has not yet approved the use of U.S. Federal Air Marshals on direct flights between Nigeria and the United States.

On May 5, 2008, in Abuja, President Yar'Adua (the late), in a message delivered by then Vice President Goodluck Jonathan to open a conference of the Committee of Intelligence and Security Services in Africa (CISSA), charged the assembled heads of intelligence and security services with developing strategies to check the spread of extremist ideologies in West Africa by external elements, and called for increased regional and global networking to meet the threat. Ambassador Emmanuel Imohe, Director-General of Nigeria's National Intelligence Agency (NIA), also took a leadership role at the meeting, calling for greater cooperation and intelligence sharing, particularly given the region's porous borders. On May 14, 2008, the Nigeria Police Force announced the deployment of units from its newly created Antiterrorism Squad (ATS) to Lagos, Abuja, Port Harcourt, and Kano, reportedly as a result of an alleged terrorist threat. On May 27, 2008, Malam Kasimu Umar, leader of an extremist Shia group in Sokoto, and 112 members of his sect, were sentenced by the Sokoto Upper Sharia Court to eight years imprisonment on weapons charges, resisting arrest, public incitement, and "inciting contempt of religious creed," in connection with violence in the aftermath of the July, 2007 assassination of a renowned Islamic preacher Malam Umaru Dan Maishiyya, a crime whose motive has never been determined.

From September 8–12, 2008, members of the Nigerian Armed Forces, as well as authorities from customs and immigration and other relevant civilian agencies, participated in a USG security seminar on protecting the maritime domain. During the September 17–22, 2008 visit of the USS Elrod, under the auspices of the Africa Partnership Station, a joint exercise was successfully conducted with the newly operational Regional Maritime Awareness Capability (RMAC) system in Lagos. Progress continued on the establishment of an additional RMAC station in the east. Nigerian military personnel attended operational and strategic counterterrorism training in the United States and Germany under the auspices of the Trans-Saharan Counterterrorism Partnership. Twelve Nigerians attended a U.S.-sponsored Post-Blast Investigation Training course in August, 2008, while 20 participated in a Maritime Port and Harbor Security Management course in September, 2008.

On November 2, 2008, the Nigerian Police Force announced the deployment of ATS units to strategic locations in the Federal Capital Territory, as well as Rivers, Lagos, and Kano States. On November 7, 2008, the Nigerian federal government elevated its threat level over potential sabotage of national infrastructure in a confidential memo that was subsequently leaked to the *Nigerian Tribune* newspaper.

A member of the Intergovernmental Anti-Money Laundering Group in Africa, Nigeria's mutual evaluation report was discussed and adopted by the plenary body in May, 2008. Nigeria's Financial Intelligence Unit (FIU) is the only Egmont member in the sub-region, and has volunteered to sponsor four additional FIUs in the sub-region for membership. Actions taken by the Nigerian authorities in 2008 regarding the Economic and Financial Crimes Commission have led to concerns about the effectiveness of this institution and its continued sustainability.[21]

South Africa

South Africa has stated its reluctant opposition to AFRICOM. South Africa sees itself as a sole hegemon of Sub-Saharan Africa. But, South Africa's opposition to AFRICOM will not deter AFRICOM'S mission or deployment, since that organization's interests lie in West Africa and the Horn, not southern Africa, per se. The African National Congress's (ANC) consolidation of power has allowed South Africa to push for a Southern Africa Development Community (SADC) peacekeeping force based in South Africa with the intent of deploying such a force anywhere on the continent.[22] South Africa has little influence outside of SSA. It has not involved itself in the Horn, or elsewhere on the continent.

It is also noteworthy that South Africa does not wish to engage the Chinese in what Mbeki has characterized as a "neo-colonial" relationship.[23] This statement may have been a warning to AFRICOM to keep a light footprint in SSA.

South Africa supported efforts to counter international terrorism and shared financial, law enforcement, and limited intelligence information with the United States. Some analysts believe that elements and support systems for Al-Qaeda and/or other extremist groups have a presence within South Africa's generally moderate Muslim community, but it was unclear to what extent foreign terrorist groups have a presence in South Africa. In 2007, the Department of the Treasury designated South African nationals Farhad and Junaid Dockrat as Al-Qaeda financiers and facilitators, subjecting them to U.S. sanctions.

Border security challenges, socio-cultural attitudes, and document fraud negatively affected the government's ability and efforts to pursue and intervene in counterterrorism initiatives. South African identity and travel documents generally included good security measures, but because of poor administration, lack of institutional capacity, and corruption within the Department of Home Affairs, which is responsible for immigration services, thousands of bona fide South African identity cards, passports, and work/residence permits were fraudulently issued.

South Africa is the only Financial Action Task Force member in Africa and has one of the three Egmont-member Financial Intelligence Units in the region. It is also a member of Eastern and Southern Africa Anti-Money Laundering Group (ESAAMLG) and as such, has served as a resource for other ESAAMLG members.[24]

Ethiopia and Somalia

Before leaving Washington, the Bush administration extended aid to Somalia for its counterterrorism efforts. This aid, however, did not include direct U.S. assistance other than occasional striker hits at know terrorist targets.[25] By accepting U.S. aid, the Somalis are announcing to the Ethiopians that their aid alone—the presence of about 20,000 troops—is insufficient, but not unwelcome. Ethiopia needs to push its national security envelope into Somalia to forestall threats from that country. But, such Ethiopian operations in Somalia also endanger the possibility of peace talks or reconciliation aimed at isolating Somali Islamists.[26]

In Somalia, the Al-Qaeda link is weak. The inter-clan rivalry stems much of the foothold Al-Qaeda would like to make in the Puntland region where most of the piracy occurs.[27] However, the geography of the Puntland makes this region salient given its proximity to Yemen.[28]

The Government of Ethiopia, facing a deteriorating security environment in Somalia that resulted in increased threats to its own security, and in support of the internationally recognized Transitional Federal Government of Somalia, battled insurgents and extremists that were formerly affiliated with the Council of Islamic Courts, including the Al-Qaeda-affiliated al-Shabaab factions. Until they announced their military withdrawal from Somalia in late 2008, Ethiopian forces provided critical support to the African Union Mission in Somalia (AMISOM) peacekeeping force, which was also targeted by extremist elements. In addition, Ethiopian forces countered individuals affiliated with organizations that attempted to conduct attacks inside Ethiopia.

Ethiopia's location within the Horn of Africa made it vulnerable to money-laundering activities perpetrated by transnational criminal organizations, terrorists, and narcotics traffickers. However, the government has yet to establish an anti-money laundering/combating the financing of terrorism (AML/CFT) regime. Although passage of the AML/CFT regime stalled in 2007, the government pressed forward to pass an existing draft, and requested the participation of USG officials involved in prior technical assistance programs to work with Ethiopian central bank officials and local technical consultants in order to finalize the AML/CFT law before submission to parliament. In addition, the government requested that USG officials help draft AML/CFT training manuals for the Ethiopian banking sector. The manuals will be part of the establishment of a Financial Intelligence Unit at the National Bank of Ethiopia.

Ethiopia's National Intelligence and Security Service (NISS), with broad authority for intelligence, border security, and criminal investigation, was responsible for overall counterterrorism management. Federal and local police counterterrorism capabilities were primarily focused on responding to terrorist incidents. In November, 2008, the Ethiopian government's House of People's Representatives ratified the Protocol to the Organization of African Union (OAU) Convention on the Prevention and Combating of Terrorism. Ethiopia was an active participant in African Union (AU) counterterrorism efforts, served as a focal point for the AU's Center for Study and Research on Terrorism, and participated in meetings of the Committee of Intelligence and Security Services of Africa (CISSA).[29]

Other considerations: Africom[30] and the U.S. military priorities in Africa

Security assistance programs are a high priority in Africa for the Obama administration, a State Department official said on February 9, 2009, in remarks at the African Center for Strategic Studies in Washington, D.C. According to Phil Carter, the then acting assistant secretary of state for African Affairs, the decision to create a U.S. Africa Command, also known as AFRICOM, "marks the beginning of a new era where African security issues can be addressed from an Africa-centric perspective, and AFRICOM is a new type of command that will focus on building African regional security and crisis response. Its objective is a more secure Africa."[31]

Secretary Carter then went on to list four priorities for the Obama administration in Africa. The first is providing security assistance programs that are critical to securing the objective of a peaceful African continent. According to him:

> We are working with our African partners to build capacity at three levels: (1) at the level of the African Union, (2) at the sub-regional level, and (3) at the level of individual states. At the level of the AU, we are supporting the Strategic Planning and Management Unit at AU headquarters in Addis Ababa with advisors and equipment. At the sub-regional level, we have provided assistance to peacekeeping training centers in Senegal, Ghana, South Africa, Mali, and Kenya. The United States provides a peace and security advisor at ECOWAS headquarters, and continues to support the ECOWAS logistics facility in Freetown, Sierra Leone.[32]

The second priority on the continent is promoting democratic systems and practices—the United States is engaged in supporting the rise of freedom and democracy on the continent. From the U.S.' perspective, it is not enough to just end wars, but the U.S. must move beyond post-conflict transformation to consolidate democracies. Moreover, the U.S. must work with African societies on the critical issues of governance, transparency, and accountability as a means of helping establish pluralistic communities where open political dialogue is the channel for reform and progress. During the past two decades, progressive democratic reform has adapted to local values, customs, and practices throughout Sub-Saharan Africa. Outgrowths of democratic, well-governed states, which adhere to the rule of law, support the will of their people, and contribute responsibly to the international system, are developing. One U.S. think tank that has studied Africa, Freedom House, has determined that "three quarters of African countries are now democratizing."[33]

The third foreign policy priority is promoting sustainable and broad-based, market-led economic growth. While Sub-Saharan Africa has experienced impressive growth rates in recent years, Africa can still be characterized as a rich continent in an impoverished state. The United States must help its African partners to raise income levels, promote sustainable growth that benefits all in a society, opens markets for African exports, reduces barriers to investment, and identifies opportunities and comparative advantages.[34]

The fourth U.S. foreign policy priority in Africa is promoting health and social development. As the leading cause of death on the continent, disease is one of the greatest challenges to Africa's future. Rising to meet this challenge, the United States, through public health initiatives targeting the prevention, care, and treatment of disease, is partnering with Sub-Saharan nations to fight HIV/AIDS, tuberculosis, and malaria.[35]

Security, democracy, markets, and health—these are the pillars of the Obama administration's policy toward Africa, but security still ranks first as it did with the Bush administration. The creation of AFRICOM is evidence that the security interests of the US in the continent were not being met. America's strategic concerns in Africa that AFRICOM will address are:

- fostering maritime security and stability in the oil-rich Gulf of Guinea region, where Nigeria exercises considerable influence;
- combating piracy off the coast of the Horn of Africa (U.S. Naval warships have long conducted counter-piracy operations in this area);[36]
- denying sanctuary to international terrorist organizations;
- undermining the spread of radical Islam in the Horn of Africa and across North Africa.[37]

Conclusion

The two drivers of US policy in Sub-Saharan Africa are anti-terrorism and natural resources, principally oil. From an African lens, however, the Obama administration is expected to, perhaps even must, give greater consideration to the continent's issues and concerns given his Kenyan heritage. But other issues such as the current global economic recession and interactions with and by players such as Russia, China, Iran, Iraq, and Afghanistan, *inter alia*, push Africa to the side once again.

But, it is significant that the U.S. Army War College's Key Strategic Issues List for 2007 did not mention the "Long War," or "GWOT," *at all*! The following year's list, however, puts "GWOT" at the top of the list of concerns and the "stability and security role of Africa's regional powers: Nigeria, Ethiopia, Kenya, and South Africa" are listed as sixteenth or last.[38] As Statfor contends:

> [T]he anti-terrorism campaign in the sub-Sahara is one of subtle manipulation rather than overt intervention. In some respects, it is similar to U.S.-backed military operations in Latin America. The United States is again

taking charge in fighting terrorism in Africa, but its nearly "hands off" approach focuses on using local security forces and intelligence efforts to identify and rout out suspected Islamist militants. This influence over local governments and regional powers is achieved through a combination of indirect military aid, U.S. military training, and joint small-scale raids.[39]

Islam is the predominant religion on the continent, ranging from Tunisia in the north to as far south as the Central African Republic—in addition to the Horn of Africa. U.S. military involvement in this region, although little publicized, is widespread. The United States has had some Special Forces involvement—targeted raids, training, or both—in African nations as varied as Mauritania, Mali, Niger, Liberia, Algeria, Nigeria, Chad, Kenya, Ethiopia, Cameroon, Botswana, South Africa, Ghana, Tanzania, Egypt, Tunisia, and Djibouti. Indirect U.S. military involvement—financial and equipment aid—can be seen in Sudan, Uganda, Rwanda, Morocco, Cote d'Ivoire, Equatorial Guinea, Senegal, Angola, Zambia, Benin, Burkina Faso, Burundi, Cape Verde, Central African Republic, Comoros, both Congos, Eritrea, Gabon, Guinea, Guinea Bissau, Lesotho, Madagascar, Mauritius, Mozambique, Namibia, Sao Tome, Seychelles, Sierra Leone, and Togo.

One of the darker by-products of security assistance to Sub-Saharan Africa is the proliferation of African mercenaries onto the world scene, as well-trained professional soldiers, who seek to profit from their unique skills. African guns-for-hire are showing up in Iraq, for example. On the continent itself, rival regimes and domestic foes have often employed these shady "soldiers of fortune" for their own ends. Calls have gone out for the United States and others to take steps to curb the military export business; but, so far no substantive action has been taken.

Regardless of these minor setbacks and obstacles, putting African security forces on the front lines of Western military operations is the tactic of choice for the United States and other international powers—who can take the anti-terrorism fight to the continent without getting bogged down in the sectarian violence that is rife throughout Africa. It serves the practical purpose of gaining allied governments, provides future inroads into African intelligence, and prevents the political quagmires resulting from sending thousands of troops to a chaotic and ill-defined battlefield. Additionally, it gives a number of African governments, who otherwise would be left to wander in the geopolitical wilderness, a chance to be heard.[40]

Before taking the reins at the Department of State, Senator Clinton made these remarks before the Senate Foreign Relations Committee: "The foreign policy objectives of the Obama administration in Africa are rooted in security, political, economic and humanitarian interests."[41] Moreover, she noted that the Obama administration's foreign policy objectives for Africa also include

> combating Al-Qaeda's efforts to seek safe havens in failed states in the Horn of Africa; helping African nations to conserve their natural resources

and reap fair benefits from them; stopping the war in the Democratic Republic of the Congo; [and] ending autocracy in Zimbabwe and human devastation in Darfur. Additionally, the United States will support African democracies like South Africa and Ghana, which just had its second peaceful change of power following democratic elections.[42]

The salient issues in American policy makers' minds towards this region remain anti-terrorism and natural resources. Geographically, this means West Africa and the Horn. The rest of Sub-Saharan Africa is still virtually undetectable, or "blipless," on US warning scopes. From Bush to Obama, there is consistency in American foreign policy regardless of the party in power. The key Sub-Saharan states during the Bush administration were Ethiopia, Nigeria, and South Africa. Angola, while not a partner with the United States, is an emerging regional hegemon. These four key states will undoubtedly also underlay the Obama administration's policy in Sub-Saharan Africa.

The Obama administration's intent in this war is to continue the progress made under the Bush administration, but center the focus on the Asian subcontinent. The primary success of the surge under President Bush was to convince the Jihadists that the U.S. presence was real and not transitory. Since 2001, the hope of the Jihadists of re-establishing the caliphate by massive uprisings in the Islamic world has failed. In its place, two governments have been overthrown, the Shia are moving slightly towards a more cooperative frame of mind with the Americans, and the new corporate headquarters of Al-Quaeda, Pakistan, is teetering on the abyss of becoming a failed state run by the military instead of becoming an Islamic government.

While Africa has only been viewed on a tertiary screen of U.S. counter-terrorist policy, three Sub-Saharan nations—Ethiopia, Nigeria, and South Africa—were Washington's anchors under the Bush administration. The current Obama administration has now added another nation, Angola, to that list. These four nations will serve as the cornerstone of American policy in a region that is of relatively minor counter-terrorist importance—at the moment. What may be an Obama break in such policy consistency might be found in the current administration's evolving counterterrorism policy and future events that may precipitate action. That is the subject for future analysis.[43]

Notes

1 Stratfor Global Intelligence, "Annual Forecast 2009: War Recession, and Resurgence," www.stratfor.com/forecast/20090128_annual_forecast_2009_war_recession_and_resurgence_introduction (accessed September 6, 2010). See also, "Annual Forecast 2010," www.stratfor.com/forecast/20100101_annual_forecast_2010 (accessed September 6, 2010).
2 Stratfor Global Intelligence, "Africa: Constraints on FDI in the Sub-Sahara," www.stratfor.com/ analysis/africa_constraints_fdi_sub_sahara (accessed September 6, 2010).
3 Tomas A. Bailey, *A Diplomatic History of the American People*, 10th ed. (Englewood Cliffs, NJ: Prentice Hall, 1970), pp. 210–11, 215–16.

4 Robert W. July, *A History of the African People*, 2nd ed. (New York: Charles Scribner's Sons, 1970), p. 316. See also, Abeodu Bowen Jones, "The Republic of Liberia," in J. F.A. Ajayi and Michael Crowder (eds.), *History of West Africa*, Vol. II (New York: Columbia University Press, 1973), pp. 310, 312.

5 Ibid., pp. 312–15. July, *A History*, op. cit., p. 316.

6 Bowen Jones, "The Republic of Liberia," op. cit., p. 315. July, *A History*, op. cit., p. 416.

7 Bowen Jones, "The Republic of Liberia," op. cit., p. 332. July, *A History*, op. cit., pp. 522–24.

8 Bowen Jones, "The Republic of Liberia," op. cit., p. 335.

9 Bailey, *Diplomatic History*, op. cit. See also Charles W. Kegley, Jr. and Eugene R. Wittkopf, *American Foreign Policy* (New York: St. Martin's Press, 1979); Norman A. Graebner, *An Uncertain Tradition: American Secretaries of State in the Twentieth Century*, (New York: McGraw-Hill, 1961); Thomas G. Paterson, J. Garry Clifford, and Kenneth J. Hagan, *American Foreign Policy*, Vols. I & II (Lexington, MA: D. C. Heath, 1977); Thomas G. Paterson (ed.), *Major Problems in American Foreign Policy*, Vol. II (Lexington, MA: D. C. Heath, 1978); John Spanier, *American Foreign Policy Since World War II* (New York: Praeger, 1962).

10 Melvin Gurtov, *The United States Against the Third World* (New York: Praeger, 1974), pp. 41–49.

11 M. K. Dziewanowski, *Russia in the Twentieth Century*, 6th. Ed. (Upper Saddle River, NJ: Prentice Hall, 2003), pp. 339–42.

12 Stratfor Global Intelligence, "Africa: Constraints on FDI in the Sub-Sahara," op. cit.

13 Ibid.

14 Ibid.

15 Stratfor Global Intelligence, "Angola: Net Assessment," www.stratfor.com/analysis/angola_net_assessment (accessed September 6, 2010).

16 Stratfor Global Intelligence, "Africa: Diamond Prospectors Eye New Supplies," www.stratfor.com/analysis/south_africa_diamonds (accessed September 6, 2010).

17 Stratfor Global Intelligence, "Geopolitical Diary: Angola and the United States Make Amends," www.stratfor.com/node/138538/geopolitical_diary/20090521_geop olitical_diary_angola_and_united_states_make_amends (accessed September 6, 2010).

18 Office of the Coordinator for Counterterrorism, U.S. Department of States, Chapter 2," Country Reports: Africa Overview, U.S. State Department, www.state.gov/s/ct/rls/crt/2008/ 122412.htm (accessed September 6, 2010).

19 Stratfor Global Intelligence, "Africa: Diamond Prospectors Eye New Supplies," www.stratfor.com/analysis/south_africa_diamonds (accessed September 6, 2010).

20 Stratfor Global Intelligence, "Nigeria: Opposition to AFRICOM Ends, December 14, 2007," www.stratfor.com/analysis/nigeria_opposition_africom_ends (accessed September 6, 2010).

21 Stratfor Global Intelligence, "The Obama Administration and Sub-Saharan Africa," www.stratfor.com/analysis/20090211_part_4_obama_administration_and_sub_saharan_Africa (accessed September 6, 2010).

22 Office of the Coordinator for Counterterrorism, "Chapter 2. Country Reports: Africa Overview," U.S. State Department, www.state.gov/s/ct/rls/crt/2008/122412.htm (accessed September 6, 2010).

23 Stratfor Global Intelligence, "The Obama Administration and Sub-Saharan Africa," op. cit.

24 Stratfor Global Intelligence, "South Africa, U.S.: Dueling for Hegemony in Africa", www.stratfor. com/south_africa_u_s_dueling_hegemony_Africa (accessed September 6, 2010).

25 Office of the Coordinator for Counterterrorism, "Chapter 2. Country Reports: Africa Overview," US State Department, www.state.gov/s/ct/rls/crt/2008/122412.htm (accessed September 6, 2010).

26 Stratfor Global Intelligence, "South Africa, U.S.," op. cit.

27 Stratfor Global Intelligence, "Somalia: The Islamist Insurgency and U.S. Aid," www.stratfor.com/analysis/somalia_islamists_insurgency_and_u_s_aid (accessed September 6, 2010).
28 Stratfor Global Intelligence, "Somalia: A Weak Link Between al Quaeda and Somali Pirates," www.stratfor.com/analysis/20090417_somalia_weak_link_between_al_qaed a_and_somali_pirates (accessed September 6, 2010).
29 Office of the Coordinator for Counterterrorism, "Chapter 2. Country Reports: Africa Overview," op. cit.
30 Ibid.
31 Stratfor Global Intelligence, "The Obama Administration and Sub-Saharan Africa", op. cit.
32 Phil Carter, "Policy Statement: US Policy in Africa," *United States Africa Command*, AFRICOM, www.africom.mil/getArticle.asp?art=2617&lang=0 (accessed September 6, 2010).
33 Ibid.
34 Ibid.
35 Ibid.
36 Stratfor Global Intelligence, "Geopolitical Diary," op. cit.
37 Stratfor Global Intelligence, "United States: The US Navy and Africa," www.stratfor.com/analysis/united_states_u_s_navy_and_Africa (accessed September 6, 2010).
38 Antulio J. Echevarria II, "2007 Key Strategic Issues List (KSIL)," *Strategic Studies Institute*, U.S. Army War College, www.strategicstudiesinstitute.army.mil/ pubs/display.cfm?pubID = 796 (accessed September 6, 2010); "Key Strategic Issues List, July 2008," *Strategic Studies Institute*, U.S. Army War College, www.strategicstud iesinstitute.army.mil/ pubs/display.cfm?pubID=860 (accessed September 6, 2010).
39 Stratfor Global Intelligence, "Africa Net Assessment: Sub-Saharan Oil and Arms," www.stratfor.com/africa_net_assessment_sub_saharan_oil_and_arms. (accessed September 6, 2010).
40 Ibid.
41 Charles W. Corey, "Hillary Clinton Outlines Obama Africa Policy," *United States Africa Command*, AFRICOM, www.africom.mil/getArticle.asp?art=2493&lang=0 (accessed September 6, 2010).
42 Ibid.
43 Donovan C. Chau, "U.S. Counterterrorism in Sub-Saharan Africa: Understanding Costs, Cultures, and Conflicts," *Strategic Studies Institute*, U.S. Army War College, www.strategicstudiesinstitute.army.mil/pubs/display.cfm?pubID=821 (accessed September 6, 2010); Robert Berschinski, "AFRICOM's Dilemma: The 'Global War on Terrorism' 'Capacity Building,' Humanitarianism, and the Future of U.S. Security Policy in Africa," *Strategic Studies Institute*, U.S. Army War College, www.strategic studiesinstitute. army.mil/pubs/display.cfm?PubID=827 (accessed September 6, 2010).

Part II
The U.S.' threat perception

3 The U.S. war on terrorism and the dynamics of threat perception in West Africa

Pita Ogaba Agbese

Introduction

In general, threats are conceptualized as impending danger or harm. Events or actions that constitute a potential source of harm or danger are also considered as threats. Thus, from a national security perspective, we can conceive of a threat as an event or process that has the capacity or potential capacity to cause grave danger and destruction to a large number of people and properties. An event or process that may fundamentally alter or transform a state's way of life can also be construed as a threat. A threat may manifest quite suddenly or it may be in the offing for a very long time. Similarly, the recognition of a threat or a potential threat may be immediate or it may come too late.

Since the first duty of a state is the protection of its citizens, political leaders have enormous tasks to assess potential threats and devise effective strategies of countering them. Both threat assessments and the design of effective strategies to counter threats and potential threats require the ability to correctly perceive the threats in the first place. Being aware of the threat or danger is as important as formulating effective strategies against it. Complicating the task of accurately determining the nature of sources of national threats is the fact that states now operate in a complex, rapidly changing and interconnected international environment. Second, threats to national security in the contemporary international system are multidimensional. They include terrorism, financial and economic crimes, natural disasters, and the dangers of weapons of mass destruction.

Focusing on West Africa for evidence, this chapter analyzes the dynamics of U.S. threat perceptions. It examines factors and indicators that the United States views as threats to its national security interests in West Africa. The analysis was undertaken against the backdrop of the United States' ongoing war against terrorism. The chapter contends that the attacks against the United States in September 2001 transformed the dynamics and processes of American threat perceptions. Globally, the attacks enlarged the geographical scope of U.S. threat perceptions and from then on, regions of the world such as West Africa that were hitherto marginal to American security concerns became places of strategic interest in American security calculations. How seriously does the United States view threats to its national interests in West Africa?

Threat assessment and threat perception in the United States did not begin after September 11, 2001 but the terrorist attacks against the US that day have since changed the dynamics of U.S. threat perceptions. As Karlyn Bowman has aptly observed, "For the public and policymakers alike, the attacks of September 11, 2001 thrust security issues to the front ranks of national discourse where they are likely to remain for some time to come. The memories of September 11 connect those issues powerfully to national political affairs."[1] Similarly, writing on threat perception and the public's outlook on national security in the United States, Frank Graves has noted that:

> Undeniably, North American societies have changed indelibly since September 11, 2001. Despite some fluctuations and controversies, the public now views security and safety as among the most important criteria for guiding national policy. Throughout 2004 and into 2005, we saw a great deal of volatility in terms of overall confidence in the Canadian federal government. In stark contrast, marks for the federal government's direction in the security field remained consistently positive.[2]

What then, does the United States view as fundamental threats to its national security? How did the attacks of September 11, 2001 shape the contours and contexts of American threat perceptions? What does the United States perceive as threats to its national security interests in West Africa? By what yard stick does the U.S. measure such threats? Did such threats exist prior to the 2001 attacks or were they only made manifest as a result of the attacks? Do the threats constitute part of the dynamics of the events of September 2001 or merely a fallout of the U.S. response to the attacks?

In its review of the strategic environment under which the United States operates, the 2009 National Intelligence Strategy of the United States of America noted that the U.S. "faces a complex and rapidly changing national security environment in which nation-states, highly capable non-state actors, and other transnational forces will continue to compete with and challenge U.S. national interests."[3] The document went on to identify the major security challenges to the U.S. Among states, entities, and other factors specifically identified as major security issues for the United States were the following: Iran, North Korea, China, Russia, violent extremist groups, insurgents, transnational criminal organizations, failed states and ungoverned spaces, the global economic crisis, climate change and energy competition, rapid technological change, and pandemic disease. Iran was considered a major challenge to U.S. security objectives in the Middle East and elsewhere "because of its nuclear and missile programs, support of terrorism, and provision of lethal aid to U.S. and coalition adversaries."[4] As for North Korea, it was highlighted as a threat to peace and security in East Asia because "of its sustained pursuit of nuclear and ballistic missile capabilities, its transfer of these capabilities to third parties, its erratic behavior, and its large conventional military capability."[5] The document acknowledged that China and the United States had many common interests but nonetheless, its "increasing natural resource-focused diplomacy and military modernization are among the factors making it a complex global challenge." Similarly, while approvingly noting Russian and U.S. partnership in important initiatives such as securing fissile material and combating nuclear terrorism, the Intelligence Strategy argued that Russia "may continue to seek avenues for reasserting power and influence in ways that complicate U.S. interests."[6]

Since the terrorist attacks against the United States in 2001, the U.S. government has viewed radical Islamic ideology as a fundamental threat to America. For instance, the September 2006 National Strategy for Combating Terrorism boldly asserts that:

> America is at war with a transnational terrorist movement fueled by a radical ideology of hatred, oppression, and murder. Our National Strategy for Combating Terrorism ... recognizes that we are at war and that protecting and defending the Homeland, the American people, and their livelihoods remains our first and most solemn obligation.[7]

The National Intelligence Strategy equally recognizes violent extremist groups as a major threat to U.S. national security interests. It argued as follows:

> Violent extremist groups are planning to use terrorism—including the possible use of nuclear weapons or devices if they can acquire them—to attack the United States. Working in a number of regions, these groups aim to derail the rule of law, erode societal order, attack U.S. strategic partners, and otherwise challenge U.S. interests worldwide.[8]

Both the National Strategy for Combating Terrorism and American political leaders such as President George W. Bush and President Barack Obama have emphasized that the war against radical Islamic extremism is not a war against Islam as a religion. Islam as a religion is not considered a threat per se, but from the U.S. perspective, unscrupulous Muslim leaders such as Osama bin Laden have perverted the teachings of Islam to promote hatred, violence, and bigotry. In the words of the National Strategy:

> Our terrorist enemies exploit Islam to serve a violent political vision. Fueled by a radical ideology and a false belief that the United States is the cause of most problems affecting Muslims today, our enemies seek to expel Western power and influence from the Muslim world and establish regimes that rule according to a violent and intolerant distortion of Islam. As illustrated by Taliban-ruled Afghanistan, such regimes would deny all political and religious freedoms and serve as sanctuaries for extremists to launch additional attacks against not only the United States, its allies and partners, but the Muslim world itself. Some among the enemy, particularly al-Qaida, harbor even greater territorial and geopolitical ambitions

and aim to establish a single, pan-Islamic, totalitarian regime that stretches from Spain to Southeast Asia.[9]

In his speech to the U.S. Congress in the wake of the September 11 attacks, President Bush also described those who carried out the attacks as people who "practice a fringe form of Islamic extremism that has been rejected by Muslim scholars and the vast majority of Muslim clerics; a fringe movement that perverts the peaceful teachings of Islam."[10] Bush distinguished between the vast majority of Muslims who are peaceful and go about their normal business with the "terrorists [who] are traitors to their own faith, trying in effect, to hijack Islam itself." Bush reiterated that in declaring war on Islamic extremism, the U.S. was not trying to wage a war against Islam. As he put it, "the enemy of America is not our many Muslim friends. It is not our many Arab friends. Our enemy is a radical network of terrorists and every government that supports them." Bush also went on to reassure Muslims that the United States respected the Islamic faith. As he put it, Islam "is practiced freely by many millions of Americans and by millions more in countries that America counts as friends. Its teachings are good and peaceful, and those who commit evil in the name of Allah blaspheme the name of Allah."

In his speech to university students in Cairo in 2009, President Obama also reiterated that the United States was not at war with Islam. He noted that historical factors such as colonialism, the Cold War, and globalization had created tensions between the United States and Muslims around the world and that

> violent extremists have exploited these tensions in a small but potent minority of Muslims. The attacks of September 11, 2001 and the continued efforts of these extremists to engage in violence against civilians has led some in my country to view Islam as inevitably hostile not only to America and Western countries, but also to human rights. All this has bred more fear and more mistrust.[11]

Nonetheless, the president emphasized that "America is not—and never will be—at war with Islam. We will, however, relentlessly confront violent extremists who pose a grave threat to our security—because we reject the same thing that people of faiths reject: the killing of innocent men, women, and children." President Obama also noted that Islam was an integral part of the fabric of the United States' society, pointing to the fact that Morocco was the first nation in the world to recognize the United States, and that there was a mosque in every state of the U.S. He also noted that there were over 1,200 mosques in the United States.

From the way the United States sees it, the danger posed by Al-Qaeda and other extremist Islamic groups is in several folds: First, as President Bush noted in his speech to Congress after the 2001 attacks, the terrorists hate the United States and all that it stood for and they aimed to destroy America. In Bush's own words:

They hate what they see right here in this chamber: a democratically elected government. Their leaders are self-appointed. They hate our freedoms: our freedom of religion, our freedom of speech, our freedom to vote and assemble and disagree with each other. They want to overthrow existing governments in many Muslim countries such as Egypt, Saudi Arabia and Jordan. They want to drive Israel out of the Middle East. They want to drive Christians and Jews out of vast regions of Asia and Africa.

Second, terrorists constitute a threat to the United States through their very method of dealing with opponents: Indiscriminate violence. Again, Bush put this very graphically, noting that the "terrorists kill not merely to end lives, but to disrupt and end a way of life. With every atrocity, they hope that America grows fearful, retreating from the world and forsaking our friends. They stand against us because we stand in their way." Reiterating virtually the same point, the National Strategy for Combating Terrorism argued that for terrorists:

> violence is not only justified, it is necessary and even glorified—judged the only means to achieve a world vision darkened by hate, fear, and oppression. They use suicide bombings, beheadings, and other atrocities against innocent people as a means to promote their creed. Our enemy's demonstrated indifference to human life and desire to inflict catastrophic damage on the United States and its friends around the world have fueled their desire for weapons of mass destruction. We cannot permit the world's most dangerous terrorists and their regime sponsors to threaten us with the world's destructive weapons.

In addition to accusing Islamic extremists of aiming to establish a "totalitarian regime," the US also considers them a threat to the United States because they do not accept the principle of "peaceful co-existence with those who do not subscribe to their distorted and violent view of the world. They accept no dissent and tolerate no alternative points of view. Ultimately, the terrorist enemy we face threatens global peace, international security and prosperity, the rising tide of democracy, and the right of all people to live without fear of indiscriminate violence."[12] Moreover, Islamic terrorists, the U.S. declared, seek to "create and exploit a division between the Muslim and non-Muslim world and within the Muslim world itself."[13]

Violent extremist groups are considered dangerous not just because they use violent means to kill and maim innocent citizens but the "hate-filled" ideology that they preach may draw new followers to their causes. Thus, the United States, according to the National Strategy for Combating Terrorism, must wage a "battle of arms" as well as a "battle of ideas" against the terrorists and "their murderous ideology." The "War on Terror" thus has two phases: A short-run phase and a long-run phase. The first phase involves militarily defeating radical extremists, denying them safe haven, ensuring that they do not acquire weapons of mass destruction, strengthening security and cutting off sources of their funding. The document declared however, that "winning the War on Terror means winning the battle of ideas. Ideas can transform the embittered and disillusioned either into murderers willing to kill innocents, or into free peoples living harmoniously in a diverse society."[14]

Finally, from the perspective of the U.S. government, the danger of Islamic terrorism is not just that it constitutes a "threat to our way of life" (of a free and open society) and principles but that it is equally a danger to civilization and to American global preeminence. In the American thinking, the threat posed by Al-Qaeda is aimed at supplanting Western values. In this thinking, Al-Qaeda singled out the United States for its position as the leading Western nation. The United States as the undeniable champion of Western and democratic values therefore has a responsibility to thwart the threat. In effect, it was imperative for the United States, as the leading Western nation, to assume global leadership in the struggle against terrorism. As President Bush put it: "[O]ur responsibility to history is clear: to answer these attacks and rid the world of evil."[15] Thus, while the U.S. would naturally assume the leadership of the war against terrorism, the threat posed by terrorism is not a threat to the U.S. alone. President Bush reiterated the American belief that the 2001 attacks were directed against the world as a whole. As he argued, "this is the world's fight. This is civilization's fight. This is the fight of all who believe in progress and pluralism, tolerance and freedom."[16]

As noted above, the U.S. identifies insurgencies, transnational criminal organizations, the global economic crisis, failed states and ungoverned spaces, climate change and energy competition, pandemic diseases and rapid technological change as major challenges to U.S. national security. Insurgents are considered dangerous because they "are attempting to destabilize vulnerable states in regions of strategic interest to the United States." The danger of transnational criminal organizations to the United States springs from their potential to penetrate and corrupt strategically vital markets. Their potential to "destabilizing certain states; and providing weapons, hard currency, and other support to insurgents and criminal factions" equally make them a source of threat.[17]

Failed states and ungoverned spaces worry the United States because they "offer terrorist and criminal organizations safe haven and possible access to weapons of mass destruction (WMD), and may cause or exacerbate starvation, genocide, and environmental degradation."[18] On the other hand, the current global economic crisis is considered a threat to the United States because it could accelerate and weaken U.S. security by fueling political turbulence. In some developing economies, a sustained slowdown could induce social and political instability, while in others it could erode support for market-oriented liberal democracy and create openings for authoritarianism.[19]

According to the National Intelligence Strategy, in view of the fact that "violent extremist groups—primarily Al-Qaeda and its regional affiliates, supporters, and the local terrorist cells it inspires—will continue to pose a grave threat to U.S. persons and interests at home and abroad," a core mission of the national intelligence community is to "understand, monitor, and disrupt extremist groups that actively plot to inflict grave damage or harm to the United States, its people, interests, and allies."

Threat perception: the factors and processes

As Christopher Lerory has correctly noted, "it is the perceptions of threat, rather than the true, statistical incidence of it, that drives public opinion."[20] Several factors shape national perceptions of threats. A state, group, or entity is likely to be regarded as a threat if it has had a past history of endangering other states, persons, or objects. In other words, threats may be deemed credible on the basis of past successful violent acts. Thus, nations or groups that had engaged in previous acts of illegitimate violence are likely to be viewed as more threatening than other states or entities. Threats may also be assessed on the basis of the presumed intentions of the adversary. If it is amassing armaments, for instance, its behavior may be read by its adversaries as a prelude to an attack or an attempt to prepare itself for launching a future aggression. This is well illustrated by the on-going nuclear stand-off with Iran. Despite the Iranian government's repeated denials that it was building nuclear weapons capability, the U.S. insists that Iran cannot be trusted. The U.S. government believes that Iran is developing nuclear weapons capability and has the intention of building them. Moreover, in U.S. thinking, if Iran does acquire such weapons, it has full intentions of using them.

A political culture could be considered threatening in and of itself. In effect, the contention here is that a national security threat may be inferred simply from the nature of the political culture. For example, the United States believes that a totalitarian society and extremist Islamic ideology in and of themselves constitute a danger to the U.S. Thus, viewed from this perspective, threats to the U.S. are inherent in certain political cultures—those that are antithetical to the U.S. political culture. Accordingly, since totalitarianism stands in contradistinction to the U.S. political culture of freedom and democracy, it is *ipso facto* a mortal danger to the United States. On the other hand, the democratic peace thesis is built on the premise that the democratic political culture abhors aggression against a fellow democratic state.

The nature of the political leadership—particularly the individual leaders' proclivities for evil—is considered a source of threat as well. For instance, certain political leaders are seen as evil tyrants who are predisposed to despicable behavior. Saddam Hussein was depicted by the Bush administration as an evil tyrant who possessed nuclear and biological weapons and would not hesitate to use them against the United States. Moreover, Hussein was alleged to have had links with the Al-Qaeda network. A majority of Americans viewed him as a threat to the United States. Successfully overthrowing Hussein after the U.S. invasion of Iraq in 2003 was thus deemed a victory in the American war against terrorism.

There may be an increased perception of vulnerability of attacks against soft targets during major events such as the Olympics Games and the Super

Bowl. The annual opening of the United Nations' General Assembly, which brings dozens of heads of states and governments to New York every September, is considered a very tempting target for violent terrorist attacks. As such, security is beefed up during the summit. Similarly, terrorists may perpetrate acts of violence during general elections as the public's attention tends to be more focused during the competition among politicians for votes. Perpetrators of violence could use the spectacle of elections to demonstrate the impotence of the contending politicians to provide public security. Their principal aim is likely to be directed at undermining the legitimacy of the political leaders.

Anniversaries of terrorist events or other calamities also tend to accentuate threat perceptions. This is so because they serve as a reminder of what had happened in the past and thus the possibility that the events in question may be repeated. Since the public may once again be reminded of the events, those who had perpetrated them may seize upon the reminder of the events as an opportunity to prove their power and invisibility.

It should be noted that a sense of vulnerability itself sharpens or increases threat perception. Government attempts to reduce vulnerability by stationing extra security, issuing high alerts, providing extra airport screening exercises may, instead of providing reassurance of security to citizens, increase their sense of an impending doom. Government's response to threats may either accentuate or decrease the public's fears about the threat. Government's response to threats can also create fear and a sense of foreboding about the threats when it raises threat levels. The terror alert itself may be even scarier than the potential violent actions of terrorists that the alert system is warning the public about. Governments may deliberately exacerbate fears about terrorism or other forms of threats for political reasons. Governments may deliberately exaggerate the capability of terrorists to project power and, at the same time, underestimate their own power to withstand the terrorist attacks. Governments may downplay threats to allay the public's concerns or as a signal in a shift in diplomatic relations. For instance, India is currently underplaying the Chinese threat. Threats may also be created where none actually exist. A perfect example was the Bush administration's false claims over weapons of mass destruction in Iraq to justify the attack on Iraq and the subsequent overthrow of Saddam Hussein. Threats may be used to justify domestic political repression and the suppression of dissent.

Threats may have actual geographical sources or they may lack geographical specificity. In the past, threats could be located at particular geographical locales. This is no longer the case. Particular kinds of threats may be associated with specific areas of the globe. For example, sea piracy has lately been largely confined to Southeast Asia and East Africa. Proximity to the source of threat increases the level and magnitude of threat perception. There may also be a predisposition to enmity between two states. That is why certain nations are viewed as threats by others. Threat perceptions affect both domestic and international politics. At the international level, it shapes how states interact with one another. At the domestic level, political candidates could structure an entire campaign on the supposed menace of their country's foes. During the Cold War, some U.S. politicians accused their competitors of being soft on communism. Specific factors such as national reputation, power, wealth, past history, and geographical locations shape threat perceptions.

New technologies may increase vulnerabilities and thus, creating new forms of threats, anxieties and perceptions of threats. The U.S. now has a Cyber Warfare Operations Center that was created in response to concerns over cyber threats. Other factors that may shape the dynamics of threat perception among the public include the accuracy of assessment of the threats, how the threat is sold to the public, the immediacy of the threat, its lethality, and how the threat assessment is translated into a useful policy response.

Predicting threats and preparing adequate responses to them have been made particularly difficult in the contemporary international system because of peculiar characteristics of modern global threats. Contemporary threats are multifaceted and multidimensional, cannot be isolated to any specific geographical region and no amount of preparedness can totally eliminate every form of threat. Other principal features of the current international context of security threats include the following: Threats are interrelated and inter-connected—a threat of one kind can accentuate or magnify other forms of threats; a small number of people can inflict enormous damage; the lethality of modern weaponry is unprecedented and this accentuates anxiety over threats; no nation, no matter its high defense expenditures, is immune from global security threats.

A United Nations report on global threats, challenges and change that was prepared for the UN Secretary-General in 2004 noted the specific features of contemporary global threats in the following words:

> [T]hreats recognize no national boundaries, are connected, and must be addressed at the global and regional as well the national levels. No State, no matter how powerful, can by its own efforts alone make itself invulnerable to today's threats. And it cannot be assumed that every State will always be able, or willing, to meet its responsibility to protect its own peoples and not harm its neighbors.[21]

The report went on to define a threat to international security as "any event or process that leads to large-scale death or lessening of life chances and undermines States as the basic unit of the international system." It contends that the contemporary international system faces "six clusters of threats." These are as follows:

1   Economic and social threats, including poverty, infectious diseases, and environmental degradation.
2   Inter-state conflict.
3   Internal conflict, including civil war, genocide, and other large-scale atrocities.

4   Nuclear radiological, chemical, and biological weapons.
5   Terrorism.
6   Transnational organized crime.

Noting the mutual vulnerability of all states, the report drew attention to how poor states can affect the security and welfare of more powerful and richer states. As it argued, "the security of the most wealthy State can be held hostage to the ability of the poorest State to contain an emerging disease."[22]

U.S. perceptions of national security threats in West Africa

As noted earlier, the 2009 National Intelligence Strategy of the United States of America lists violent extremist groups, insurgencies, transnational organized criminal organizations, failed states and ungoverned spaces, pandemic diseases, climate change and energy competition, and rapid technological change as the principal global concerns and challenges to U.S. national security. Similarly, the 2008 U.S. National Defense Strategy listed additional security threats to the United States to include hostile states armed with weapons of mass destruction, rising regional powers, space and cyber threats, and the inability of states to police themselves effectively. West Africa seems to harbor many of these security concerns of the United States. The sub-region has had many failed states: Liberia, Sierra Leone, Chad, etc. Guinea Bissau has virtually been transformed into a narco-state in the mold of some Latin American states. Nigeria, the largest and most powerful state in West Africa, is on the verge of state failure. It shares many of the characteristics of failed states: Government being unable to provide for the welfare and security of its citizens; the collapse of public institutions and infrastructure such as schools, hospitals, roads, electricity, and water supply. As is typically characteristic of failed states, corruption is rife in Nigeria, there is public disdain for officials and institutions of governance and governments seem unconcerned about the poverty and general plight of the populace. Massive revenues from oil have papered over the huge cracks in the fabric of the nation's governance architecture but the fundamental inability of the state in Nigeria to function efficiently and effectively is an open secret. While the failed states of West Africa are not likely to "offer terrorist and criminal organizations ... weapons of mass destruction," they have contributed to political instabilities, mass starvation, drug and human trafficking, and huge refugee flows.

The West African sub-region has thousands of square miles of ungoverned, mal-governed, and under-governed spaces. Much of Sahel (the region of West Africa between the Sahara desert and the savanna vegetation zones) is a vast area of land that is not effectively controlled by any state in West Africa. As the U.S. fears, such a place could offer safe haven to extremist groups to engage in terrorist training and characteristics. The fact that states in the sub-region have been unable to effectively police their borders gives a concrete reality to U.S. concerns about ungoverned, misgoverned, under-governed, and ungoverned spaces in West Africa.

The United States is also concerned about political instability as a breeding ground for terrorism. As the National Strategy to Combat Terrorism has noted, "spoilers can take advantage of instability to create conditions terrorists can exploit."[23] West Africa has been a hotbed of political instabilities for a long time. Civil wars have been fought in Nigeria, Chad, Liberia, Ivory Coast, Sierra Leone, etc. In addition, West Africa has had more military coups than any other sub-region in Africa. The sub-region is just emerging from the throes of decades of military dictatorships. In addition to civil wars and military interventions in politics, pangs of political instabilities that West Africa has suffered from have included ethnic and communal violence and religious crisis.

Francis Langumba Leili has drawn a linkage between political instabilities in West Africa and the proliferation of small arms and light arms. As he noted:

> West Africa has for many years been the most unstable subregion on the continent. Since 1960, of the 15 member states that make up the Economic Community of West African States (ECOWAS), most have been through several military coups, 37 of which were successful. One causative factor for such unprecedented insurrection is the movement of small arms and light weapons (SALW) throughout the sub-region. The uncontrolled movement of SALW has exacerbated conflicts and brought destruction, untold hardship, poverty and underdevelopment.[24]

As a result of incessant political turmoil and violence, the West African sub-region is awash in small arms and light weapons. Lisa Misol, testifying before the U.S. Congress on the dangers of small arms proliferation in West Africa argued as follows:

> The conflict-ridden West African sub-region is a showcase of uncontrolled SALW proliferation. Vast quantities of arms have flooded the region despite their rampant misuse by state and non-state actors alike. The widespread availability of small arms to abusive actors poses a threat of unprecedented magnitude to West Africa, far greater than that of HIV/AIDS in terms of its socio-economic and human consequences. Because of this proliferation, the fabric of the sub-region itself is rapidly changing, and West Africa is moving toward self-destruction.[25]

Baffour Dokyi Amoa has argued that the issue of small arms in Africa "is a matter of life and death. It is not an exaggeration to say that small arms have contributed to the political disintegration of many African countries. The effects of the proliferation of small arms are felt by many Africans."[26] Similarly, Michael Fleshman contended that small arms "are filling African graves in ever-increasing numbers—from the killing fields of Burundi and the Democratic Republic of Congo to the streets of Lagos and Johannesburg."[27] Rachel Stohl has drawn attention of the possibility that terrorists could take advantage of West Africa's porous borders and the large supply of small arms to wreak terrorist violence on innocent people. As she pointed out:

> Controlling the flow of small arms is an integral part of the efforts underway to fight terrorism. Terrorist networks will continue to thrive if the root causes of their actions are not addressed, and if the flow of the tools of their trade are not hindered. From disarming ex-combatants and destroying surplus stockpiles of weapons to prevent their theft or diversion, to maintaining strict criteria for small arms exports and incorporating strict end-use monitoring, controlling the proliferation of small arms is essential to prevent these deadliest of weapons from ending up in the hand of terrorists. The porous borders in West Africa have allowed the Algerian terrorist group Salafist Group for Call and Combat (GSPC) to operate within the region. While West Africa is not the origin of well established terrorist networks, the stockpiles of small arms available in the region are attractive to terrorist groups hunting for cheap, easily available weapons to conduct their activities.[28]

Since the September 11, 2001 terrorist attacks on the United States by members of the Al-Qaeda radical Islamic organization, the U.S. has feared that Muslims, especially young Muslims, would be amenable to the radical version of Islam that Al-Qaeda was articulating. Given this perspective, the United States is bound to be concerned about West Africa. The sub-region has many Muslims some of whom have clearly been radicalized. While there is no direct evidence that violent local Muslim organizations in West Africa have linkages with Osama bin Laden's Al-Qaeda, nevertheless, violent Islamic organizations such as Boko Haram in Nigeria may have patterned themselves after Al-Qaeda in terms of their aspirations and operational structures.

U.S. dependence on imported oil is escalating, and West Africa is increasingly becoming an important producer of crude oil. Although West African oil is important to U.S. national security, as it seeks to cultivate alternative suppliers (in place of relying on Middle Eastern oil), West African oil is not without its problems. Fueled by genuine grievances, sheer criminality, and political thuggery, oil-producing zones of West Africa such as the Niger Delta are in open rebellions against the state and multinational oil corporations. The Nigerian government loses billions of dollars in revenues as a result of sabotage of oil facilities, kidnapping, oil bunkering, and violence against oil workers. Francis Langumba Keili painted a very vivid picture of the crisis in the Niger Delta. As he pointed out:

> In Nigeria, the country's oil-rich Delta State has seen conflict since 2003 involving well-armed militia groups motivated by economic interest in stolen crude oil. These groups use a range of sophisticated weapons such as semi-and fully automatic rifles, alongside more traditional weapons to carry out deadly and paralyzing attacks on oil and gas installations. They have killed scores of security officials, damaged oil facilities and

infrastructure, and shut down oil production. They have also taken foreign oil workers hostage. Hundreds of people have been killed in the
violence which has also resulted in the displacement of thousands and the
destruction of hundreds of properties.[29]

Insurgencies and criminal activities in petroleum-producing areas threaten the
disruption of oil and other resources produced in the region. In the case of
Nigeria, the federal government recently announced an amnesty program for
militants to surrender their weapons in return for education, job training, and
jobs. Some top leaders of the Niger Delta militant groups along with their followers have since surrendered their weapons but it remains to be seen if this
will provide a lasting solution to the crisis. Skepticism that the amnesty would
work springs from several sources. First, there are three categories of militants
in the Niger Delta. The first category is made up of those genuinely concerned about the inequity in the distribution of the proceeds from oil and the
environmental devastation associated with petroleum prospecting, production,
and distribution. Category two consists of young men recruited as political
thugs by rival political gangs and groups and the third category is made up of
those who capitalize on the real grievances of the oil-producing communities
to engage in brigandage and sheer criminality. It is clear that the amnesty
program has not gone far enough to address many of the issues that the first
set of militants is raising. Militants in this first category are not going to accept
the amnesty program. For those in the third category, it is not clear how the
monetary inducements of the amnesty program would outweigh the millions
of dollars in the illegal sale of oil. Moreover, many of these young men have top
government officials who serve as their godfathers. Since these are powerful
but shadowy figures, the amnesty as it stands would not serve their interests.

Compounding the problem of restlessness of the oil-producing communities
is the fact that the United States is in competition with China for African oil
and other natural resources. Unlike the United States, China does not publicly excoriate its African crude oil suppliers for their human rights abuses. In
addition, China's investments in natural resource extraction are usually accom-
panied by substantial economic aid for infrastructural development. This is
bound to be a strong appeal to the African suppliers.

The National Strategy for Combating Terrorism has argued that terrorism
springs from four sources: Political alienation; grievances that can be blamed
on others; subcultures of conspiracy and misinformation; and an ideology
that justifies murder. The first of these, political alienation, is rampart in West
Africa. The National Strategy for Combating Terrorism has pointed out that

transnational terrorists are recruited from populations with no voice in
their own governments and see no legitimate way to promote change
in their own country. Without a stake in the existing order, they are vulnerable to manipulation by those who advocate a perverse political vision
based on violence and destruction.[30]

Many people, particularly young men and women of the sub-region, have been alienated from their governments. They do not feel any attachment to states that fail to educate them and provide jobs and skills-training programs. They are also alienated from states that are unconcerned about their economic and social plights. Moreover, citizens know that when they try to participate in self-governance through the electoral process, their votes do not count as victory in political competition is a function of the ability of politicians to rig elections.

Threats posed by West Africa to U.S. economic interests are largely in the form of internet fraud. Fraudulent West Africans (nicknamed 419ers after Section 419 of the Nigerian Penal Code) would send letters or email to unsuspecting people in the United States or elsewhere in the economically developed countries claiming that they had stolen large sums of money and would like to deposit the money in the potential victim's bank account. For his trouble, the letter would promise to give the recipient up to 30 percent of the sum. The fraudster would then ask the recipient to send him some money that he would use to bribe top government officials to release the large sum of money.

Conclusion

Given its power, wealth, and global reach, the United States faces numerous security threats and challenges. Among these, as seen by the United States, are violent transnational extremist groups, hostile states armed with weapons of mass destruction, the proliferation of weapons of mass destruction, pandemic diseases, inability of states to police their borders effectively, competition for resources, transnational criminal organizations, and under-governed, misgoverned, and ungoverned spaces. As shown above, many of these factors are present in West Africa. The United States has recognized the presence of these destabilizing factors as threats to its national security interests. It has been trying to counter these threats through military cooperation agreements with West African governments; support for democracy and electoral reforms; training on civil–military relations for West African soldiers (under the Trans-Saharan Security Symposium). Other policy instruments that have been designed by the U.S. in response to its perceived security threats in West Africa are public sector reforms to reduce the scope and magnitude of corruption, and judicial reforms to help institutionalize the rule of law.

While the U.S. intelligence community has identified numerous security challenges to U.S. security interests in West Africa, it is not clear that the American public at large is persuaded of the urgency or the magnitude of the threats. The perception gap of security threats in West Africa between the attentive elites and the masses has several implications. First, U.S. policy makers do not have a large pool of financial resources with which to respond to the security threats. Second, many of the identified security threats in West Africa constitute a potential danger first and foremost to West Africans themselves, and only an indirect threat to the United States. In other words, it is West Africans themselves who are the primary victims of the threats in the region.

Any harm to the U.S. in the region is merely an ancillary harm to the greater danger to West Africans themselves.

The U.S. does not have a West African Saddam Hussein through which it could personify the evil and dangers emanating from West Africa. Without such a person and in view of the fact that the dangers posed by the security threats are not imminent, it is difficult to mobilize the American public behind U.S. security options in West Africa.

American financial commitments to combating threats to its security interests do not match the magnitude of the professed threats. For instance, the United States has spent tens of billions of dollars on Afghanistan but only a few hundred million dollars in all of West Africa. This little spending on what the U.S. deems to be major security issues in the region raises doubts on whether these are real threats after all.

Notes

1 Karlyn Bowman, "U.S. Public Opinion and the Terrorist Threat," in *One Issue, Two Voices* (Washington, D.C./Ottawa: Woodrow Wilson International Center for Scholars and the Canada Institute, 2005), p. 2.
2 Frank Graves, "The Shifting Public Outlook on Risk and Security," in *One Issue, Two Voices*, op. cit., p. 11.
3 The National Intelligence Strategy of the United States of America (Washington, D.C.: Office of the Director of National Intelligence), p. 3.
4 Ibid.
5 Ibid.
6 Ibid.
7 National Strategy for Combating Terrorism (Washington, D.C., September 2006), p. 1.
8 The National Intelligence Strategy, op. cit., p. 3.
9 National Strategy for Combating Terrorism, op. cit., p. 5.
10 See President George W. Bush's Speech to a Joint Session of Congress, September 20, 2001.
11 President Barack Obama's Speech in Cairo, June 4, 2009.
12 National Strategy for Combating Terrorism, op. cit., p. 6.
13 Ibid., p. 5.
14 National Strategy for Combating Terrorism, op. cit, p. 7.
15 See President George W. Bush's speech at the National Cathedral, Washington, D.C., September 14, 2001.
16 President George W. Bush's Speech to the U.S. Congress, September 20, 2001.
17 The National Intelligence Strategy of the United States, op. cit., p. 4.
18 Ibid., p. 4.
19 Ibid.
20 Christopher J. Lerory, "Threat Perceptions in the United States and Canada: Assessing the Public's Attitudes toward Security and Risk in North America," *One Issue, Two Voices: Issue Four* (Washington, D.C./Ottawa: Woodrow Wilson International Center for Scholars and Canada Institute, 2005), p. 1.
21 *A More Secure World: Our Shared Responsibility: Report of the Secretary-General's High-Level Panel Report on Threats, Challenges and Change* (New York: United Nations, 2004), p. 1.
22 *A More Secure World*, op. cit., p. 19.
23 National Strategy for Combating Terrorism, op. cit., p. 16.

24 Francis Langumba Keili, "Small Arms and Light Weapons Transfer in West Africa: A Stock-taking," *Disarmament Forum*, No. 4, 2008, p. 3.
25 See Testimony of Lisa Misol, "Small Arms and Conflict in West Africa," U.S. Congressional Human Rights Caucus, May 20, 2004.
26 Baffour Dokyi Amoa, "Small Arms and Conflict in Africa," *The Patriotic Vanguard*, September 26, 2006.
27 Michael Fleshman, "Counting the Costs of Gun Violence," *Africa Recovery*, Vol. 15, No. 4, December 2001, p. 1.
28 See Rachel Stohl's testimony, "The Legacy of Illicit Small Arms: Devastation in West Africa," before the U.S. Congressional Human Rights Caucus: Briefing on Small Arms in West Africa, May 20, 2004.
29 Francis Langumba Keili, "Small Arms and Light Weapons," op. cit., p. 9.
30 National Strategy for Combating Terrorism, op. cit., p. 9.

4 The crisis in Nigeria's Niger Delta region

Implications for the U.S. war on terror

Idowu Okheren Ejere

Introduction

The overwhelming effect of the September 11, 2001 attack on the World Trade Center (WTC) invoked renewed interest on the concept and perception of security. Political analysts, academics, policy makers, and even ordinary citizens have begun to conceptualize security in more than military or other conventional terms. With the globalization of the trade in arms and the expansion of the scope of what constitutes "threat" or "insecurity," it is now widely accepted that a myriad of factors and forces can precipitate instability, insecurity, extremism, violence, and conflict.

Historical evidence shows that threat can emerge from regions that have suffered neglect, marginalization, and poverty over time and that the build up of animosity can result into full blown conflicts that may take several forms including guerrilla warfare. Increasingly, discourses on security are beginning to emphasize human and social dimensions that focus on living standards, access to food, health care and infrastructure, public policies, quality of leadership, and resource management. As can be gleaned in the case of Nigeria's Niger Delta region, where there is clearly a disconnect between resource endowment and human development, conflicts can emerge from the absence of basic human needs, bad governance, bad leadership, illiberal democratic environments, and the mismanagement of resources and opportunities. Though the revenue accruing from oil over a 35-year period has led to an increase in government expenditure, the poor management of available resources has precipitated a decline in overall productivity, thereby leaving the standard of living no better today than it was in the oil boom years. The net result is gross income inequalities, mass poverty, unemployment, political instability, urban decay, infrastructural dilapidation, deindustrialisation, corruption, economic and financial crimes, ethnic divisions and conflicts. Embedded in these consequences of poor management and leadership is insecurity, instability, uncertainty, and violence.

Nigeria became the world's most oil dependent country in 2000, when its earnings accruing from crude oil export reached 99.6 percent of its total export earnings. Yet the Niger Delta region, whose abundant endowment of oil resources contributes about 40 percent to Nigeria's gross domestic product (GDP) and accounts for more than 80 percent of government earnings, records the lowest human development index in the country. The combination of oil wealth in the midst of extreme poverty and deprivation in the Niger Delta region has led to a crisis of social unrest characterized by vandalization of foreign and national oil exploration facilities and kidnap and abductions of foreign and indigenous oil workers (for ransoms) by restive youths fighting against oppression and for the control of their resource wealth. This has further exacerbated the issue of security in the region, which hitherto has been attributed largely to inter- and intra-ethnic conflicts.

Historical neglect and the failure of public policies in the Niger Delta region have compelled the youth in the region to take up arms against transnational oil corporations (TNOCs) engaged in oil exploration in the region as well as federal government security operatives and the armed forces stationed in the region. The devastating effects of the guerrilla warfare raging against the Nigerian government and TNOCs have led to oil spillages, thereby leading to the loss of billions of dollars in foreign exchange earnings, devastation of the environment including loss of farmlands and water systems in a region that is Nigeria's food basket where the predominant sources of livelihoods are farming, fishing, and hunting. Forced curfews have also led to the inability of people to move about, destroyed social life, ruined small businesses, and constrained traditional patterns of free associations in society. The contradictions in the Niger Delta region have affected oil production and exploration, foreign exchange earnings, policy making and governance processes, tourism and development assistance, as well as food production causing a crisis of human insecurity in the region that threatens to tear the fabric that holds the Nigerian entity together as one whilst destroying the image of the country in the global arena. And though there have been numerous policy responses to the Niger Delta issue since the 1970s, the region remains in the news largely for issues of violence, kidnappings, ineffective policies and oil wealth mismanagement, community unrest, environmental degradation, poverty, oil bunkering, and, more recently, terrorism. Ironically, terrorist acts have now spread beyond the Niger Delta to the northern parts of the country.

The human deprivation, environmental degradation, and insecurity in the Niger Delta cannot be fully captured except when one visits the creeks to see the communities that have been devastated by years of crude oil exploration without recourse to human or environmental safety; villages razed to the ground either by explosions caused by leaking pipelines and crude oil spillages or by avenging government-backed armed forces. One also needs to see the extent of damage wrought on the TOCs and the Nigerian government and people by the various Niger Delta militia groups. The truth is that to understand the issues at stake in the region one must not neglect the perspectives of the Nigerian government and the TNOCs, on the one hand, and the perspectives of the Niger Delta people, the militant groups, and that of other Nigerian citizens, on the other. Visiting the creeks, one is confronted by indescribable environmental degradation caused by gas flaring, oil spillages, and years of deliberate neglect. Aside the cities of Port Harcourt and Calabar, there have been minimal changes in the region over the last 50 years. There are a few new architectural and physical innovations but no fundamental structural changes to the processes and patterns of production, exchange, and consumption. The quality of life in general has continued to deteriorate in spite of regime, personality, and leadership changes. To be sure, a few elites with linkages to power and oil have become fairly affluent and have used the resources accumulated to influence the political processes to the detriment of the people, the environment, and the process of sustainable growth and development. Few people in the region have access to clean water, electricity, and educational and health facilities are lacking. The people whose predominant occupation are farming, fishing, and hunting have lost their sources of livelihood as a result of seizure of lands by government, and oil spillage on farms and rivers by TNOCs and militant activities. A 2005 survey of human conditions in the Niger Delta carried out by the United Nations (UN) showed that many Niger Delta states were in neglect and life expectancy in the region was 52.7 years.

The Niger Delta has become an economic ticking bomb where rusty pipes run through villages, where in some villages there is little difference between night and day as their days have been darkened by noxious emissions caused by gas flaring and nights brightened by unending gas flares. Rapid soil depletion and loss of land caused by oil spillages have ensured that farming activities generate low productivity. Infrastructural development is lacking, except in state capitals where there are a few tarred roads, and because of the swamps and rivers the major means of transportation, which include motorcycles, speed boats and canoes, are expensive. According to a scientific document published by the Niger Delta Environmental Survey (NDES), "very little of the large windfall from the sale of oil has trickled to the aborigines, poverty is prevalent in the region and many people have been forced to migrate to other parts of the country to become part of the urban poor."[1]

The Federal Government of Nigeria has over the years set up various agencies to tackle the insistent problems of poverty, conflict, and development in the Niger Delta region. These agencies have to date failed to make any significant change in the region. The Niger Delta Board (NDB), which was set up in 1961 following the findings of the Wilkins Commission, failed to ensure even distribution of the region's wealth among the despairing ethnic groups. The inefficiency of the NDB led to the creation of the Niger Delta Rural Development Authority (NDRDA).[2]

In 1992, the Oil and Mineral Areas Development Commission (OMPADEC), was established to alleviate poverty and develop the oil producing states, but it failed woefully, and in 2000 was replaced with the Niger Delta Development Commission (NDDC). Ten years after its establishment, the NDDC is yet to make any remarkable socio-economic impact that will create jobs, alleviate poverty, and gear the region towards sustainable development (which is the crux of the region's problem), largely because it can only make tokenistic contributions to addressing the deep-seated anger, suspicion, chronic poverty, and marginalization in the Niger Delta Region.

The consequence has been the rise of militant groups who share the same animosity against the federal government and the TNOCs and non-oil producing states, especially those of Northern Nigeria. The crisis, which has been simmering for years, threatens to blow into a full-scale war, with militia groups comprising youths from different ethnic groups in the region launching several attacks against the federal government and TNOC oil exploration facilities, as well as driving their point home by kidnapping foreign oil workers including humanitarian workers in the region. Such disruptions have immediate effects on government revenues, as exploration activities are constrained, and exports decline, leading to precipitous fall in oil revenue, which accounts for 80 percent of government earnings. This has led to the rise in the cost of oil within the country causing scarcity of fuel and the relocation of foreign staff of TNOCs to safer cities with many abandoning their jobs for safety reasons. As the most visible TNOCs in the region, Shell and Chevron have been on the receiving end of most of the vandalization, resulting in the shutting down of most flow stations. Given the wide-spread impact and activities of militants in the region, and given the increasing rate at which youth were joining the militant groups, the Federal Government of Nigeria initially adopted a military approach to resolving the problem, until the declaration of the oil war by the Niger Delta People's Volunteer Force in 2009, when it became apparent that the way forward might be through dialogue. Following the recommendations of the Ledum Mittee-led Niger Delta Technical Committee, the government granted amnesty to militant groups that surrendered under the amnesty agreement.

Against this backdrop, the focus of this chapter is to examine the nature and dynamics of the crisis in Nigeria's Niger Delta region, and its implications for the U.S. war on terrorism. This chapter explores two interrelated questions: (1) what are the implications of the Niger Delta crisis for Nigeria's national security? And (2) how does the Niger Delta crisis affect the U.S. war on terror?

The Niger Delta region: a background

The Niger Delta region is located in the South-South area of Nigeria with the land and water area spanning over 20,000 kilometers, earning it the position of the world's third-largest delta. The region is divided into four ecological zones, namely: Freshwater zone, mangrove swamp zone, low rainforest zone, and coastal inland zone—2,370 kilometers consist of river creeks and estuaries, 8,600 kilometers are covered by stagnant swaps, while mangrove swamps extends over 1,900 kilometers. With a highly diverse environment, supportive of different species of terrestrial and aquatic flora and fauna, as well as human life, the region is the most ecologically sensitive region in Nigeria.[3] Historically, the region consisted of Edo, Delta, Akwa-Ibom, Rivers, Cross River, and Bayelsa states until 2000, when President Olusegun Obasanjo's administration

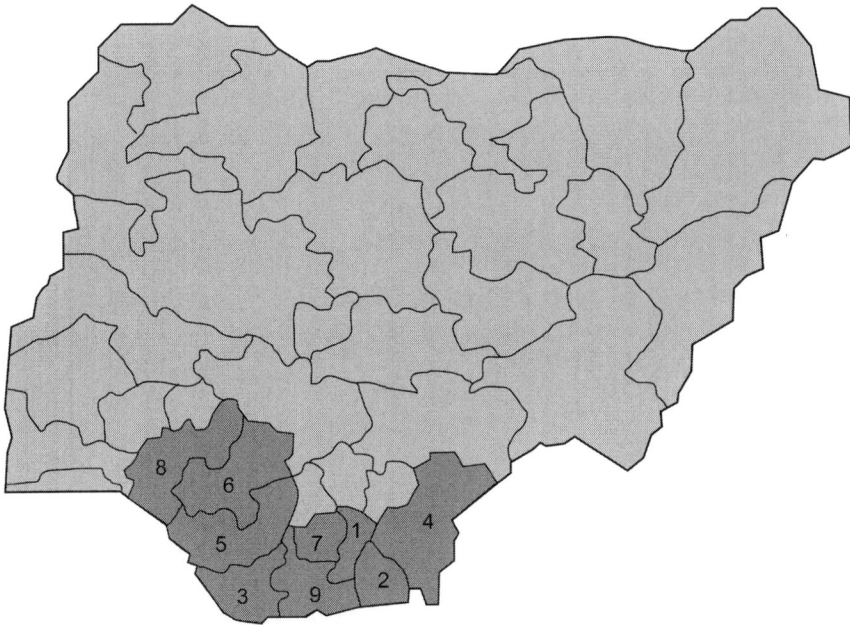

Figure 4.1 The map of Nigeria showing the states in the Niger Delta region: (1)Abia,
(2) Akwa Ibom, (3) Bayelsa, (4) Cross River, (5) Delta, (6) Edo, (7) Imo, (8)
Ondo, and (9) Rivers
Source: http://upload.wikimedia.org

added Abia, Imo, and Ondo states bringing the number of the Niger Delta
states to nine.

The Niger Delta is a heterogeneous, multicultural, ethnically diverse region;
it makes up 7.5 percent of Nigeria's total landmass, and is home to an estimated
31 million people from 41 different ethnic groups, more than 23 percent of
Nigeria's total population.[4] The predominant ethnic groups in the region are
the Ikales, Ilajes, Binis, Urhobos, Itsekiris, Itsokos, Egbema, Ogba, Ekpeyes,
Itshans, Ndoni, Degema, Growhia, Okpo, Ibibios, Efiks, and Ohajis, among
others, and 75 percent of them live in rural areas and their major economic
activities are fishing, farming, and hunting. The region is endowed with oil and
gas and is one of the highly productive oil exporting regions in the world.[5]
The bowels of the Niger Delta yield two million barrels of crude oil per day
with the Delta, Bayelsa, and Rivers states alone accounting for 75 percent of
Nigeria's total oil production and 50 percent of federal government revenues.[6]

The crisis in the Niger Delta predates the Nigerian post-colonial state and
it has always been based on resource control, though the emergence of militant groups has added a new dimension to the crisis. It is dominantly a civil
agitation against the political economy of oil and the neglect of the region.
The region has been a source of contestation for resources since the sixteenth
century when it served as an outlet for the slave trade. The struggles have in

general been responses to the exploitation, oppression, and marginalization of the region in the socio-economic and political chessboard of Nigeria. Whether it was led by King Jaja of Opobo, Ovonramwen Nogbasi of the Benin Empire, Isaac Adaka Boro of the Ijaw Nation, Ken Saro Wiwa of the Movement for the Survival of Ogoni Peoples (MOSOP), or the numerous young militants that dot the region, the issues have always been the same: Resource control, sustainable development, environmental protections, local input into the pattern of development, and better living conditions.

The region later became a major producer of palm oil, which was as important back then as oil is today, and conflict arose out of struggle for the control of palm oil fields. The struggle for the emancipation of the people of the Niger Delta in contemporary times started in 1951, when the National Convention of Nigerian Citizens (NCNC) tried to break away from Nigeria to join Cameroon, due to a perception of not belonging to eastern Nigeria. The people felt that they were overlooked by the federal government because they did not belong to any of the three major ethnic groups. The second phase of the Niger Delta crisis was just before the Nigerian Civil War when a Nigerian student activist, Isaac Adaka Boro, declared an independent Niger Delta region during the first military regime in 1966. The third phase of the crisis began in 1993, when the military regime of General Sani Abacha executed playwright and human rights activist Ken Saro-Wiwa and eight other activists following the killing of eight Ogoni chiefs in the complex and complicated struggle for the emancipation of the region. The fourth phase of the crisis began in 1999 under the democratic dispensation of the former President Olusegun Obasanjo. The current phase, the fifth, started with the amnesty program of the late Umaru Musa Yar'Adua administration, which was focused on finding a peaceful way out of the violence in the region.

As indicated earlier, with the discovery of oil in the region, the people have suffered displacement, environmental degradation, deprivation, and human rights abuses that have stirred up deep-seated resentment against the federal government and the TNOCs engaged in oil exploration and exploitation in the region. The major grouse of the people is that despite the revenue that their oil wealth provides for the federal government and the rest of the country they live in poverty and lack basic infrastructure, at least when compared with non-oil producing areas, especially the new Federal Capital Territory of Abuja. It is on record that whenever youth from the region have cause to visit the Federal Capital city of Abuja, they often return to the region feeling alienated, angry, and convinced that there was too much inequality in the ownership and control of oil resources. They also complain that they receive no compensation for the environmental degradation caused by the exploration and exploitation of their resources and that they are marginalized and oppressed by the federal government. Before independence, the derivation formula for natural resources in Nigeria was 100 percent revenue control by the region where the resource is derived. However, under the 1963 Constitution it was reduced to 50 percent allocation to the region with 30 percent and 20 percent going to other regions and the federal government respectively. Later the derivation formula was reduced to 13 percent as captured in the 1999 Constitution of the Federal Republic of Nigeria. In spite of this constitutionally defined allocation, the federal government still exercised full control over oil resources and revenues and presided over the disbursements. Since the return to civilian rule in 1999 the people have been agitating for an increase in the revenue allocation formula under the struggle generally tagged "resource control."

Military forces have been stationed in the region for over 15 years to safeguard oil production facilities and foreign oil workers. These government forces have not failed to be high-handed in the execution of their duties and there have been incidences and reports of rapes and extrajudicial killings. Villages and towns like Odi have been completely razed to the ground by military men acting on instructions from the federal government. The worst hits are women and children under the age of five whose mortality rate is highest. The testimonies made before the Oputa Panel in 2000 exposed the extent of the horror and violence that the people endured under the Rivers State Security Task Force and associated bodies where thousands of ordinary people were assaulted, raped, maimed, and killed.

Framing the crisis in the Niger Delta

Several theoretical perspectives have been used to describe the conflict in the Niger Delta. Some analysts see the disconnection between the natural resource wealth of the Niger Delta and the prevalent situation of poverty and strife in terms of the *resource curse*. The idea that natural resources might be more of a curse than a blessing as espoused by Auty (1993) suggests that "natural resources might be a handicap to development rather than a blessing, because most resource rich countries tend to have lower economic growth."[7] Indeed, there is a profound discrepancy between the Niger Delta oil wealth and the human development level of the region. And at the heart of this discrepancy is the persistent failure of government policies, mismanagement, and corruption. The federal government has failed to ensure the revenue accruing from the exploitation and sale of oil is used to develop not only the region it is derived from but the entire country.

Mohdavy (1970) contends that "oil producing states are typical *rentier states*."[8] These are countries that depend on the substantial amounts of revenue they receive from Transnational Corporations (TNOCs) for the exploration and exploitation of their natural resources.[9] The primary aim of rentier policy is to reduce taxation but increase state spending to foster development especially in terms of infrastructure and technology. In other words, the rentier state depends less on taxation and other domestic activities to generate revenue or foreign exchange as it collects huge rents from foreign interests with little or no inputs into the process. However, resource rents tend to bring about corruption because there is no transparency in the management of revenues accruing from economic rents, and the state may not be accountable to the people because they pay little or no tax. The consequence is that it affects the long-term economic growth of the rentier state and breeds dissatisfaction that may lead to conflict. In many instances, rentier states are despotic and tend to promote underdevelopment for the majority and affluence for the few.

Evidences from Africa and Latin America show that countries with little or no natural resources have a lower propensity for conflict than countries that are richly endowed with natural resources. Whereas countries with an abundant endowment of natural resources face a 0.5 percent probability of conflict, countries with natural resources face a 26 percent probability of civil conflict out of 23 percent.[10] Nigeria's rentier economy makes it vulnerable to conflicts arising over resource control and revenue allocation. Folarin (2008) agrees that resource abundance may cause conflict when there is lack of diversification of the economy, especially if the resource is readily available and can be sold without processing.[11] Hence there may be no incentive to invest in manufacturing or infrastructural development.

Sala-I-Martin (2004) noted in an IMF survey that "no where are all the pathologies associated with oil as clearly manifest as in Nigeria."[12] The Nigerian Civil War (Biafran War of secession), Africa's biggest civil war, in the late 1960s, which led to about one million deaths, was in part an attempt by the eastern, predominantly Igbo, region to gain control over oil resources.[13] The mismanagement of the windfall from the sale of oil during the oil boom years contributed to poor growth and staggered development outcomes as oil became the single most important source of foreign earnings for Nigeria while other sectors were abandoned.[14] For the dominant elites, the oil boom was an opportunity for primitive accumulation and the pursuit of luxury. It was thus easy to ignore agriculture, initiate a dependent food policy, and abandon the processes of nation-building. The curse and greed element of the Niger Delta's and Nigeria's resource endowment is further exacerbated by the process of bad governance, largely incompetent leadership, misplaced priorities, institutional decay, and policy dislocations. From 1970 upwards, Nigeria's political elites put in place authoritarian structures and policies to enable them to centralize control of strategic resources including oil.[15] The rent-seeking behavior of the government banished the majority of ordinary Nigerian citizens from policy making and revenue allocation processes, especially the minorities. These self-serving and ambiguous strategies are not driven by the needs of the people and the consequence has been social unrest and agitations in the Niger Delta and elsewhere.

According to Ihonvbere (2000a), "the Nigerian state continues to be directly responsible for reproducing the country's deepening socio-economic and political contradictions because neither the custodians of state power nor public institutions have adjusted to new pro-people strategies of growth and sustainable development."[16] Ihonvbere is of the view that the constitution of the state and accumulative patterns of the custodians of state power have combined to precipitate a preference for lucrative but non-productive activities at the expense of deploying oil rents to the construction of institutions and structures that promote growth and development. It is this combination of policy failure, insensitivity, and oppression that has precipitated youth reaction in the Niger Delta region.

Reaction from the youths

Civil groups in the Niger Delta region have been suppressed by authoritarian civil leaderships and military dictatorships, but the global wave of democracy has allowed these groups to re-emerge as important actors in governance and the struggle to privilege democracy. In the Niger Delta, these actors are the youths. The development of Nigeria from pre-colonial to post-colonial periods has been attributed to the role played by the youths. The Nigerian youths, who fall within the ages of 18 and 35, are characteristically daring, vibrant, and active with useful energies and they constitute the most volatile segment of society who are most threatened by the state of affairs in the country.[17] From political machinations and marginalization to unemployment and rising school fees, the youths are the most affected in the socio-economic and political downturn of the country. General unemployment, lack of a viable youth development policy and the economic downturn have thrown the youth into anti-social vices. Thus, they have become agents of thuggery, political intimidation, armed robbery, religious and ethnic conflicts.

The specter of youth restiveness in the Niger Delta has grown in proportion in the last 15 to 20 years. Armed youth insurgency first occurred in the Niger Delta in 1966, but it was crushed by the military. From 1997 to date, it has remained persistent and has grown daily with more youth groups joining their peers in the creeks and resorting to violence and the use of arms. The militarization of the conflict followed the emergence of youth movements as a vanguard for the struggle for resource control in the 1990s.

The first contemporary activist group, Movement for the Survival of Ogoni People (MOSOP) led by Ken Saro Wiwa, produced a militant faction called the National Youth Council of Ogoni People (NYCOP). The youth groups appropriated arms and armed confrontations as the main instrument of struggle, when dialogue failed, especially after the flat rejection of the Ogoni Bill of Rights by the federal government. This has led to the emergence of militias, pirates, and armed gangs that operate from different hideouts in the swampy waterways and creeks. After MOSOP came several groups such as the Ijaw Youth Council and several declarations such as the Ogbia Declaration, the Oron Bill of Rights, the Kiama Declaration, the Itsekiri Bill of Rights all aimed at articulating the realities, and yearnings of the peoples, of the Niger Delta. Unfortunately, these were also ignored.

The Niger Delta Youth, professionals, and intellectuals tried to follow a trend set by Ken Saro Wiwa by internationalizing their predicaments and demands through the Commonwealth of Nations, the United Nations, and international non-governmental organizations in Europe and North America. These efforts also yielded nothing, as evidenced by the fact that the Nigerian government ignored them. It was the failure of all overtures to the federal government, the lack of new policy initiatives towards the region, growing political and leadership insensitivity to the pains of the ordinary Niger Deltans, that compelled the youth of the region to take up arms against a state they perceive as corrupt, insensitive, oppressive, and lacking in compassion towards their plight. Foremost among the youth militant groups are the Movement for the Emancipation of the Niger Delta (MEND) and the Niger Delta People's Volunteer Force (NDPVF), Ijaw Youth Council (IYC), Egbesu Boys of Africa (EBA), Council for Ikwerre Nationals (CIN), Urhobo Progressive Union (UPU), Itsoko Development Union (IDU), among others. The youths have been able to transform from loosely organized movements to strong very well-armed militias with political ambitions and super-enhanced capacities.

For Ihonvbere (2000b), the plight of the youths arises from the situation into which they were born.[18] Poverty has been the key problem predisposing the youths to militancy in the region, and they believe they have been exploited by the federal government. In fact, as Folarin (2008) has pointed out, the militants who elevated the Niger Delta crisis to its present state are the children from the region, who were denied qualitative education, in the 1970s and 1980s. Many youths whose families have lost their sources of livelihood have been rendered jobless and have been forced by the prevailing situation to take up guerrilla warfare as the way to draw national and international attention to their plight. Today, the militant groups have reached the next stage and they want their concerns to be addressed, they want the world to know how the government is utilizing the money accruing from the oil derived in the region, and they want the leaders and TNOCs to be held accountable for the situation in the Niger Delta. The major means of agitations have been through guerrilla warfare, vandalism, and hostage taking.

Regardless of its original justification, the current militancy in the region appears to have been perverted, misdirected and criminalized by opportunists, who are motivated by economic profiteering through hostage taking and illegal oil bunkering with external commercial networks. Of course, "copycat groups," essentially criminals, have infiltrated the groups, formed new groupings and are terrorizing businesses, governments, and citizens of the region. These new groups consist of youths from other parts of the country that are developing and exploiting new business opportunities in illegal activities within the Niger Delta from sales of small arms to the kidnapping of non-oil workers. As to the original militant groups, they have succeeded to a very large extent in protecting their identities, articulating their objectives, identifying their targets, and remaining focused on their goals. The number of times they humiliated Nigeria's security forces and their abilities to operate from several camps without conflicts demonstrate very clearly that they were not nonentities. Numerous interviews with their leaders, the established chain of command, their press releases, and special statements show that they remained committed to the main agenda of resource control, good governance, and development of the region.

To be sure, as in many other situations worldwide, while some are genuinely motivated by a justice agenda, some are opportunists using the crisis as a cover for their illegal bunkering, proliferation and sale of small arms, some don't have any family roots in the region. And contrary to popular belief that the militants are disparate collections of different factions with mixed agendas, most of them are educated, experienced, and disciplined. There has emerged a new crisis of rule in the region as a number of states, local governments, and communities have been rendered helpless by militant activities, which have increased insecurity and intra-community violence. This has affected businesses very adversely and increased the cost of governance and socio-economic transactions.

The implications for the U.S. war on terrorism

The overarching implication of the rise of youth militancy is that it has exacerbated the already tense atmosphere and thrown the region into chaos, grinding oil exploration almost to a standstill. In 2008 alone, there were more than 50 attacks on oil production facilities, resulting in shutdowns and spillages with consequent losses in revenue estimated at about $20.7 billion. This amount is exclusive of another $3 billion lost to oil bunkering over the first seven months of 2008 alone.[19]

The crisis in the region has attracted international attention not only because of the humanitarian issues, but also for its impact on international oil prices, and the fear that the creeks may be a nest for terrorist activities. For example, on September 27, 2004, the NDPVF declared an oil war against the Nigerian government and attacked oil production facilities, virtually stopping oil production in the region. Following this announcement, world oil prices rose past $50 per barrel for the first time. Globalization and the growth of technology has enabled satellite, mobile phones, and modern electronic facilities that have brought the world closer and enabled reaching one end of the world quicker and faster than ever before. In turn, this has allowed the Niger Delta militants to form short- and long-term alliances with other militant groups within and outside the region to carry out operations against TOCs and government installations, as well as to facilitate oil bunkering and buying and the proliferation of small arms, which has sustained the crisis.

Another major derivative for international and national security concern is that the region may be a cove for radical terrorist activities. A CIA report in 2000 stated that the region was a breeding ground for militants, and warned of the catalytic effects of militia/terrorist collaboration. As is well known, international terrorist groups usually seek recruits and partners in crime from such unsteady, unstable, and violent zones around the world. As well, in their desperate search for resources, allies, and weapons, elements in the leadership of the militant groups may reach out to terrorist groups and leaders in other parts of the world. Either way, American investments and citizens would be affected and resources meant for development would be diverted to security and military campaigns with far-reaching implications.

At the moment, it would appear as if the U.S. government is treating the Niger Delta problem as a small internal affair. Maybe it is. However the scale of destruction of lives and properties so far dictates a new perception and understanding. It is essential that best practices in non-combat peace-building methods be introduced through local NGOs to facilitate the processes of reconciliation, rehabilitation, and reconstruction. The cost of ignoring the depth of anger amongst the youth in the region may be much higher than what may be needed to ensure and assure peace today.

The crackdown from the government has been immediate and crushing. Most of the people killed in Odi, in one case, were youths. Also, most of those, who were massacred by the military in Yenagoa in 1998, were youths. And when the youths made the Kaiama Declaration that same year, the town of Kaiama was attacked by the Nigerian military, resulting in the killing of several youths. This state-centric notion of the federal government informs the militarization of the region that has led to the destruction of many communities, and the loss of thousands of lives in the region. What has become obvious is that attacks on communities and militant camps and facilities have only hardened the groups and attracted recruits. Though the new amnesty program has calmed nerves somewhat, it is not addressing the fundamental issues. This means that in large measure the security threats in the Niger Delta may have gone under, but are certainly not eliminated.

Conclusion

The Niger Delta people have a basic fundamental right to self-determination. But, there are too many contradictions, negative coalitions, and entrenched interests that are benefitting from present balances to allow for progressive change. Although, there is an ongoing constitutional review process in Nigeria, but, once again, the legislators are carefully avoiding the contentious issues relating to the Niger Delta. Clearly, time was fast running out for the Nigerian state, when it reversed course and accepted the amnesty option as a way out of the resistance and violence in the region.

A major reason for the problems in the Niger Delta is that there is no political process there. Leadership is fragmented and mostly unreliable and corrupt. The political parties have compromised the process and institutions of governance, and local leaders, at least until very recently, had no qualms in betraying their peoples. The real issue in the region has always been in the implementation of the various projects by the state, local, and federal government agencies in the region. The recent release of N200 billion by the Federal Executive Council, to execute 44 projects, ranging from the construction of roads to the provision of electricity amongst other things, will show if the state governments will betray their people yet again or if they will use this opportunity, however little, to finance the pressing needs of the people, especially those in the rural areas. The region needs capacity building in order to have an effective non-violent political movement that is focused on justice, equity, and collective development. Thus, the solution is true federalism (as against the corrupted version currently in place) and democracy where the minorities are provided for.

The Nigerian state, through the federal government and its institutions, must begin the radical processes of socio-economic and political restructuring and repositioning in the Niger Delta. It must put the present and future of the youth in its priority focus to ensure that the distractions and attractions of militancy are diluted, if not eliminated. The government and its agents must take responsibility for their actions in the region and make amends by listening to the grievances of the people, lay the issues on the dialogue table, and then constitute a transparent body to be overseen by development experts, and not technocrats or politicians, to ensure sustainable development in the Niger Delta region *within a specified period of time.* In spite of current processes of amnesty and organized dialogue, the government must recognize that it is not all over with militancy. The failure of the amnesty program could easily encourage the return of experienced and very angry militants to the creeks.

Human lives should be the index of development in the Niger Delta region rather than by the quantum of money that is pumped into failed development projects. Considering the revenue accruing daily from the exploration and exploitation of resources from the region, education, health, and youth development are crucial to the transformation of the people, from the agitation for rights and justice through armed conflict to a new relationship in which the people readily cooperate with the government for development and security. Emphasis should therefore be placed on the need for educational facilities with free education, including school uniforms, stationery, and examination fees. Also, attention should be given to the number of youths, who are gainfully employed by TNOCs in host communities, with clear and sustainable training, retraining, and skill acquisition programs made available in all local government areas. Furthermore, there should be a focus on health care facilities to reduce mortality rates, especially infant mortality and maternal health care, along the deadlines established by the Millennium Development Goals (MDGs). Policies that promote women's empowerment should be put in place, as women and children bear the brunt of the crisis far more than the men or youths. Environmental issues should be prioritized in collaboration with communities, youth groups, and non-governmental organizations, in order to protect host communities in the region. TNOCs should be held accountable and responsible in cases of oil spillage, which usually can be avoided if oil facilities are serviced and regulated to avoid catastrophes like the Jesse fire. The state governors should be held accountable for the underdevelopment of the communities in their respective states, and yearly quarterly reviews should be done by an independent federal government agency. This way, human life will be the measure of development, and the figures of budgetary allocations will not remain provocative abstract terms to the people of the region.

Infrastructural development is one thing that is clearly lacking in the region, and this has been at the core of the protests by youth groups and NGOs. Due to the terrain, as most communities are hidden in the creeks, the people need means of communication with the outside world. This includes road networks, bridges, speedboats and canoes, as well as motorcycles. The general idea has been that it will cost a lot to construct roads and bridges in the region because of the terrain, but that should not be an issue because a fortune is derived from the region. What is lacking in the area of infrastructure is political will, and the recent disruption of development works by the militants, who are bent on grinding activities in the region to a halt, attest to how seriously they take this factor. In this regard, the federal, state, and local governments, as well as the traditional leaders and youth councils need to work together. This will ensure that the most pressing needs of the people are attended to and sustainable development is achieved in the long run.

Oil companies are not aid agencies, yet they have social responsibility. Ultimately it is the duty of the federal government to develop the region and ensure that TNOCs operating in the region comply with international environmental standards. The youths should not forget that the fight is on their land, and they stand to lose more in the long run and destroy that which they are trying to protect, if the crisis persists. If they have been compelled to take to militancy, they should embrace new options for dialogue and collaboration without abandoning their essential demands for justice, equity, good governance, federalism, and social justice.

A Technical Committee appointed by the president made recommendations for action relating to the region over a year ago, but so far, no action has been taken. The amnesty offered to the militants as a way to end the crisis and pursue holistic development through the NDDC and the new Ministry of the Niger Delta has opened new options for dialogue. MEND and other militant groups have eventually agreed to negotiation, the surrender of weapons, and a post-amnesty program is being discussed and implemented. Of course, serious questions continue to abound: Will the federal government keep to its promise? Will the process not be corrupted by bureaucrats and politicians? Has enough been done to win the sympathy and support of all stakeholders? Is Nigeria drawing lessons from best practices around the world to prevent a return to violence in the region? Will the processes of disarmament, demobilization, and reintegration adequately cater for the militants, especially the unskilled and those already addicted to extra-legal modes of survival? Will there be any scapegoating in the future? Will the ongoing constitution review process address issues of revenue allocation, resource control, community ownership, and the rights of the youth to education, employment, and basic human needs in justiciable provisions? Why are some ex-militants returning to the creeks?

The questions above would inform a study of the amnesty and post-amnesty politics in the Niger Delta in the very near future. Suffice to conclude that unless the post-colonial Nigerian state is democratized, and the custodians of state power appreciate the importance of human security while reforming and repositioning public institutions, we may not have heard the last of the restive youth and militant groups in the Niger Delta region of Nigeria. In a fragile sociopolitical environment, even a regional crisis could spread across the entire nation with very far-reaching implications for the sub-region and continent. The United States would do well to support the processes of demilitarization, democratization, and restructuring in the Niger Delta, so as to prevent it from becoming a breeding and recruiting ground for terrorists with ambitions to operate beyond the borders of Nigeria.

Notes

1 United Nations, *World Economic and Social Survey: Financing for Development* (New York: United Nations Publication Section, 2005), p. 2.
2 Ajiboye Olanrewaju Emmanuel, Jawando Jubril Olayiwola, and Adisa Waziri Babatunde, "Poverty, Oil Exploration and Niger Delta Crisis: The Response of the Youth," *African Journal of Political Science and International Relations*, 3 (5), 2009, pp. 224–32.
3 Etiosa Uyigue and Matthew Agho, *Coping with Climate Change and Environmental Degradation in the Niger Delta of Southern Nigeria* (Benin-City: Community Research and Development Center [CREDC], 2007), p. 1.
4 Joy Ogwu and Ray Olaniyan, *Nigeria's International Economic Relations: Dimensions of Dependence and Change*, 2nd ed. (Lagos: Nigerian Institute of International Affairs, 2005).
5 Akinjide Osuntokun, *Environmental Problems of the Niger Delta* (Lagos: Ebert Foundation, 2002).
6 Africa Network for Environmental and Economic Justice, *Oil and Poverty in the Niger Delta* (Abuja: ANEEJ, 2004).
7 Richard M. Auty, *Sustaining Development in Mineral Economies: The Resource Curse Thesis* (London: Routledge, 1993).
8 Douglas Yates, *The Rentier State in Africa: Oil Rent, Dependency and Neo-colonialism in the Republic of Gabon* (Trenton, NJ: Africa World Press, 1996), p. 1.
9 Kenneth Omeje, *Extractive Economies and Conflicts in the Global South. Multi-Regional Perspectives on Rentier Politics* (Aldershot: Ashgate Publishing, 2008).
10 Paul Collier and Anke Hoeffler, "Greed and Grievance in Africa's Civil Wars," *Quarterly Journal of Economics*, 115, 2002, pp. 755–89.
11 Teslim Kola Folarin, *Resolving the Niger Delta Crisis*, http://allafrica.com/stories/200807040994.html (accessed November 17, 2010).
12 Xavier Sala-I-Martin, *How Oil Demon Captured Nigeria's Soul* (Washington, D.C.: The International Monetary Fund, 2004), p. 1.
13 Nancy Birdsall and Arvind Subramanian, "The Resource Curse," *Australian Financial Review*, September 10, 2004.
14 Arvind Subramanian and Xavier Sala-I-Martin, *Tackling the Resource Curse: Illustrations from Nigeria* (Washington, D.C.: The International Monetary Fund Survey, 2004).
15 Oronto Douglas, Ike Okonta, Imieari Von Kemedi and Micheal Watts, *Oil and Militancy in the Niger Delta: Terrorist Threat or another Columbia*, Niger Delta Economics of Violence Working Paper No. 4 (Berkeley, CA: Institute of International Studies, University of California at Berkeley, 2004), p. 5.
16 Julius Ihonvbere, *Africa and the New World Order* (New York: Peter Lang Publishing, 2000), pp. 21–23.
17 Nneoyi I. Ofem and A. R. Ajayi, "Effects of Youth Empowerment Strategies on Conflict Resolutions in the Niger-Delta Region of Nigeria: Evidence from Cross River State," *Journal of Agriculture and Rural Development*, 6 (1&2), 2008, p. 5.
18 Julius Ihonvbere, *Recipe for Perpetual Crisis: The Nigerian State and the Niger Delta Question, Boiling Point: The Crisis in the Oil Producing Communities in Nigeria* (Lagos: Committee for the Defense of Human Rights, 2000).
19 Chikeze Amanze-Nwachukwu, "Nigeria: Niger Delta Country Loses U.S. $24 Billion in Nine Months," *This Day*, April 9, 2009.

Part III

The U.S.' counter-terrorism policy and strategies

5 Global terrorism and U.S. counter-terrorism policy in West Africa

Russell D. Howard

Introduction

This chapter's purpose is to explore the threat of global terrorism in West Africa and U.S. counter-terrorism policy in the region. Somewhat unique to U.S. political rhetoric is the misuse of the term "war." Perhaps due to a sense of urgency or out of need for motivation, American politicians give "warfare status" to non-warlike circumstances. Examples include the Johnson administration's "War on Poverty" and the Reagan administration's "War on Drugs." By any definition, neither were wars: They were not waged against states (the characteristic that marks the primary definition of war in the *Merriam-Webster Dictionary*),[1] nor were all the elements of power at America's disposal used to fight them. Similarly, the so-called "war on terrorism" is not a war by any definition. The U.S. is neither threatened by nor engaged in conflict with any state or single entity. Instead, the primary threats to the U.S. and the West are transnational, non-state actors such as Al-Qaeda, who attack globally and pursue the acquisition of weapons of mass destruction (WMD).

The American public certainly does not consider itself to be at war. Historically, Americans have displayed an extraordinary degree of resourcefulness and self-sacrifice in times of war.[2] The best example of that tradition is the Second World War, when the war effort became an immediate extension of America's national will and purpose.[3] Today, says Stephen Flynn, "We are breaking with that tradition. Our nation faces grave peril, but we seem unwilling to mobilize at home to confront the threat before us."[4] For example, at the height of the Second World War, the United States committed roughly 36 percent of its gross domestic product (GDP) to the war effort and had more than 12 million men and women in uniform. Presently, less than 4 percent of U.S. GDP is committed to defense,[5] and of the 2.2 million men and women presently in uniform, 839,000 are in the National Guard and Reserve.[6] Unlike during the Second World War, when consumer goods were rationed and America's productive capacity was focused on the war effort, today there are no shortages or rationing, and goods and services for the consumer market continue to be produced without restraint, even during the present time of economic stress.

The United States' traditional allies do not view the current struggle as a war, either. The United Kingdom stopped using the term "global war on terrorism" in April 2007. According to Hilary Benn, Great Britain's International Development Secretary, "In the UK, we do not use the phrase 'war on terror' because we can't win by military means alone … and because this isn't us against one organized enemy with a clear identity and a coherent set of objectives."[7] To many countries that have had terrorism problems for decades— including the United Kingdom, Spain, and France—a "war on terror" suggests a military operation to achieve a solution. However, these countries largely prefer police operations as a means to achieve political solutions to terrorism—an approach that has been successful in many cases. More important, several European countries are home to large Muslim diasporas that, like their counterparts in their regions of origin, are not enamored with the term "global war on terrorism." U.S. allies such as the U.K. and France have to calibrate their willingness to be "coalition partners" with the hostility such a partnership raises within the sizeable Muslim communities in both countries.

When first articulated by President Bush before a joint session of Congress on September 20, 2001, the term "war on terrorism" was clearly meant to galvanize the American people. This term—along with other phrases like "axis of evil" or "you are either with us or against us"[8]—were intended to rally the American public to the task at hand, and they worked. However, when the American President and Congress speak, the whole world—not just the primary American audience—listen. These terms, meant to boost American resolve and morale, were interpreted very differently by non-Americans. For example, many Muslims in Africa—as many as 70 percent in Egypt, Indonesia, Morocco, and Pakistan—perceived the so-called "war on terror" as "trying to weaken and divide the Islamic world."[9]

It seems logical that, if the U.S. and its allies are not fighting a war, they should not call it a war. Instead, they should call it what it is: A campaign against Islamic extremists who threaten the United States, its friends and allies. The U.S. and other at-risk nations cannot underestimate the threat; it is extremely serious and made more so by asymmetric characteristics very different from more traditional, state-centric threats. However, to defeat Islamic extremists, the United States will require the support of its friends, its allies, and the American public—few of whom believe (or act like) the country is at war.

Terrorism: A background

"Global terrorism"

The term "global terrorism" is widely misunderstood and misused. While terrorism and terrorist activity have increased in the last decade—particularly the Islamist Salafi-jihadist variety—the notion that "global terrorism" is a unified effort directed at the United States and the West is overstated. Clearly, Al-Qaeda's networks of independently operating terrorist organizations and cells have had global presence and reach. Since 9/11, Al-Qaeda and like-minded operatives hailing from 54 nations have been arrested in 102 countries. Thousands more have been killed. At Al-Qaeda's peak in 2004, it maintained operational cells in an estimated 40 to 70 countries.[10] However, Al-Qaeda and like-minded extremist groups do not hold a monopoly on international terrorist activity, nor have they controlled some of the world's most active terrorist organizations, such as the Revolutionary Armed Forces of Colombia (FARC), the Irish Republican Army (IRA), Basque Homeland and Freedom (ETA), or the Kurdistan Workers Party (PKK). While Hamas and Hezbollah have similar ideologies and have occasionally cooperated with Al-Qaeda, they are neither directly controlled by nor been official members of the Al-Qaeda network.

Al-Qaeda's present strength and influence are subjects of debate. Some experts, including Rohan Gunaratna, report that Al-Qaeda's ranks have been depleted to about 200—down substantially from the 3,000 to 4,000 estimated members immediately after 9/11. According to Gunaratna, the remaining Al-Qaeda members are mostly Arabs operating in the Federally Administered Tribal Areas (FATA) of Pakistan.[11] Assistant Treasury Secretary David S. Cohen recently told a joint conference of the American Banking Association and American Bar Association that Al-Qaeda may be in its worst financial shape in years. According to Cohen, "by targeting donors, fundraisers and facilitators of terrorist groups in the U.S. and abroad," the Treasury Department has been able to "partially choke" the flow of money to Al-Qaeda and other terrorist organizations, including Hamas and Hezbollah.[12] The department's anti-terrorism efforts, he says, have been particularly successful against Al-Qaeda, "which made four public pleas for funds during the first six months of 2009, including a June appeal when a group leader complained that a money shortage was hurting recruitment and training."[13] Cohen concluded that "Al-Qaeda is in its weakest financial condition in several years, and that, as a result, its influence is waning."[14]

However, other experts, such as leading catastrophe risk firm Risk Management Solutions (RMS), disagree. According to RMS, claims of Al-Qaeda disruption "have been dramatically overstated."[15] Although some high-ranking Al-Qaeda members have been eliminated, says RMS, the organization has been able to replace losses and, along with like-minded Salafi-jihadist terrorist organizations, remains active on a global scale.[16] Furthermore, according to an August 2009 RMS report, the Al-Qaeda-led Salafi jihadist threat emanating "from conflict zones such as Iraq, Afghanistan, Pakistan, Somalia, Algeria, India (Kashmir), and Russia (Chechnya)" is now spilling over and destabilizing neighboring regions and countries.[17]

While Gunaratna, Secretary Cohen, and RMS may debate Al-Qaeda's numbers and organizational viability, all agree that Al-Qaeda has perhaps actually expanded its global influence by forging closer relationships with like-minded Salafi jihadist groups. According to Gunaratna, these groups have grown dramatically in number, from a few in 2001 to more than 30 today, thus exponentially increasing the number of associated Al-Qaeda groups.[18] RMS notes that despite progress in Iraq, "macro terrorism attacks perpetuated" by

Al-Qaeda-influenced terrorist groups "have increased to 340 attacks globally [in 2009], compared to 326" in 2008.[19] Secretary Cohen's claims reflecting major strides in disrupting Al-Qaeda's funding network are qualified by the statement that several other like-minded terrorist groups, particularly the Taliban in Afghanistan, "are much stronger financially than Al-Qaeda," and that these other terror groups continue to pose "serious threats" to the United States and its interests around the world.[20]

Africa and global terrorism: A background

The model of expansion by forging relationships favored by Al-Qaeda is evident in Africa. While Al-Qaeda has been very specific about its objectives and opportunities in Africa, the like-minded Salafi jihadist groups have actually conducted most of the operations on the continent in the past several years. Clearly, Al-Qaeda is interested in Africa. In 2006, Al-Qaeda sympathizer and operative Abu Azzam al Ansari (part of the Zarqawi network, he was arrested in Saudi Arabia in 2007) wrote and released a work originally named "Al-Qaeda is Moving to Africa," which was re-released in 2007 under the title "Al-Qaeda Organization and the African Continent: Past, Present and Future."[21] This document is illustrative of Al-Qaeda's interest in Africa and provides thoughtful and realistic analysis of the opportunities, challenges, and limitations for its expansion on the continent.

Al Ansari's piece highlights Africa's importance to Al-Qaeda and notes its successes in North and East Africa. For example, the text proudly cites the U.S. embassy bombings in Kenya and Tanzania, the expulsion of Americans from Somalia, the network's involvement in Sudan, and attacks by Al-Qaeda and like-minded groups in Mombassa, Jerba/Tunisia, Casablanca, Sharm al-Sheikh, and Sinai.[22] However, the article also explains that Al-Qaeda does not have a prominent role in other parts of Africa, including West Africa, despite the fact that conditions for successful expansion exist.

What are those conditions? According to al Ansari, "the political and military conditions in most of the African continent, as well as the broad weaknesses of its governments and the internal fighting and corruption of its regimes, should ease the ability of the Mujahidin [Salafi-jihadists] to move, plan, and organize themselves" without being detected.[23] Other exploitable conditions include ethnic conflicts and civil wars, which provide opportunities for operatives to easily move among African countries, and easy access to inexpensive weapons and other military equipment.[24] Finally, al Ansari's article explains that a prominent advantage for the Mujahidin in Africa is the "general condition of poverty and the social needs prevalent in most African countries," which allows operatives to provide much-needed goods and services, gaining favor and the chance to post influential operatives in key areas.[25] In all, al Ansari considers Africa a "gold[en] opportunity" for Al-Qaeda's unfettered activity and expansion.[26]

Most intelligence analysts, security experts, academics, "Africa watchers," and counter-terrorism experts would agree with al Ansari's assessment.

Certainly, Al-Qaeda in the Islamic Maghreb (AQIM) and al Shabab in Somalia have taken advantage of the conditions in North and East Africa to conduct terrorist operations. However, the Salafi jihadist variety of terrorism practiced by Al-Qaeda—the central focus of this chapter—has had little success in expanding into West Africa to date. Why is this, and will the situation change? Will Al-Qaeda and like-minded terrorist groups expand their operations into West Africa? And if they do, what will their chances be for success? What other terrorist organizations operate in the region and what is their connection, if any, with Al-Qaeda? How can the United States ensure that Al-Qaeda and like-minded groups do not gain a foothold in West Africa?

Al-Qaeda's Africa experience: An overview

The continental level

In a testimony before the Senate Armed Services Committee, General William Ward, head of U.S. Africa Command (AFRICOM), said that over the past three years Al-Qaeda has increased its influence dramatically across Northern and Eastern Africa. Two groups figure prominently in his analysis: Al-Qaeda in the Islamic Maghreb (AQIM) in North Africa and al Shabab in Somalia.[27]

Worried traditional Islamic African leaders appear to agree with Ward's assessment. At a March 2009 meeting of Islamic leaders concerned with the extremism of Al-Qaeda and likeminded groups held in Timbuktu, Mali, these leaders explained that bin Laden's organization arrived in Africa in 2007, when the group integrated an Algerian extremist organization previously called the Salafist Group for Preaching and Combat (GSPC). Under Al-Qaeda's cooperative influence, GSPC became AQIM, and then CIA Director Michael Hayden called this group "a serious and growing threat."[28] Since then, AQIM has started trafficking in weapons and established a base in northern Mali.[29] This Al-Qaeda-related group "carried out a string of killings, bombings and other lethal attacks against Westerners and African security forces" in mid-2009.[30] Between June 1 and July 15, 2009, the group "claimed responsibility for killing a British hostage in Mali and an American aid worker in Mauritania, murdering a senior Malian army officer in his home, and ambushing a convoy of nearly two dozen Algerian paramilitary forces," raising fears that AQIM may be on the verge of even deadlier attacks.[31]

According to General Ward and as reconfirmed recently by military intelligence chief Lieutenant-General Michael D. Maples, al Shabab's influence is also on the increase. Al Shabab continues to distribute propaganda highlighting its shared ideology with Al-Qaeda, suggesting, Maples said, that "a formal merger announcement is forthcoming."[32] The al Shabab connection is particularly troublesome because the Salafi jihadist group is actively recruiting American citizens. According to an FBI report, young men of Somali descent have been vanishing from Minnesota and other midwestern states and heading for Somali terrorist training camps run by al Shabab, which means "the Youth" in Arabic.[33] One of them has already carried out a suicide bombing in Africa, and others are believed to be forming terrorist cells to hit targets in Europe and the United States. According to some experts, a possible union with Al-Qaeda makes that scenario even likelier.[34]

Other Al-Qaeda-affiliated groups in Africa include the Egyptian Islamic Jihad (EIJ; formerly known as Islamic Jihad or the Jihad Group), the Moroccan Islamic Combatant Group (GICM), and the Libyan Islamic Fighting Group (LIFG). EIJ has reportedly fully merged with Al-Qaeda and has been "involved with most of the terrorist attacks on the United States in the last two decades," with its operatives instrumental in both World Trade Center attacks.[35] GICM is suspected of orchestrating the 2004 Madrid bombings, which killed at least 190 people, and of being involved in the 2003 Casablanca attacks, which killed more than 40.[36] LIFG, founded in 1995 by veterans of the war against Soviet forces in Afghanistan, has also been linked to Al-Qaeda. In May 2008, Colonel Gaddafi "released 90 imprisoned members, saying they had reformed."[37]

According to the West Point Combating Terrorism Center's (CTC) Harmony Project analysis, Al-Qaeda almost certainly continues to maintain cells in Kenya, which is riddled with corruption and has a marginalized Islamic minority along the Swahili coast and the border with Somalia. In fact, the Harmony Project forecasts Al-Qaeda-sponsored terrorism in Kenya as being a greater threat than al Shabab in Somalia. CTC analysis contends that Al-Qaeda operatives continue to

> move about the country freely, establish businesses in Mombasa, Nairobi, and Lamu, operate Islamic charities, find local brides, rent light aircraft to come and go from Somalia, hold meetings, communicate with Al-Qaeda figures outside the country, transfer money, stockpile weapons, and engage in years of undetected reconnoitering of possible targets.[38]

However, of all the Al-Qaeda-affiliated groups, AQIM is the closest and most dangerous to West Africa. According to *The Times* of London, Western intelligence and diplomatic sources concur that AQIM's mission is to "create an arc of influence throughout North Africa by spreading Osama bin Laden's 'brand' through fusion of disparate fundamentalist groupings."[39] According to AQIM leader Abu Musab Abdel Wadoud, the group's "commitment to jihad extends far beyond North Africa."[40] In a prepared statement to the Western media in the summer of 2008, he declared, "We see that it's our duty to join Al-Qaeda so that we can have our fight under one flag and one leadership in order to get ready for the confrontation."[41]

The West African sub-region

Because Islam is the fastest-growing religion in West Africa, and the economic and social environment is conducive for terrorist recruitment and activity, many experts presume that there is a linkage between West African Muslims and terrorists. And that those anti-Western Muslims may provide sanctuary to terrorists.[42] The truth is that, other than confirmed involvement that Al-Qaeda is engaged in the West African diamond trade and speculation that it has also entered the drug business, there seems to be very little evidence of Al-Qaeda or other Salafi jihadist activity in West Africa.

Al-Qaeda's relationships with known diamond-smuggling regimes in West Africa are collaborated by the FBI and the UN.[43] Terrorist involvement in the diamond trade, "begun under the protection of former Liberian strong-man Charles Taylor, continues despite international efforts to curb it."[44] It is known that Al-Qaeda has smuggled diamonds from Sierra Leone and sold them in Liberia.[45] It has also been reported that Al-Qaeda purchased between $30 million and $50 million worth of diamonds from the former Liberian President Charles Taylor during the eight months prior to 9/11. So, it appears that Al-Qaeda was involved in two-way diamond trade with Taylor playing middle man.[46] Interestingly, Hezbollah has been using diamonds from West Africa to finance its activities since its inception, successfully embedding its financial structure in the diamond trade.[47] Perhaps most concerning is that "Al-Qaeda operatives plugged into the same [Hezbollah] network, bridging the divide between Shiite and Sunni Muslims."[48]

Al-Qaeda's foray into West Africa's lucrative drug trafficking has been a matter of speculation for some time. This supposition is not without merit, as Al-Qaeda's history in Afghanistan drug trafficking operations is well documented. For example, former drug czar General Barry McCaffrey, who consulted with U.S. and NATO officials in July 2008, wrote in a recent report that Al-Qaeda and the Taliban "are principally funded by what some estimate as $800 million a year derived from the huge $4 billion annual illegal production and export of opium/heroin and cannabis."[49]

Certainly, the lack of infrastructure, weak political systems, ineffective security forces, and inefficient justice systems, which have "left West Africa vulnerable to drug cartels, [have] also made it susceptible to the possibility that terrorists could further infiltrate the region."[50] However, it has been "difficult to obtain concrete evidence that the illegal drug trade in West Africa is financing terrorism."[51]

Case study: Nigeria

Some experts contend that Nigeria faces terrorist threats in the north, from Muslim extremists intent on driving all Western "infidel influences" out of the region, and in the south, where a mix of separatists, criminal gangs, and economic insurgents have been attacking the nation's oil infrastructure for profit and political gain.[52] However, in both circumstances, terrorism may not be the causal factor.

Douglas Farah, a noted Africa expert, insists that Al-Qaeda-allied groups are operating in northern Nigeria.[53] According to Farah, "there is a large and radicalized Muslim population in northern Nigeria, where 12 of the states (out of 36 in all) have imposed Sharia law."[54] Radicalization, says Farah, "is mixed with a deep sense of historic grievance against the south and the central government, as well as antagonism toward the sizable Christian minority."[55] Farah does agree that not all Muslims in the north are radicalized or seeking violent means to overthrow the state; however, the leaders of the new, self-proclaimed Nigerian Taliban—believed to be "direct descendants of the previously-active Nigerian Taliban that emerged in 2003"—are.[56] In fact, "the Islamist fighters are thought to belong to a group known as Boko Haram, which means 'western education is a sin'."[57] The group's goal is to implement Sharia law throughout Nigeria, a country of 150 million people.[58]

A Muslim leader of the northern Nigerian state of Sokoto disagrees with Farah. Neither Al-Qaeda nor the Taliban movement exists in Northern Nigeria, said the Sultan of Sokoto, Alhaji Muhammadu Sa'ad Abubakar, in a November 2007 meeting at the U.S. Institute of Peace in Washington, D.C.[59] The Sultan, who claims to be constantly briefed on such sensitive matters, said that none of the emirs or district heads in his state had reported such activity, and he dismissed recent terrorist activity in the area as the "handiwork of … misinformed extremists" rather than the work of an organized branch of Al-Qaeda or the Taliban.[60]

Putting aside disagreement over the level of organized extremism in Nigeria, conflict between Muslims and Christians in the country should be taken seriously. Violence between the two groups has been significant in the northern, predominantly Christian Plateau State—in 2001, the capital city of Jos was the site of religious clashes that led to 1,000 deaths, and a state of emergency was declared in 2004 when Christian militias killed 200 Muslims.[61] Both were destabilizing events requiring Nigerian military intervention. However, the cause of the violence may have anthropological underpinnings, and be more about economics than religion or terrorism. This type of violence is essentially a competition for resources between those that see themselves as indigenous to an area and those they view to be more recent settlers.[62] In the case of Plateau State, which borders the Muslim north, Christian Tarok farmers are regarded as indigenous, and the cattle-herding, Hausa-speaking Muslims are seen as the newer settlers.[63] Desertification in the Sahara—which is expanding at a rate of several kilometers per year and affects most northern Nigerian states[64]—puts pressure on Muslim cattle herders to seek other pasturelands, threatening the livelihoods of Christian farmers and often resulting in violent conflict. It seems that anthropological causes, not religious friction or terrorism, could be the key dependent variable causing violence in Nigeria.

In southern Nigeria, the Movement for the Emancipation of the Niger Delta (MEND) has challenged the central government and the oil companies in the Niger Delta since 2006. Based on Osama bin Laden's goals for Africa, some believe that a MEND-Al-Qaeda relationship is likely. As one observer argues:

> Although the majority of Muslims live in the northern region of Nigeria, the presence of Islamic extremism in the country presents an unsettling possibility that the extremist movement could reach the Niger Delta. If it

does, there's a strong possibility that the MEND may form a temporary alliance with Islamic radicals, if only to receive logistical support or training. This temporary union would most likely take the form of an objective-oriented alignment between radical Muslims and the MEND.[65]

MEND's behavior since 2006 suggests that this assessment is incorrect. MEND's goals and objectives have nothing to do with religion or Salifi jihadist ideology. Instead, the group is the largest and best known of several regional insurgent groups that rail against the Nigerian government and the oil industry, which they believe has harmed the region and led to grave injustices for its people.[66]

MEND is comprised of several smaller groups, resulting in a "highly coordinated but largely faceless organization ... with no single or distinct structured leadership."[67] While the number of active MEND members is unknown, estimates range from a few hundred to several thousand, and the group and its affiliates reportedly have access to more than 100 boats and thousands of small arms.[68] Their tactics—destruction of pipelines, kidnappings, and raids[69]—are well documented in the press and have been the subject of documentary films.[70] MEND does have the ability to conduct multiple coordinated attacks, as demonstrated in January 2007, when the group freed its leader, Sobomabo George, from prison in Port Harcourt while simultaneously conducting diversionary attacks in other locations that resulted in the release of 125 other prisoners.[71] According to General Ward, oil theft by armed militants is a "significant problem" in the Niger Delta, with some studies estimating a 20 percent reduction in Nigerian oil exports "due to banditry fostered by lingering societal and political grievances."[72] Ward said: "Theft of oil within the country costs the state untold revenues that could be used to improve services for the population."[73]

If one considers oil workers civilians, then MEND does engage in "the willful targeting of civilians with violence and or the threat of violence for political purposes," which is the common definition of terrorism. That said, it is still unclear whether MEND is a terrorist group in the traditional sense. It is certainly not a Salafi jihadist group aligned with Al-Qaeda. Many insurgents, guerrillas, irregular warfare groups, and even states resort to terrorist tactics on occasion, but they are not all considered terrorist groups. Instead, "MEND's ultimate goal is to expel foreign oil companies and non-indigenous Nigerians from the Niger Delta," which is comprised primarily of farmers and fishermen of the Ijaw ethnic group, whose "main grievance is that the local population continues to live in poverty, while the government and foreign oil companies seize all the wealth from the region."[74] Some have also taken up arms with the MEND, but despite speculation to the contrary, there is no evidence that MEND insurgents have any association with Al-Qaeda or other Salafi jihadist groups.

Opportunities for Al-Qaeda expansion in West Africa?

Despite the "golden opportunities" for terrorist expansion in West Africa, Al-Qaeda and like-minded groups have not yet made great inroads in the region. Corruption, poverty, lack of education, poor infrastructure and governance, porous borders, and other factors are helpful for Al-Qaeda infiltration in West Africa—so why hasn't Al-Qaeda been more successful in the region? Three reasons come to mind. First, Salafi jihadist ideology (doctrine) may not be compatible with West African traditions. While Islam is the fastest-growing religion on the African subcontinent, "mystical and often syncretic variants" of Sufism are the predominant strains of Islam in West Africa.[75] Non-liberal sects such as Wahabbism, which is more in line with Al-Qaeda ideology, have found a growing audience throughout the continent,[76] but do not seem to resonate in much of West Africa.

Second, Nigerian insurgents are more aptly described as partaking in a local struggle rather than one between extremists/jihadists and the West.[77] While some may classify Muslims in Nigeria as members of the jihadist movement, the reality is that groups like MEND are actually spearheading local insurgent or terrorist activities against specific entities—"an indication that West African militants may not be interested in the global Islamic struggle but in their local causes."[78]

Third, Al-Qaeda is a predominantly Arab organization, and many West Africans do not trust Arabs. It is part of their culture and dates from slave-trading days. While Arab the slave traders' primary area of operation was East Africa, it is not lost on West Africans that Arabs traded as many as 14 million Africans between the seventh and twentieth centuries.[79] In a modern example, Darfur illustrates the racial schism between northern Muslim Arabs and southern Christian and indigenous Africans. The deep racial and ethnic animus in the savage attacks sponsored by the Sudanese (Arab) government on black African ethnic groups has been made clear by the United Nations, Amnesty International, the International Crisis Group, and myriad news reports from the long border between Sudan and Chad, where more than a quarter of a million Sudanese refugees have fled.[80]

U.S. counter-terrorism policy in West Africa

The Trans-Sahara Counterterrorism Partnership (TSCTP) is the U.S. government's current "multi-faceted, multi-year strategy" to address terrorist threats in North and West Africa.[81] The primary goals of the program are to "enhance the indigenous capacities of governments in the pan-Sahel (Mauritania, Mali, Chad, and Niger, as well as Nigeria and Senegal), to confront the challenge posed by terrorist organizations in the region, and to facilitate cooperation between those countries and [the U.S.'s] Maghreb partners (Morocco, Algeria, and Tunisia) in the global war on terror."[82] Launched in 2004, TSCTP replaces the U.S. State Department's Pan-Sahel Initiative (PSI), which was initiated in 2002, as a Sahel-specific program to "protect borders, track movement of people, combat terrorism, and enhance regional cooperation and stability."[83] Its goals supported two U.S. national security interests in Africa: "[W]aging the war on terrorism and enhancing regional peace and security."[84] The TSCTP has similar goals but aims to engage "with more countries than PSI, with a greater emphasis on helping to foster better information sharing and operational planning between regional states."[85] Both programs were the responsibility of European Command (EUCOM) and run by Special Operations Command Europe (SOCEUR). Presently, the follow-on TSCTP program is operated under the AFRICOM initiative, and run by Special Operations Command Africa (SOCAF).

TSCTP is designed to strengthen regional capacity in counter-terrorism, security cooperation, democratic governance, rule of law, and military professionalism—all of which will ultimately benefit U.S. bilateral relationships with each of the cooperating states in the region.[86] Key aspects of the TSCTP training include basic marksmanship, planning communications, land navigation, patrolling, and medical care. Additionally, civil–military relations, civil–military operations, security sector reform, and interagency cooperation are other important training and education priorities.[87] According to the U.S. Department of State, TSCTP's main elements include:

- Counterterrorism (CT) programs to create a new regional focus for trans-Saharan cooperation, including use of established regional organizations like the African Union and its new Center for the Study and Research on Terrorism in Algiers. These programs include training to improve border and aviation security and overall CT readiness.
- Continued specialized Counterterrorism Assistance Training and Terrorist Interdiction Program (TIP) activities in the trans-Sahara region and possible regional expansion of those programs.
- Public diplomacy programs that expand outreach efforts in the Sahel and Maghreb regions, Nigeria, and Senegal and seek to develop regional programming embracing this vast and diverse region. Emphasis is on preserving the traditional tolerance and moderation displayed in most African Muslim communities and countering the development of extremism, particularly in youth and rural populations.
- Democratic governance programs that strive, in particular, to provide adequate levels of USG support for democratic and economic development in the Sahel, strengthening those states to withstand internal threats.
- Military programs intended to expand military-to-military cooperation, to ensure adequate resources are available to train, advise, and assist regional forces, and to establish institutions promoting better regional cooperation, communication, and intelligence sharing.[88]

U.S. Army Special Operations Forces—including Special Forces, civil affairs, and psychological operations soldiers—have been the key implementers of both TSCTP and PSI. However, other staff agencies and contractors have filled some requirements due to heavy commitments of Special Operations Forces to Iraq and Afghanistan. Initial funding for the TSCTP program was $500 million, in the form of $100 million per year over five years.[89] This is much more robust than the PSI's initial funding of $6 million and $7.75 million in its first two years.[90] Despite increased funds for TSCTP, indicators of success for both programs have been scarce. Recent operations conducted by AQIM in Algeria, Chad, Mauritania, and Mali do not suggest resounding success. However, the lack of serious infiltration in other West African countries could indicate that the programs might be partially successful.

Whatever their form, the U.S. and its allies must closely observe and monitor their counter-terrorism programs in the Sahel and West Africa, because any such program can potentially be counterproductive. For example, for several years, members of the 3rd and 10th Special Forces Groups have been conducting TSCTP-type missions in Niger to modernize and build the capacity of Niger military units—particularly quick response units. Unfortunately, the loyalty of the units trained by Special Forces has been called into question, as uncorroborated reports claim that the entire Niger Rapid Intervention Company trained to conduct counter-terror operations defected *en masse* to the Niger Movement for Justice.[91]

Preliminary conclusions

Clearly, the conditions exist for successful Al-Qaeda and other Salafi jihadist expansion in West Africa. These exploitable conditions, or "golden opportunities," include poverty, corruption, poor governance, porous borders, lack of education and infrastructure, ethnic conflicts, and civil wars, to name a few. Two Al-Qaeda-related groups have increased their presence in Africa. Al Shabab has replaced the Islamic Courts in Somalia as a terrorist group capable of inflicting harm on the United States. And its ability to recruit in the U.S. and provide sanctuary to Al-Qaeda is particularly worrisome. AQIM has also flexed its muscles in the region, operating in the margins of some West African states, where the group's presence is especially troubling.

However, and surprisingly, despite the "golden opportunities" outlined by Al-Qaeda operative al Ansari, Al-Qaeda and like-minded groups have not been able to set up and operate freely in West African countries. Factors such as West African Muslims eschewing ultra-conservative religious ideologies, and historical animosities and ethnic tensions between Africans and Arabs, may be important factors inhibiting Al-Qaeda-related expansion. U.S. counterterrorism initiatives such as PSI and TSCTP may also have helped to create a less-hospitable environment for extremist groups: In addition to increasing West African militaries, police, and interagency capabilities to thwart terrorism, the programs are also designed to reduce Al-Qaeda's "golden opportunities" to gain a foothold.

Two lessons can be drawn from the activities of Al-Qaeda and other Salafi-jihadist groups in Africa. One is that these terrorists are sophisticated in their exploitation of "gray areas" where governments are weak, corruption is rampant, and the rule of law is nonexistent. The second is that West African states, with the help of the U.S. and the West, must reduce the "golden opportunities" Al-Qaeda has sworn to exploit. Letting Al-Qaeda win is not an option.

Notes

1 War is defined as "a state of usually open and declared armed hostile conflict between states or nations" in the first entry of the *Merriam-Webster Dictionary*, www.merriam-webster.com/dictionary/war (accessed December 13, 2009). Interestingly, the secondary definition from the same source is more vague, referring only to "a state of hostility, conflict, or antagonism" in general.

2 Stephen Flynn, *America the Vulnerable* (New York: Harper Collins, 2004), p. x.

3 David Halberstam, *War in a Time of Peace: Bush, Clinton, and The Generals* (New York: Scribner, 2001), p. 496.

4 Flynn, *America the Vulnerable*, op. cit., p. x.

5 "Air Force Association 2005 Statement of Policy," Air Force Association, September 12, 2004, www.afa.org/AboutUs/PolicyIssues05.asp (accessed November 28, 2009).

6 "The Air Force in Facts and Figures: 2009 USAF Almanac," *Air Force Magazine*, May 2009, 34, www.airforcemagazine.com/MagazineArchive/Magazine%20Docum ents/2009/May%202009/0509facts_fig.pdf (accessed November 28, 2009).

7 "Benn Criticizes 'War on Terror'," *BBC News*, April 16, 2007, http://news.bbc.co. uk/2/hi/6558569.stm (accessed November 28, 2009).

8 The phrase "axis of evil" was first used in President Bush's State of the Union Address of January 29, 2002; see "Bush State of the Union Address," CNN.com, http://transcripts.cnn.com/2002/ALLPOLITICS/01/29/bush.speech.txt/ (accessed December 12, 2009). The statement "you are either with us or against us" was made by Bush in a joint press conference with French President Jacques Chirac on November 6, 2001; see "'You Are Either With Us or Against Us'," CNN.com, November 6, 2001, http://archives.cnn.com/2001/US/11/06/gen.attack.on.terror/ (accessed December 12, 2009).

9 Michelle Nichols, "Muslims Believe U.S. Goal to Weaken Islam: Poll," *Reuters*, April 24, 2007, www.reuters.com/article/politicsNews/idUSN2332112320070424? feedType=RSS (accessed November 28, 2009).

10 Multiple conversations with Rohan Gunaratna, 2001–9. See also, Jerrold M. Post, "Killing in the Name of God: Osama Bin Laden and al Qaeda," in *Know Thy Enemy: Profiles of Adversary Leaders and Their Strategic Cultures*, Barry R. Schneider and Jerrold M. Post (eds), (Maxwell Air Force Base, AL: USAF Counter-proliferation Center, 2002), p. 33, www.au.af.mil/au/awc/awcgate/cpc-pubs/know_thy_enemy/ index.htm (accessed November 28, 2009); and David Kilcullen, "Countering Global Insurgency," *Small Wars Journal*, November 30, 2004, p. 4, http://smallwarsjournal. com/documents/kilcullen.pdf (accessed November 28, 2009).

11 Conversation with Rohan Gunaratna on October 24, 2009.

12 Arun Kumar, "Al Qaeda Funding Disrupted, but Taliban Much Stronger: US," *Inndo-Asian News Service*, October 13, 2009, www.thaindian.com/newsportal/ world-news/al-qaeda-funding-disrupted-but-taliban-much-stronger-us_100260192.html (accessed November 30, 2009).

13 Ibid.

14 Ibid.

15 Risk Management Solutions, "Global Terrorism Trends 2009," *Terrorism Risk Briefing*, August 2009, p. 1, www.rms.com/Publications/RMS_Terrorism_Risk_Briefing _August_2009.pdf (accessed November 30, 2009).

16 Ibid.

17 Ibid.

18 Conversation with Gunaratna, op. cit.

19 Risk Management Solutions, "Global Terrorism Trends 2009," op. cit.

20 Kumar, "Al Qaeda Funding Disrupted," op. cit.

21 Moshe Terdman, "Factors Facilitating the Rise of Radical Islamism and Terrorism in Sub-Saharan Africa," *Project for the Research of Islamist Movements (PRISM,)*

African Occasional Papers, Vol. 1, No. 1 (March 2007), p. 1, www.e-prism.org/
images/PRISM_African_Papers_vol_1_no_1 – Radicalism_in_Sub-Sahara_Africa –
March_07.pdf (accessed November 30, 2009).
22 Ibid.
23 Ibid., p. 2.
24 Ibid.
25 Ibid.
26 Ibid.
27 See "Statement of General William E. Ward, Commander, United States Africa
Command, before the Senate Armed Services Committee," U.S. Senate Armed
Services Committee, March 17, 2009, http://armed-services.senate.gov/statemnt/
2009/March/Ward%2003-17-09.pdf (accessed December 2, 2009).
28 Amil Khan, "Al Qaeda's Spreading Tentacles in West Africa Opposed by Traditional Leaders," *Telegraph*, March 28, 2009 www.telegraph.co.uk/news/worldnews/
africaandindianocean/mali/5067404/Al-Qaedas-spreading-tentacles-in-West-Africa-o
pposed-by-traditional-leaders.html (accessed December 2, 2009).
29 Ibid.
30 Eric Schmitt and Souad Mekhennet, "Qaeda Branch Steps up Raids in North
Africa," *New York Times*, July 9, 2009, www.nytimes.com/2009/07/10/world/africa/
10terror.html (accessed December 2, 2009).
31 Ibid.
32 "Haunted by Somalia," *Los Angeles Times*, March 13, 2009, www.latimes.com/
news/opinion/editorials/la-ed-somalia13–2009mar13,0,2777948.story (accessed December 2, 2009).
33 "FBI Chief: Suicide Bomber Indoctrinated in Minnesota." *Minnesota Star-Tribune,*
February 24, 2009, www.startribune.com/local/40202352.html (accessed December
2, 2009).
34 "Haunted by Somalia," op. cit.
35 Holly Fletcher, "Egyptian Islamic Jihad," Council on Foreign Relations, May 30,
2008, www.cfr.org/publication/16376/egyptian_islamic_jihad.html (accessed December
12, 2009).
36 See "Madrid Massacre Death Toll Revised," Associated Press, June 9, 2004, www.
breakingnews.ie/archives/2004/0609/world/kfojkfojidkf/ (accessed December 2,
2009; and Martin Bright, Paul Harris, Ali Bouzerda, and Emma Daly, "Horror in
Casablanca as al Qaeda toll hits 41," *Guardian*, May 18, 2003, www.guardian.co.
uk/world/2003/may/18/alqaida.terrorism2 (accessed December 2, 2009).
37 David Sharrock, "Out of Africa: A Growing Threat to Europe from al Qaeda's
New Allies," *The Times*, May 8, 2008, www.timesonline.co.uk/tol/news/world/
africa/article3876563.ece (accessed December 2, 2009).
38 The most comprehensive research effort so far on the role of al-Qaeda in the region
is now on the website of the Harmony Project Combating Terrorism Center at
West Point. Entitled *Al-Qa'ida's (mis)Adventures in the Horn of Africa*, it includes
original, mostly early,
Al-Qaeda documents. It has a heavy focus on Kenya and Somalia, and offers
relatively little information on the rest of the region. It is, nevertheless, must reading for specialists on East Africa and the Horn. It is available at http://ctc.usma.
edu/aq/aqII.asp (accessed December 2, 2009).
39 David Sharrock, "Out of Africa," op. cit.
40 Michael Petrou, "Al Qaeda in North Africa," *Macleans*, May 6, 2009, www2.
macleans.ca/2009/05/06/al-qaeda-in-north-africa (accessed December 2, 2009).
41 Ibid.
42 Cyril I. Obi, "Terrorism in West Africa: Real, Emerging or Imagined Threats?"
African Security Review, 15(3), 2006, p. 93, www.iss.co.za/index.php?link_id=32&s
link_id=4515&link_type=12&slink_type=12&tmpl_id=3 (accessed December 2, 2009).

43 Douglas Farah and Richard Shultz, "Al Qaeda's Growing Sanctuary," *Washington Post*, July 14, 2004, p. A 19, www.washingtonpost.com/wp-dyn/articles/A48221-20 04Jul13.html (accessed December 4, 2009).

44 Ibid.

45 Jakkie Cilliers, "Africa, Root Causes and the War on Terror," *African Security Review*, 15(3), 1996, p. 98, www.iss.co.za/index.php?link_id=32&slink_id=4513&lin k_type=12&slink_type=12&tmpl_id=3 (accessed December 4, 2009).

46 David H. Shinn, "Domestic or International Terrorism? A Dysfunctional Dialogue," paper presented at *Africa: Vital to U.S. Security?* Symposium, Panel on Terrorism and Transnational Threats – Causes and Enablers, National Defense University, November 15–16, 2005, p. 5, www.dtic.mil/cgi-bin/GetTRDoc?AD=ADA441210& Location=U2&doc=GetTRDoc.pdf (accessed December 4, 2009).

47 Douglas Farah and Richard Shultz, "Al Qaeda's Growing Sanctuary," op. cit.

48 Ibid.

49 I receive periodic reports from General McCaffrey in his "Adjunct Professor" capacity in the Department of Social Sciences at West Point.

50 Ejike Okpa, "West Africa: A Drug Smuggling and Terrorism Hub?" *The African Executive*, April 15–22, 2009, www.africanexecutive.com/modules/magazine/section s.php?magazine=225&sections=17 (accessed December 4, 2009).

51 Ibid.

52 James J. F. Forest and Matthew V. Sousa, *"Oil and Terrorism in the New Gulf: Framing U.S. Energy and Security Policies for the Gulf of Guinea,"* (Lanham, MD: Lexington Books, 2006), p. 122.

53 Douglas Farah, "Nigeria and al Qaeda," DouglasFarah.com, September 7, 2009, www.douglasfarah.com/article/490/nigeria-and-al-qaeda (accessed December 5, 2009).

54 Ibid.

55 Ibid.

56 Ibid.

57 Ibid.

58 Ibid.

59 Scott Gilbreath, "No al-Qaeda or Taliban in My Country: Nigerian Sultan," MagicStatistics.com, November 15, 2007, http://magicstatistics.com/category/intern ational-relationspolitics/terrorism/ (accessed December 12, 2009).

60 Ibid.

61 Konye Obaji Ori and Will Ghartey-Mould, "Nigeria: Islamists' Nationwide Sharia Demands Raise Alarm Over Deepening Religious Fissure," Afrik.com, July 27, 2009, http://en.afrik.com/article15969.html (accessed December 5, 2009).

62 Ibid.

63 Ibid.

64 Salisu Suleiman, "The Desert Encroaches," Next.com, December 11, 2009, http://234 next.com/csp/cms/sites/Next/Home/5494716–182/The_desert_encroaches-.csp (accessed December 12, 2009).

65 Kyle Dabruzzi, "A Hard Wound to MEND," *FrontPage Magazine*, November 9, 2006, http://97.74.65.51/readArticle.aspx?ARTID=1654 (accessed December 12, 2009).

66 Akpobibibo Onduku, "The Global Repercussions of Nigeria's Niger Delta Insur-gency," *Terrorism Monitor,* 6(5), 2008, www.jamestown.org/programs/gta/single/? tx_ttnews[tt_news]=5082&tx_ttnews[backPid]=167&no_cache=1 (accessed December 12, 2009).

67 Ibid.

68 Brian Lionberger, "Emerging Requirements for U.S. Counterinsurgency: An Examination of the Insurgency in the Niger River Delta Region," Thesis for the U.S. Army Command and General Staff College, Ft. Leavenworth, Kansas, 2007, p. 78, www.dtic.mil/cgi-bin/GetTRDoc?AD=ADA471380& Location=U2&doc=GetTRD oc.pdf (accessed December 12, 2009).

69 John B. Alexander, "Africa: Irregular Warfare on the Dark Continent," *Joint Special Operations University Report 09–5*, May 2009, p. 33, http://jsoupublic. socom.mil/publications/jsou/JSOU09–5alexanderAfricaIW.pdf (accessed December 12, 2009).

70 See, for example, the 2009 film *Sweet Crude*, which follows a group of local young men as they become involved in MEND's activities in the Niger Delta. More information is available at www.sweetcrudemovie.com (accessed December 12, 2009).

71 John B. Alexander, "Africa," op. cit; and Brian Lionberger, "Emerging Requirements for U.S. Counterinsurgency," op. cit., p. 80.

72 Anna Mulrine, "Al Qaeda's Terrorist Web in Africa," *U.S. News & World Report*, March 17, 2009, www.usnews.com/articles/news/world/2009/03/17/al-qaedas-terrorist-web-in-africa.html (accessed December 12, 2009).

73 Ibid.

74 Kyle Dabruzzi, "A Hard Wound to MEND," op. cit.

75 David Dickson, "Political Islam in Sub-Saharan Africa: The Need for a New Research and Diplomatic Agenda," *United States Institute of Peace Special Report*, No. 140 (May 2005), p. 3, www.usip.org/files/resources/sr140.pdf (accessed December 12, 2009).

76 Ibid.

77 Trygve B. Trosper, "West Africa's War on Terrorism: Time and Patience," Strategy Research Project, U.S. Army War College, 2009, p. 15, www.dtic.mil/cgi-bin/GetTR Doc?AD=ADA499371&Location=U2&doc=GetTRDoc.pdf (accessed December 12, 2009).

78 Kevin A. O'Brien and Theodore Karasik, "Case Study: West Africa," in *Ungoverned Territories: Understanding and Reducing Terrorism Risk* (Santa Monica, CA: Rand Corporation, 2007), p. 196 (as cited in Trosper, "West Africa's War on Terrorism," op. cit.), www.rand.org/pubs/monographs/2007/RAND_MG561.pdf (accessed December 12, 2009).

79 John J. Miller, "The Unknown Slavery: In the Muslim World, That Is, and It's Not Over," *National Review*, May 20, 2002, http://findarticles.com/p/articles/mi_m1282/ is_9_54/ai_85410331/pg_2/ (accessed December 12, 2009).

80 "Tensions High on Chad-Darfur Border as Refugee Movements Continue—UN," UN News Center, March 14, 2008, www.un.org/apps/news/story.asp?NewsID=259 74&Cr=darfur&Cr1=chad (accessed December 12, 2009).

81 Office of the Coordinator for Counterterrorism, "Chapter 5—Country Reports: Africa Overview," *U.S. Department of State Country Reports on Terrorism*, April 28, 2006, www.state.gov/s/ct/rls/crt/2005/64335.htm (accessed December 12, 2009).

82 Ibid.

83 "Pan-Sahel Initiative (PSI)," GlobalSecurity.org, www.globalsecurity.org/military/ ops/pan-sahel.htm (accessed December 12, 2009).

84 Ibid.

85 "Trans-Sahara Counterterrorism Partnership (TSCTP)," GlobalSecurity.org, www. globalsecurity.org/military/ops/tscti.htm (accessed December 12, 2009).

86 Ibid.

87 The author has made eight trips to Africa in support of these and other programs.

88 Office of the Coordinator for Counterterrorism, "Chapter 5—Country Reports," op. cit.

89 "Trans-Sahara Counterterrorism Partnership," GlobalSecurity.org, op. cit.

90 "Pan-Sahel Initiative," GlobalSecurity.org, op. cit.

91 Alexander, "Africa," op. cit., p. 36.

6 The U.S. Trans-Saharan Counterterrorism Partnership

An Evaluation

Julius E. Nyang'oro and Andrea M. Walther

Introduction

The transnational terrorist attacks of September 11, 2001 (9/11) proved that weak states could pose a great threat to U.S. security. In U.S. security policy circles, the new threat assessment substantially increased Africa's geo-strategic importance to the U.S., as the continent was seen to have a combination of extreme poverty, poor governance, religious extremism, and undergoverned territories that could offer transnational and domestic terrorists, as well as terrorist financing, a ripe environment for penetration and manipulation. The National Security Strategy (NSS), which was released in September 2002, outlined how U.S. policies would work to counter terrorism and prevent another 9/11-style attack from occurring. Furthermore, the NSS identified economic development and democratic governance as ways the U.S. could work to help build African capacity to address threats in Africa.

The Trans-Saharan Counterterrorism Partnership (TSCTP) is a three-pronged program that was created in 2005 to combat terrorism in the Sahel by doing just what the NSS directed: Enhancing democratic governance, strengthening economic development, and building African military capacity. TSCTP reflects the evolving strategy of US security policy towards West Africa post-9/11. Though TSCTP claims to embody a balanced approach to countering terrorism, we argue that several factors have led to the prioritization of the security element over the diplomatic and development components. A security policy developed in the haste of the post-9/11 threat environment, TSCTP has evolved throughout the existence of the program ostensibly to better reflect and learn from realities on the ground. This chapter is a critical assessment of TSCTP within the overall context of U.S. security policy towards the Sahel.

The U.S. counter-terrorism strategies in Africa: A survey

Background

As a result of 9/11, U.S. security engagement in Africa was significantly increased during the Bush administration. Multiple initiatives were created to focus additional resources and attention on combating the terrorist threat in the Sahel.

The establishment of a new U.S. Department of Defense combatant command (AFRICOM), devoted solely to Africa, in 2008, also reflected a serious evolution in policymakers' perceptions of U.S. strategic interests in Africa.[1] The TSCTP was created in 2004, as a direct response to the terrorist attacks on the United States on September 11, 2001. TSCTP's specific mandate is to defeat terrorist organizations by (1) strengthening regional counterterrorism capabilities; (2) enhancing and institutionalizing cooperation among the region's security forces; (3) denying support and sanctuary through strategically targeted development assistance; (4) promoting democratic governance; (5) discrediting terrorist ideology; and (6) reinforcing bilateral military ties with the United States.[2] Key agencies participating in TSCTP are the Department of State (DOS), the U.S. Agency for International Development (USAID), and the Department of Defense (DOD), with the State Department's Bureau of African Affairs as the program lead. TSCTP as a program needs to be understood as part of a larger response by the U.S. government of what it perceived as a new, more robust and expanded engagement with areas that were thought to pose a new evolving security threat.

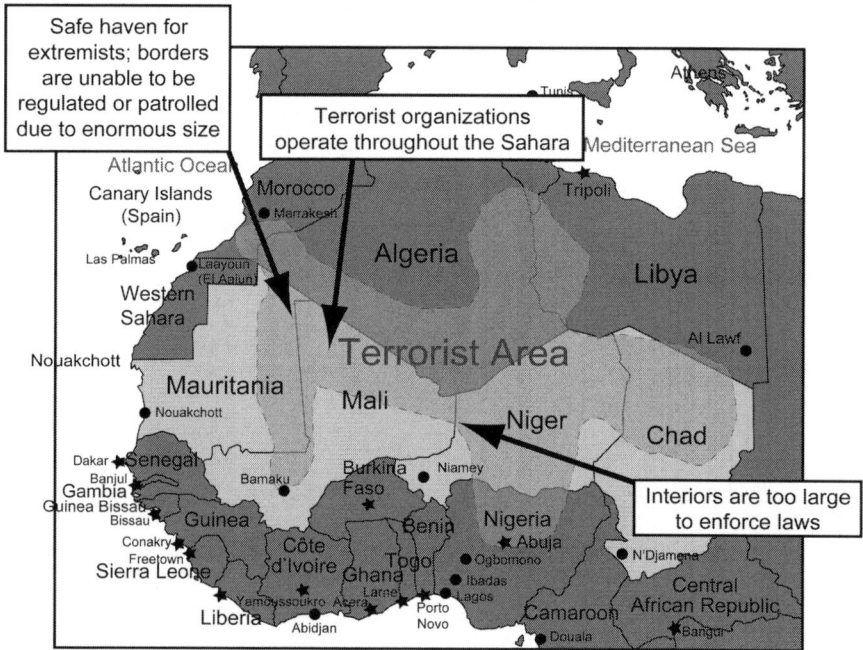

Figure 6.1 The Pan-Sahel Initiative
Source: GlobalSecurity.org, Pan-Sahel Initiative,http://www.globalsecurity.org/military/ops/images/psimap.jpg.

The Pan-Sahel Initiative (PSI)

In November 2003 a State Department-led counter-terrorism program, the Pan-Sahel Initiative (PSI), was funded with $7 million to wage the war on terrorism and to enhance regional peace and security in four countries – Mali, Niger, Chad, and Mauritania. The program worked to facilitate greater cooperation and information exchange among the governments in the region on counter-terrorism and border security issues.[3] The PSI had diplomatic and military wings to the program. The State Department conducted an extensive information campaign with host nations, with the aim of making these nations aware of the nature of the terrorist threat and the vulnerabilities each individual country faced. Special Operations Forces from U.S. European Command (SOCEUR) helped train one rapid-reaction company (about 150 soldiers), in each of the four Saharan states to enhance border capabilities against arms smuggling, drug trafficking, and the movement of trans-national terrorists.[4] Each Partner Nation received approximately 40 Toyota troop transport pickups outfitted with high-tech communications and navigation gear.[5]

The Trans-Saharan Counterterrorism Initiative/Partnership (TSCTI/P)

In 2005, the Trans-Sahara Counterterrorism Initiative/Partnership (TSCTI/P) was created as the successor program to the PSI. The U.S. State Department justified the creation of TSCTP by stating that

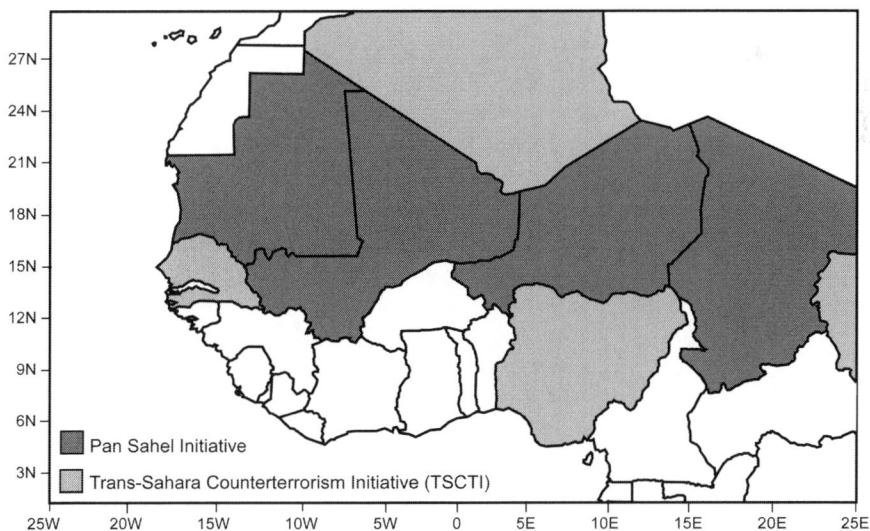

Figure 6.2 The Operation of the Pan-Sahel Initiative and the Trans-Sahara Counterterrorism Initiative (TSCTI)
Source: GlobalSecurity.org, "TSCTI," www.globalsecurity.org/military/ops/images/africa_sahel_map2.gif.

the need for TSCTP stemmed from the potential for expansion of operations by Islamic terrorist organizations in the Sahel. TSCTP was developed as a follow-on to the very successful Pan-Sahel Initiative, which focused solely on the states of the Sahel. Ongoing concern that Islamist terrorists continue to seek to create safe havens and support networks in the remote expanses of the Sahel, as well as the public affiliation of some terrorist groups with AQ, led to its formal approval by the US Government in early 2005.

(U.S. Department of State, 2006)

Additional U.S. agencies were incorporated into the program to develop a more comprehensive approach to regional security and cooperation. The State Department and USAID were tasked with addressing developing civil society initiatives, and the Department of Treasury became responsible for efforts to tighten money-handling controls in the region.

The program's name was adjusted to the Trans-Saharan Counterterrorism "Partnership" in 2007, to stress that the initiative was being conducted in conjunction with African partner nations. The name change is a reflection of the evolving strategy of "partnership" with African governments as opposed to the program being simply an "initiative" of the U.S. government. For political and diplomatic purposes, the difference in terminology is significant. The TSCTP tried to learn from the weakness of its predecessor program and incorporated and implemented a number of lessons learned. First, TSCTP's jurisdiction was expanded to cover five additional countries—Algeria, Morocco, Nigeria, Senegal, and Tunisia. It focused on building detection and response capacity for the mitigation of asymmetric threats throughout the entire region, rather than a country-by-country approach. Second, the program was awarded a five-year commitment of $500 million ($100 million per year for use in nine countries), which was a significant increase from the PSI's paltry $7 million (one-year commitment shared amongst four countries).[6]

Third, TSCTP's mandate was broadened to defeat terrorist organizations by: (1) strengthening regional counter-terrorism capabilities; (2) enhancing and institutionalizing cooperation among the region's security forces; (3) denying support and sanctuary through strategically targeted development assistance; (4) promoting democratic governance; (5) discrediting terrorist ideology; and (6) reinforcing bilateral military ties with the United States.

Fourth, the military component of the program, *Operation Enduring Freedom – Trans Sahara* (OEF-TS), was expanded to include a series of military-to-military engagements and exercises designed to strengthen the ability of regional governments to police the large expanses of remote terrain in the Sahel region.[7] The increase in funding allocated to TSCTP allowed OEFTS to train African Partner Nations at the battalion level (300 to 1,200 soldiers) rather than at the company level (62–190 soldiers). This meant that TSCTP was able to train four to six times the number of soldiers at any given time than were trained under the PSI.[8] Finally, new programs were also added, which promoted democratic governance, discredited terrorist ideology, and reinforced bilateral military ties with the U.S.[9]

Policy and program implementation

Since TSCTP's inception, the key agencies' obligations and commitments for it have amounted to approximately $353 million, primarily for (1) diplomacy, (2) development assistance, and (3) military activities. The main elements of U.S. Security Assistance programs have been:[10]

- The counter-terrorism (CT) programs to create a new regional focus for trans-Saharan cooperation, including use of established regional organizations like the African Union and its new Center for Study and Research on Terrorism in Algiers. These programs include training to improve border and aviation security and overall CT readiness.
- Continued specialized CT Assistance Training and Terrorist Interdiction Program (TIP) activities in the Trans-Saharan region and potential regional expansion of those programs.
- Public diplomacy programs that expand outreach efforts in the Sahel, Maghreb regions, Nigeria, and Senegal and seek to develop regional programming, which embrace the vast and diverse region. Emphasis is on preserving the traditional tolerance and moderation displayed in most African Muslim communities and countering the development of extremism, particularly in youth and rural populations.
- Democratic governance and development programs that strive, in particular, to provide adequate levels of U.S. government support for democratic and economic development in the Sahel, strengthening those states' ability to withstand internal threats. Development assistance examples include youth community activism, income generation, intra-faith dialogue, community outreach, conflict management through community radio, local governance, and community radio.
- Military programs intended to expand military-to-military cooperation, to ensure adequate resources are available to train, advise, and assist regional forces, and to establish institutions promoting better regional cooperation, communication, and intelligence sharing.

Post-9/11 U.S. security assessment of Africa and the Sahel

After 9/11, African stability became identified as "a near term global strategic imperative and is a high priority" in many high-profile public U.S. government documents.[11] The 2002 U.S. National Security Strategy acknowledged the strategic need to "strengthen Africa's fragile states and help build indigenous capability to secure porous borders, and help build up the law enforcement and intelligence infrastructure to deny havens for terrorists."[12] The Defense Department's 2006 Quadrennial Defense Review (QDR) highlighted the tendency of terrorist groups to take advantage of "ungoverned territories," and made note of "emerging terrorist extremist threats" in Western and Northern Africa.[13] The 2006 National Security Strategy identified that "the US recognizes that our security depends upon partnering with Africans to strengthen fragile and failing states and bring ungoverned areas under the control of effective democracies."[14]

Though immediate post-9/11 U.S. attention was focused mainly on Somalia because of the assumed connection between the collapsed state and Al-Qaeda, the Sahel was identified as having "emerged as an important staging area, training center, and a favored place [for terrorists] to target US interests".[15] The U.S. determined that the Sahel contained some of the poorest countries in the world, filled with fledgling democratic governments and weak governmental institutions that had no control over their borders. U.S. national security documents identified Africa's fragile states and porous borders as offering an attractive sanctuary to terrorists, and had great potential to become a breeding ground for terrorism.[16]

These same national security documents also identified "liberty, peace, and growing prosperity" as the longer-term aims to offset these African security threats. Potential for U.S. engagement with Africa in countering these threats was focused around both formulating economic initiatives to generate economic growth and working with partners to resolve regional conflict. Concrete steps for U.S. involvement were identified as strengthening fragile states, building indigenous capability to secure borders, and building up law enforcement and intelligence infrastructures to deny havens for terrorists. Proposals to help the continent establish cooperative security arrangements and "coalitions of the willing" amongst European and African allies to counter these threats were also created. In the most clear terms possible, U.S. national security documents expressed that the "overall path of political and economic freedom is the surest route to progress."[17]

This current U.S. security strategy hinges on three essential components: Defense, diplomacy, and development (the three Ds). The articulation of this strategy with the three components is actually a fairly recent phenomenon. In years past, while elements of the strategy may have been present in the various documents and statements by government officials, it was never coherently presented in a fashion that would make it easy to identify. The articulation of the three elements of the National Security Strategy by definition and necessity meant that the different departments of the U.S. government that were responsible for the individual elements of the strategy needed to develop a new way of doing business to reflect this combined effort.

The general African and West African context

The Sahel in general, and the four original PSI-focused countries in particular, are seen to have a combination of permissive factors and root causes that create an environment very vulnerable to terrorist activity. Permissive factors are physical, economic, institutional, and political weaknesses in African states' ability to prevent terrorists from entering and operating in their territories. Root causes are conditions that encourage individuals to lead, join, or support terrorist enterprises.

Permissive factors

Permissive factors create a supportive operating environment in the Sahel that enables existing terrorist movements to undertake operations in any given country. Sahelian permissive factors include weak militaries, which have little to no munitions and equipment, and are unable to provide sufficient border, port, and customs controls. The prevalence of organized crime and smuggling networks, which enable terrorist groups to mobilize funds, move operatives, and build networks with other armed groups is evidence of the weak militaries. Further past history of regional conflict results in tense relationships in the region at times, which has thus far made regional collaboration and information sharing difficult. The reasons most often cited for the high occurrence (and reoccurrence) of coups in West Africa include political instability, economic mismanagement, and corruption. As a result of the significant regional conflict, there is an extremely high concentration of weapons available. Thus, the threat of terrorism is just one of many security challenges Sahelian nations face, which forces the issue of terrorism to compete with other domestic security interests for political backing, funding, and attention. Finally, a lack of public information regarding the risks terrorism poses, and how it affects the African continent, makes African publics lack support towards the cause.[18]

Root causes

The presence of extreme poverty, poor governance, religious strifes, and under-governed territories, when combined, are all root causes of terrorist activity in the Sahel. The Sahelian countries are among the poorest and least food secure in the world. They are all severely underdeveloped political economies, consistently scoring very low on the UN's human development index (HDI).[19] They face numerous health challenges related to poverty, malnutrition, and inadequate hygiene and sanitation, and their health and development indicators rank among the worst in the world. The region is marked by high rates of deforestation, soil degradation, erosion and population growth, as well as by weak political and private sector institutions.[20]

Almost without exception, these countries have weak and ineffective states. They have large segments of disgruntled populations; disgruntlement is based on the fact that the states have not been able to deliver on the essentials of socio-economic development, and to a large extent the physical security of the population is also seriously threatened, with the population variously viewing the state as part of the problem if not *the* problem. In other words, there is a large governance problem. In the 1990s, approximately one-third of Sub-Saharan

African nations were deemed to have "low state capacity and unable to exercise control and authority over their rural and remote regions or their borders."[21] Though much progress has been made, West Africa has a four-decade long history of "autocratic governance, political exclusion, and unrepresentative institutions, which have given rise to the current crises which exist in the region."[22] Despite significant efforts by Sahelian governments to limit terrorist groups' access to weapons, funding, and movement, the potential for corruption remains high, and therefore one's ability to move around these obstacles is significant.[23]

Africa's Muslim population is approximately 300 million, as Islam is the fastest growing religion on the African continent. Virtually all Muslims in the Sahelian region are Sunni, and the traditional form of West African Islam is Sufi, which is known for its characteristics of tolerance and inclusivity. Though fundamentalism in the Sahel has existed for many years, it has been rather peaceful. If any violence has taken place, it has occurred as a result of local political and economic factors, rather than on a Western target.[24]

Undergoverned territories are areas in which a state faces significant challenges in establishing control and providing security for its people, a significant percentage of which is highly mobile. The events of 9/11 demonstrated that when ignored, failed or failing states as well as undergoverned territories can become physical, legal, and financial sanctuaries for global terrorist networks, international organized crime, and drug traffickers who seek to exploit the environment. There are four major factors that contribute to what makes a territory "undergoverned": (1) the level of state penetration of society; (2) the extent to which the state has control over its armed forces; (3) the extent to which the state controls its borders; and (4) whether the state is subject to external intervention by other states or outside forces. Generally speaking, weak and failing states are incapable of providing the central political good of security and traditionally have weak institutions, deteriorating or destroyed infrastructure, ineffective educational and health systems, and are extremely corrupt. It also provides the widespread conditions of poverty and hostile environment that easily give rise to feelings of alienation and radicalization. A weak state may offer sanctuary for both domestic and international terrorist groups. Thus, working to strengthen weak states that have undergoverned territories has the potential to eliminate the authority and power vacuums within which terrorism thrives.[25]

The threat of terrorism in the Sahel

As it has become clear in the last decade, terrorism is not just a Western problem; it is also very clearly an African problem that works to destabilize the Sahelian region and the continent. Even if Western "soft targets" are attacked on African soil, more Africans are affected and killed than Westerners. This became clear with the U.S. Embassy attacks in Dar es Salaam, Tanzania, and Nairobi, Kenya, in 1998. Terrorism also exacerbates political tensions and undermines economic and political development on the continent. Even the threat of potential attack works to intimidate and discourage trade, investment, and tourism. It is thus in the best interests of individual African nations, regional intergovernmental organizations, and the African Union to reduce and eliminate the permissive factors and root causes that make Africa vulnerable to terrorist activity.

Just as different U.S. federal agencies have differing objectives under TSCTP, in some respects the U.S.'s security objectives may differ from West African States' security objectives. The U.S.'s biggest concern is the confirmed presence of terrorist groups in the Sahel and their propensity to take advantage of the illicit networks present to move weapons, goods, and people, as well as conduct terrorist attacks against West African countries. Attacks will act to further destabilize one of the most conflict-prone regions in the world. Yet from the West African perspective, the largest threats in the region consist of the skyrocketing drug trade and non-traditional threats to the stability and security of the region such as food security, youth bulge, and climate change.

Figure 6.3 The Sahel region

As was outlined above, TSCTP has evolved from a partnership with four countries to the current nine. It is not clear if indeed all the nine countries have similar problems, even in their determination of the terrorist threat. It is important to point out that there are multiple kinds of terrorism. The kind that runs most rampant and has had a longer history across West Africa is domestic terrorism, not international terrorism. There is no question that Algeria has had a very serious problem with locally grown terrorism and Islamic radicalism, and Al-Qaeda in the Islamic Maghreb (AQIM) has penetrated some elements of the local radical Islam communities. It is not clear however that all the countries in the program would make the same claim. If one takes the American position of engage now or be sorry later, there is a need to have a thorough local analysis of the terrorist threat rather than simply assuming that if a country has a large ungoverned territory, terrorists are bound to show up.

But do all of these elements when combined a terrorist make? Does terrorism exist in Trans-Saharan Africa? Though at the moment the African continent is not a hotspot for terrorist activity, certain terrorist actors and groups have a history of planning and carrying out acts of terror on African soil. The Sahel–Sahara divide is a vast expanse of territory, which runs across Africa from northwestern Chad through northern Niger and Mali to Mauritania.[26]

There is evidence that terrorism is present in this region. It can be divided into three distinct but broad categories. First, transnational terror committed by Al-Qaeda, or Al-Qaeda-like groups, targets African governments or soft Western targets located in Africa. The Sahel's northern border, which leads from the Sahara desert into the North African Maghreb, is extremely porous. Transnational terrorist groups are present through many Al-Qaeda operatives and Al-Qaeda-affiliated groups in North Africa. Second, domestic terrorist groups attack African governments and Western targets to raise the visibility of their grievances, constituting a moderate to significant threat in the region. Third, terrorist financing and facilitation are also present through the collection of financial and political support for groups such as Hezbollah and Hamas.[27]

Analysis of the Trans-Sahara Counterterrorism Partnership

In the post-9/11 world, we must recognize that the U.S. became committed to the idea that terrorism was a global phenomenon, and therefore the only way to combat it was to declare a "global war on terror." This is one of the main reasons why programs in the Trans-Saharan region were started. However, Africa has experienced its own share of terrorism on the continent. While the 9/11 attacks occurred in the U.S., several African countries lost their citizens in those attacks. Further, in 1998 in two of the most devastating terrorist attacks anywhere to date, two African countries, Kenya and Tanzania, were victims of AQ attacks. Even though the targets were U.S. embassies, the overwhelming majority of the people who died or were injured were African citizens. Indeed two months after the 9/11 attacks, 16 people were killed in coordinated attacks in Mombasa, Kenya, on an Israeli owned hotel and passenger plane. These incidents proved that Africa would continue to be an environment where Western installations would be the target of terrorist attacks.

The success of TSCTP

In order to evaluate the success of the TSCTP program, inter-agency metrics need to be developed and agreed upon. There are many factors both for Africa and for the U.S., which point to the fact that TSCTP has done and continues to do many positive things. First, the creation of AFRICOM signifies an increase in strategic importance the U.S. is placing on the African continent. With the creation of AFRICOM there has been increased security, diplomatic, and development engagement with Africa.

The inter-agency nature of the TSCTP program signifies that policies are being planned across traditional stovepipes for the first time. The TSCTP countries constitute a region that is not currently a conflict zone. This program and its concepts are therefore attempting to affect the region before conflict arises. The differences between PSI, TSCTI, and TSCTP reflect a coherent transition where best practices, which appear to have attempted to take into consideration realities on the ground, were implemented from one stage to the next after action lessons learned were written, discussed, and implemented. In examining what tangible regional effects could be attributed to the success of the TSCTP program since 2002, there has been a general decrease in regional conflict and an increase in U.S.-led peacekeeping training programs available to Sahelian nations. Finally, a much greater amount of funding is going to people and places it wasn't in the Sahel. Given the extreme level of poverty in these countries, it is obvious that it should be possible to say that within the limited

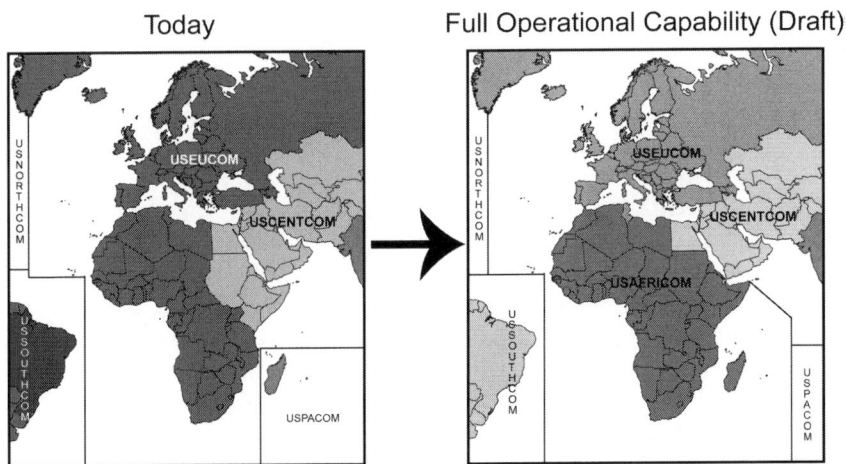

Figure 6.4 AFRICOM's Area of Responsibility
Source: U.S. Africa Command Area of Responsibility, www.globalsecurity.org/military/agency/dod/images/africom-2007.jpg

objectives of maintaining peace and stability, the U.S. is not going to solve these problems in the near-term, if at all, so these initial metrics are bearing positive results.

The criticisms of TSCTP—programmatic issues

As can be expected in programs of this magnitude and size, there are bound to be some shortcomings. This criticism it should be noted is not just from scholars or people who are simply opposed to the presence of Americans on African soil, particularly in the "global war against terror," but also by agencies such as the Government Accountability Office (GAO) in terms of the implementation of the program. To quote the GAO: On a purely technical implementation level, "several factors have hampered the key agencies' implementation of TSCTP activities, in some cases limiting their ability to collaborate in working to combat terrorism."[28] There are therefore two issues to be addressed: Implementational challenges and programmatic challenges.

On the programmatic level, it is clear that agencies lack a comprehensive, integrated strategy for their TSCTP activities, and the documents used in planning the activities do not prioritize proposed activities or identify milestones needed to measure progress or make improvements. Because of diplomatic protocol, disagreements about whether DOS should have authority over DOD personnel temporarily assigned to conduct TSCTP activities in partner countries have led to DOD suspension of some activities, for example in Niger. As the GAO report notes, DOD does not really want its personnel to be under the state's jurisdictional authority even on a temporary basis: The person who pays the piper calls the tune! To date most of the money to finance TSCTP activities has come from DOD.

Another shortcoming emanates from the bureaucratic and strategic interests of the participating agencies. DOS, USAID, and DOD each have differences in strategy and planning. DOS and USAID have long-term objectives and planning structures whereas DOD utilizes short-term planning as it has quicker access to money. This causes inconsistent funding streams in DOS' and USAID's distribution of funds for TSCTP on a year-to-year basis. From one year to the next this can result in huge discrepancies of programmatic funding. Furthermore, each department utilizes different measures of effectiveness and metrics for success. Although the agencies measure activities' outputs, such as the number of foreign military personnel trained, they do not measure their activities' outcome in combating terrorism – for instance, any decrease in extremism in the targeted countries. Another factor is the enormous difference in resources—related to both finance and personnel between DOD and DOS, which includes USAID.

But we think that there is a much more serious problem with the thrust of the program if one looks at it from the viewpoint of the three Ds. If we examine the five main elements of the program, it quickly becomes obvious that the main emphasis is on the defense (security) elements and less on the development and even less on the diplomatic elements. One can understand this, however, if we examine where the program's funding is coming from. If we make the assumption that even though this program is supposed to be an interagency effort, the main funder of the program is DOD. It is therefore not surprising that (1) the security elements of the program are emphasized; (2) there is a gap between national security policy and security programs being implemented on the ground; (3) the majority of the security-focused funding is utilized on "hard" train-and-equip exercises, efforts to enhance regional cooperation, and developing regional intelligence- and information-sharing capacity; and (4) authorities have been transferred to DOD once vested exclusively in civilian agencies. The danger of this reality and approach is that when we go back and look at the "root" and "permissive" causes, there is a need to emphasize development first, diplomacy second, and defense third. TSCTP's focus on countering terrorism may make this program appear to Africans as part of the U.S. agenda (and not an African security priority), making African governments' reactive behavior therefore open to manipulation.

Implications of this assessment

Implication of USG 3D imbalance

There are many concrete negative implications to having such a massive imbalance between the budgets of the Defense Department and the State Department, which necessitates further analysis. The defense budget dwarfs that of civilian agencies for global engagement by a factor of approximately 17 to one.[29] First, control of development assistance resources happens to be a critical element of the Defense Department's policy shift towards Africa. Between 2002 and 2005, the Pentagon increased its control of development assistance six-fold, from 5.6 percent to 21.7 percent,[30] while the percentage controlled by USAID shrank from 65 percent to 40 percent.[31] This is because the Defense Department has been granted temporary authority by Congress to provide "non-traditional security assistance" for prevention purposes, with guidelines for use in environments where civilian actors have difficulty operating or where civilian capacity is weak.

Second, there is also a large imbalance in the human resources allocated to the two departments. The increase in Defense Department personnel assigned to AFRICOM is occurring at a time when the State Department and USAID offices on the continent are both grossly understaffed and underfunded as a result of the heavy personnel and budgetary demands at the U.S. embassies in Iraq and Afghanistan. Although the U.S. military (including the Coast Guard and the reserve component) has over 2.5 million uniformed personnel and over 10,100 civilian employees, the State Department and USAID together only have 8,521 permanent employees.[32]

A third point of note is that the motives for implementing development-related projects differ greatly between the Defense Department and USAID.

For example, if USAID conducted an assessment of health needs in Niger, the project proposal would be evaluated based on how well it would serve the population most in need of particular supplies and assistance. However, a Defense Department assessment would evaluate how a donation of medical supplies could best support U.S. national security objectives. Further, in addition to differences in mandate, there is a difference in competency. Personnel assessing and implementing these programs possess distinct backgrounds, training, and skill sets based on where they work. USAID has a clear advantage in this regard and may make a different decision. For example, in a country such as Niger, which has a per capita income of $280 (in 2007) the decision of where and when to donate large amounts of supplies has serious ramifications.[33] The differing mandates and skills of each department alter how such a decision is made and the outcome that is reached.

In summation, over the past decade, the Defense Department has seen an increase in the amount of resources at its disposal to contribute to the promotion of security and development in Africa. However, while resources have dramatically increased, DOD does not have appropriately trained staff members to be making the qualified decisions necessary to identify and program the aid.

Implications of TSCTP 3D imbalance

Combating and overcoming current global threats necessitates a comprehensive national security strategy, which incorporates balanced tools of diplomacy, defense, and development. Though a key goal of the 2006 US National Security Strategy is "to promote economic development and the expansion of effective, democratic governance so that African states can take the lead in addressing African challenges," the strategy currently seems to be only supported on paper not financially or programmatically.[34]

It is necessary to examine what programs have been put into place and what financial support they receive, in order to determine the effectiveness of current U.S. policies and programs. Overall, there are four key pillars involved in the democratization process that would have to be synchronized in order for the U.S. Strategy to be successful: (1) justice and reconciliation efforts, which work to create legitimate legal systems; (2) social and economic well being initiatives, which work to create essential social and economic services; (3) governance and participation programs, which create legitimate political and administrative institutions; and (4) security-focused efforts, which work to create a safe and secure environment and legitimate security institutions. Over the past eight years, different programs have been created in each of these pillars, which together formulate U.S. foreign policy towards Africa.

A closer examination of U.S. foreign policy to Sahelian countries suggests that military and security concerns dominate this policy. By having a security-focused policy, the U.S. is signaling to Sahelian countries that the way to get the attention of U.S. policy makers in terms of support is through their militaries. Yet, as TSCTP works to create highly trained and equipped militaries, and foreign assistance to TSCTP countries is increasingly security focused, an unhealthy civil–military balance seems to be developing with the military gaining ground in the imbalance. This ultimately leads to a degradation (rather than a stabilization) of governmental and security institutions within a given country. Weak governance capacity increases the potential for African nations to embellish the threats they face to ensure continued U.S. aid and support. Weak governance and a civil–military imbalance may also increase the potential for incidents of state terrorism or other types of domestic unrest to occur. Where security forces are not monitored by legitimate civilian authorities, abuse of power and infringements of human rights threaten human security.[35] This chain of events could result in a downward spiral of destabilization and conflict, the exact opposite of what security and counter-terror programs aim to achieve.

A Malian example will help us to illustrate the problem. In Mali, the largely nomadic Tuareg population in the north of the country has had a long-running problem with Malian authorities due to a consistent lack of governmental attention and resources on the areas in the north. This has resulted in heightened militarization of desert areas, fears that the Tuareg may be cooperating with and becoming radicalized by AQIM, and the tendency of the Malian and U.S. to therefore blur the lines between the Tuareg and AQIM threat. The presence, training, and collaboration of U.S. and Malian troops have given the two groups common grounds for opposition and protestation. The situation that has resulted is a dangerous combination: A strong and well-equipped Malian military, a weak civilian government likely to exaggerate the terrorist threat to justify continued funding, an active domestic extremist group, and the presence of AQIM in the north. In examining the recent spike in both domestic unrest and AQIM activity in the north, as well as rumors of documented Tuareg/AQIM collaboration circulating, it appears that TSCTP has in some ways been counter-productive, and has led to resentment and encouraged the very extremism it was intended to prevent.

One other casualty of the emphasis on defense as opposed to diplomacy and development is security sector reform, which falls under the general domain of governance. Because of the U.S. preoccupation with terrorism, there is evidence that Americans are less enthusiastic about implementing security sector reform, as long as the African partner is demonstrating commitment to the CT cause. This indeed has been the case with Mauritania in more recent months. It is clear that the Mauritanian armed forces committed a cardinal sin in terms of SSR by intervening in politics in 2007. Even the African Union (AU), not known for applying strict standards in upholding many principles, suspended Mauritania from participating in AU activities as a result of this action. Yet, Mauritania continued to be an active partner of the US in the "war against terror." This is a very bad precedent, because the West African subregion historically has experienced the most coups in all of Africa, and it should not be a surprise if some military officers get tempted to play a role in politics. Mauritania also attempted to influence the opinion of the international community via international media outlets by claiming that the grounds for launching the coup were due to the fact that the former democratically elected government (arguably the nation's first democratically elected government ever) wasn't tough enough on radical Islamic terrorists operating within the country. The current instabilities in Niger and Guinea with those countries' militaries flexing their muscles should also be a great concern for political stability in the region.

Terrorism in the Sahel—a wrong calculation?

The West African sub-region therefore has all the elements—"root" and "permissive" causes, which make it vulnerable to security threats, including terrorism. However, there is a need for caution because the mere existence of these elements does not translate into the fact that terrorists and terrorism exists. Perhaps it may be worth noting that in the U.S. calculation the combination of extreme poverty, poor governance, ungoverned territories, and Muslim majority countries does not equal conditions vulnerable to terrorist activity. But the opposite may also be true that the combination of these factors could be a dangerous mix that may lead to undesirable results. Perhaps by not linking all of these elements under an umbrella of terrorism, the underlying systemic issues could be addressed in a better and more substantive manner. Furthermore, by taking the focus off of terrorism and increasing funding and focus for issues such as counter-narcotics trafficking, the U.S. could make better inroads with partner nation governments by supporting African security priorities.

The majority of the Muslim communities in this region practice moderate and accommodating versions of Islam. And indeed, as the case of Mauritania and Mali have shown, local populations have been reluctant to welcome AQIM in their midst. It is therefore important for the U.S. to take note of this fact, as it deals with the partner states to make sure that military cooperation between the U.S. and the partners does not actually work as an incentive for local young people to join in the cause of anti-Americanism. A more differentiated approach of assessing an individual country's needs might be better than painting the entire region with one broad brush.

Recommendations for TSCTP

TSCTP policy recommendations

Our analysis suggests that a more cohesive and balanced set of U.S. democratization programs is needed on bi-lateral, regional, and international levels towards Africa in general, and West Africa in particular. First, this would entail a stark increase in programmatic funding for the non-security pillars: Democracy and governance, health and education, and economic and social. Capacity building within existing institutions in each of these pillars is extremely important as it will ensure that African governments are capable of handling the issues and threats that are confronting them. Increasing State Department and USAID diplomatic presence in embassies in the sub-region would help African countries work step by step to ensure that enhanced democratization programs are successful. This is especially important within the security realm, as it is imperative that the capacity of the security institutions match the increased skills and equipment that African militaries are receiving from U.S. counter-terrorism programs.

Second, the primary security focus of TSCTP should prioritize SSR. SSR is "about designing and implementing a series of activities geared towards the security of a state and its people; the justice system; and the governance of security sector institutions."[36] It should be provided for those responsible for democratic control of the security sector, such as civilian governments, democratically elected parliaments, civil servants, and monitors within civil society.

Increased technical support for ECOWAS would help the region develop and implement a common ECOWAS-backed SSR for the West Africa sub-region, which would boost the legitimacy of such a program in each of the different countries there within. It would also provide a good sense of what the sub-region wants from SSR. Enhanced support for regional peacekeeping training organizations and programs may also be an avenue for success. In addition to maintaining support for elevated levels of UN and AU peacekeeping capacity, via the U.S. African Contingency Operations and Training and Assistance program (ACOTA) and the Global Peacekeeping Operations Initiative (GPOI), continued support via the development of the African Standby Brigades, an innovation under the new AU security architecture, is a good step. Furthermore, the U.S. should extract commitments from African nations that they participate in regional centers for capacity building of armed forces in exchange for U.S. involvement and programs. We see these steps as working to enhance more regional security cooperation.

At the international level, the U.S. should enhance multi-lateral support to UN peacekeeping missions and crisis response capacity. The U.S. can accomplish this via increased support of the UN Regional Center for Peace and Disarmament (UNREC) based in Togo, which boasts SSR programs in 12 post-conflict countries in Africa.[37] It can also work to better support the UN Security Council's Counter-Terrorism Committee (UNCTC), which works with international partners to assist member states in their implementation of the UN Security Council Resolution 1371.[38] The UN Office of Drugs and Crime also has a Terrorism Prevention Branch that works to help partner nations fully implement the 12 international counter-terrorism conventions.[39] Additional support could also be given to the G8's Counter-Terrorism Action Group (CTAG), which was established in 2003 to act as a donor forum of counter-terrorism assistance.

Recommendations for successful departmental and interagency implementation of TSCTP

There are many different concrete steps that can be taken on both the departmental and interagency levels to enable TSCTP to have more impact and achieve more of the results that it sets out to attain. On the departmental level, DOD needs to focus on emphasizing its long-term commitment and strategy towards Africa. Increased funding for Foreign Area Officer (FAO) type programs and the creation of a regional rotational system to generate officer experience are two possible options for building its cadre of African specialists. DOS needs to prioritize increasing its diplomatic and development presence in embassies throughout the subregion. Although this may be more wishful thinking on our part then practical at the moment, it would greatly behoove the reputation and effectiveness of USAID to become an independent federal department agency, so that it can do development with the goal of alleviating world poverty rather than development as a tool of U.S. foreign policy.

On the interagency level, first, as was discussed above, more balanced financial and personnel resources between DOS, USAID, and DOD need to be allocated. Increased support for TSCTP programs and mission need to be communicated both horizontally throughout each department from the Home Office to the Combatant Command/Regional Office to the Country Team/Embassy as well as vertically throughout each department's chain of command. More coordinated planning strategies, both temporal and structural, need to be established between the three departments. Since individuals within TSCTP programs are now working across departmental lines for the first time, increased DOS/DOD/USAID staff informational training opportunities and exchanges need to be developed to augment each department's understanding and knowledge of each other. Finally, the creation of advancement opportunities for each department to incentivize exchange tours of duty in other departments is critical to developing inter-departmental awareness, understanding, and synergy.

Conclusion

The presence of poor governance, ungoverned spaces, poverty, and religious extremism in Sahelian Africa raises the critical problem of the role that the region may play in international terrorist activity. The socioeconomic and ideological underpinnings of this emerging terrorist threat highlight the need for sustained solutions on political, economic, social, and security levels. As a response to September 11, 2001, the 2002 US National Security Strategy aimed to build African capacity to counter these threats, primarily through supporting economic development and strengthening democratic governance. The US created the Trans-Saharan Counter-Terrorism Partnership (TSCTP) to work with targeted northwest African countries to eliminate terrorist safe havens and reduce the potential for religious radicalization.

The TSCTP, however, does not adequately support the policy outlined in the National Security Strategy to counter the threat of terrorism in the Sahel. Though TSCTP aims to embody a balanced approach to countering terrorism, many factors elevate the security element over the program's diplomatic and development components. The security focus of US counter-terrorism programs may have inadvertently increased the exact religious radicalization of local groups and collaboration with terrorist organizations that the US designed TSCTP to eradicate and prevent.

Notes

1 U.S. Africa Command (AFRICOM), www.africom.mil/ (accessed September 3, 2010).
2 U.S. Africa Command, "The Trans-Sahara Counterterrorism Partnership," www. africom.mil/tsctp.asp (accessed September 3, 2010).
3 Lawrence Cline, "Counterterrorism Strategy in the Sahel," *Studies in Conflict & Terrorism*, 30(10), 2007, p. 873.
4 "Pan Sahel Initiative," GlobalSecurity.org, www.globalsecurity.org/military.ops. pan-sahel.htm (accessed September 3, 2010).
5 John Davis, "The Bush Model: US Special Forces, Africa, and the War on Terror," in John Davis (ed.), *Africa and the War on Terrorism* (Aldershot: Ashgate Publishing, 2007), p. 152.
6 Jamie L. Wood, "Trans-Saharan Conference Focuses on 'Expanding Partner Nation Capacity-Building,'" March 27, 2008, www.africom.mil/getArticle.asp? art=1707 (accessed September 6, 2010).
7 Lauren Ploch, "Africa Command: US Strategic Interests and the Role of the US Military in Africa," *Congressional Research Service*, RL 34003, January 5, 2009, p. 19.
8 A battalion is composed of four to six companies (300 to 1,000 soldiers), http:// usmilitary.about.com/od/army/l/blchancommand.htm (accessed September 6, 2010).
9 U.S. State Department, "Africa Overview," Country Reports on Terrorism, April 30, 2007, www.state.gov/s/ct/rls/crt/2006/82730.htm (accessed September 8, 2010).
10 Ibid., Trans-Sahara Counterterrorism Partnership (TSCTP).
11 James Jones, Statement before the Senate Armed Services Committee, March 7, 2006.
12 The White House, *The National Security Strategy of the United States of America*, (Washington, D.C.: The White House, 2002), pp. 10–11.
13 U.S. Department of Defense, *Quadrennial Defense Review Report*, February 6 (Washington, D.C.: U.S. Department of Defense, 2006), pp. 33, 12.
14 White House, *The National Security Strategy of the United States of America* (Washington, D.C.: The White House, 2006), p. 37.
15 Ted Dagne, "Africa and the War on Terror," *CRS Report RL 31247*, January 17, 2002, p. 1.
16 Davis, "The Bush Model," op. cit., p. 151.
17 White House, *The National Security Strategy of the United States of America*, March (Washington, D.C.: The White House, 2002), p. 1.
18 Andre Le Sage, *African Counterterrorism Cooperation: Assessing Regional and Sub-regional Initiatives* (Washington, D.C.: Africa Center for Strategic Studies, 2007), pp. 8–11.
19 Human Development Report Statistics, http://hdr.undp.org/en/statistics/ (accessed September 10, 2010).
20 U.S. Agency for International Development, *Sub-Saharan Africa*, www.usaid.gov/ locations/sub-saharan_africa/ (accessed September 8, 2010).
21 Joshua Forrest, "State Inversion and Non-State Politics," in Leonardo Villalon and Phillip Huxtable (eds), *The African State at a Critical Juncture* (Boulder, CO: Lynne Rienner Publishers, 1998), p. 45.
22 Ismail Rashind, "West Africa's Post-Cold War Security Challenges," in Adekeye Adebajo and Ismail Rashid (ed.), *West Africa's Security Challenges: Building Peace in a Troubled Region* (Boulder, CO: Lynne Rienner Publishers, 2004), p. 387.
23 Davis, "The Bush Model," op. cit.

24 Editor, "Islamist Terrorism in the Sahel: Fact or Fiction?" International Crisis Group's Africa Report No. 92, March 31, 2005.
25 Angela Rabasa *et al. Ungoverned Territories: Understanding and Reducing Terrorism Risks* (Santa Monica, CA: The Rand Corporation, 2007), p. xvi.
26 From here on forward in this chapter, the Sahel–Sahara divide will just be referred to as "the Sahel."
27 Le Sage, *African Counterterrorism Cooperation*, op. cit., pp. 34–35.
28 U.S. Government Accountability Office, "Countering Terrorism Actions Needed to Enhance Implementation of Trans-Sahara Counterterrorism Partnership," GAO-08-860, July 2008, p. II.
29 Mark Malan, "US Civil–Military Imbalance for Global Engagement; Lessons from the Operational Level in Africa," *Refugees International,* July 2008, p. II.
30 Stephen J. Morrison and Kathleen Hicks, *Integrating 21st Century Development and Security Assistance* (Washington, D.C.: Center for Strategic and International Studies, 2008), p. vi.
31 Malan, "US Civil–Military Imbalance," op. cit.
32 Ibid., p. 1.
33 World Bank, "Niger at a Glance 2007," www.devdata.worldbank.org/AAG/ner_aag.pdf (accessed September 9, 2010).
34 White House, *The National Security Strategy of the United States of America,* March (Washington, D.C.: The White House, 2006), p. 37.
35 David Nii Addy, *The Challenges of Developing a Policy Agenda for Security Sector Reform and Governance in West Africa,* Accra: Kofi Annan International Peacekeeping and Training Center, June 5–6, 2007.
36 John Mark Opoku, *The Challenges of Developing a Policy Agenda for Security Sector Reform and Governance in West Africa,* Accra: Kofi Annan International Peacekeeping and Training Center, June 5–6, 2007.
37 United Nations Regional Center for Peace and Disarmament, www. unrec.org (accessed September 10, 2010).
38 United Nations, *United Nations Counter-Terrorism Committee,* www.un.org/sc/ctc/ (accessed September 10, 2010).
39 United Nations, *Terrorism Prevention, by the UN Office on Drugs and Crime,* International Relations and Security Network, www.isn.ethz.ch/isn/Digital-Library/IR-Directory/Detail/?ord549=grp1&ots591=CAB359A3-9328-19CC-A1D2–8023E6 46B22C&lng=en&id=89272 (accessed September 10, 2010).

7 The Mauritanian military and the U.S. war on terrorism

Boubacar N'Diaye

Introduction

In 2009, Mauritania's head of state, General Mohamed Ould Abdel Aziz, seems to have made the strategic choice to enter into negotiations with a nebulous group of Salafists, nearly 70 of whom are in the country's prisons charged with various terrorist offenses. The negotiations are conducted by high-level government officials and Islamic scholars. For a country that, until recently, vehemently denied even the existence of extremists within its borders, this is a major development. For a head of state who had, only a year and a half ago, overthrown in a military coup the only democratically elected president the country has ever known, under the pretext that he was soft on terrorism, this indeed comes as a shocker. In Mauritania, terrorism has most certainly ceased to be a taboo subject, and is finally treated as a major challenge by the state and its institutions. Indeed, even as these overtures were made to Islamists, some of whom allegedly committed terrorist acts, the parliament debated and passed (in a confused atmosphere) an anti-terrorist law. This legislation introduced by the government significantly increased the powers of the security forces and toughened certain dispositions of a 2005 anti-terrorist law. In short, after a particularly tumultuous year and a half, and certainly since terrorism claimed its first victims directly in June 2005, Mauritania seems to have entered a new phase in facing the phenomenon of terrorism and religious extremism.

Because of its location, underlying societal dynamics, the fragility of its institutions, the Islamic Republic of Mauritania is likely to be confronted with religious extremism for the foreseeable future. For many reasons discussed below, Mauritania's approach to fighting terrorism over the last several years, its role in the U.S.-led Global War on Terror (GWOT), and how the GWOT affected the country, its society, and the working of its institutions are instructive. These variables can contribute immensely in our efforts at better understanding this phenomenon and its consequences. They most certainly hold valuable lessons for students of the threat of terrorism, its impact on the political dynamics within countries such a Mauritania and their security policies. Of all its institutions, it is, without a doubt, its armed and security forces and their saga in this endeavor that will be of singular interest. However, in a country like Mauritania, given the political and societal backdrop against which the GWOT reached its shores, this means also going beyond the strict workings of the military, to examine the relations between the security sector as a whole and the political system, and indeed society at large. The central contention of this study is that, against the resurgence of the terrorist threat, to appreciate the role the military—and those who control it—has been playing in the U.S. GWOT, it is critical to understand the dynamics within Mauritania's socio-political system. Only such an understanding may avoid for the U.S. unintended and adverse consequences and counterproductive outcomes in its counter-terrorist policies in Northwest Africa and the Sahel region more generally.

Little-known Mauritania has often fallen through the cracks in analyses of political phenomena on the continent. An appropriate starting point of an examination of the role of its military in the GWOT must therefore be a brief presentation of its relevant socio-political background. Then Mauritania's security sector is presented right before examining its role in the country's terrorist threat and in the U.S.-led GWOT. The analysis focuses on the underlying political, socioeconomic dynamics of the military's role, the resulting misuses and manipulations that surrounded the terrorist threat, the main actors, and regional and international dimensions. A concluding section examines the outcomes, prospects, and proffers recommendations.

Socio-political background

Long before "Islamic" became, with the Iranian revolution, a suspect and somewhat worrisome adjective (from the perspective of many Westerners) and then an outright forbidding one (after September 11, 2001, again, from the perspective of the average Westerner, and many others), there was a perfectly innocuous, non-threatening Islamic Republic of Mauritania (the very first of the kind in Africa). Then the "Islamic" was only as a matter of fact avowal, since 100 percent of its population was Muslim. Then it did not even matter. Very few in Africa, let alone in Europe or the United States, could situate it on the map. Quite often when "Mauritania" is uttered, the typical reaction was (still is) "oh yeah, Mauritius, in the Indian Ocean!"

Straddling West Africa and the North African Maghreb, Mauritania is arguably one of the least-known countries in Africa. A brief historical background focusing on the country's postcolonial evolution and the sociopolitical context of the terrorist threat and counterterrorism is therefore always useful. According to World Bank data, Mauritania had an estimated 3.22 million people in 2008, a life expectancy of 57 years, and with a GNI per capita of 840 dollars (2007)[1] is one of the poorest countries in the world despite being generously endowed in natural resources, recently including oil. Mauritania is also characterized by a stark income inequality with colossal fortunes amassed by mostly individuals, generally relatives of the head of state of the moment coexisting with squalor and destitution in the slums of Nouakchott and other large cities.

Recurring droughts, economic mismanagement, and the effects of various international economic crises have installed a sense of permanent precariousness and human insecurity.

All Mauritanians share the same religion, (Sunni Maliki) Islam, but are made up of three major ethno-cultural groups. The first group (referred to as "Negro-Mauritanians") is comprised of four essentially sedentary black ethnic groups (the *Halpulaar*, the *Soninke*, the *Wolof*, and the *Bambara*) who live mainly in the south and east and in urban centers. They make up about one-third of the total population. Mauritania's recent political history has been marked by cyclical attempts by these groups, who feel disenfranchised, to assert their (non-Arab) cultural identity, and an insistent claim to a more equitable share of political and economic power. The second group is the nomadic Arab-Berber (*Beydane* meaning "White" or "light skinned" Maur) ethnic groups, who live mainly in the north, center, and in the east of the country. Arab-Berbers, divided in more than 150 ethnic groups, also make up about one-third of the population. Though their elites are sometimes locked in bitter rivalries, they dominate all institutions, in particular the military, and monopolize all facets of political and economic power. They identify more with the Arab world and, in general, insist on the Arab and Islamic character of Mauritania. Over the years, this monopoly on power led to a depiction to the outside world of Mauritania as an exclusively Arab country, accentuated in recent years by deliberate policies to reduce ties with West Africa. Finally, the *Haratines* and *Abeed*, most certainly the largest group, are (freed or still enslaved) descendants of enslaved black Africans, who identify culturally and psychologically with their former or current *Beydane* masters with whom they share the same language (the *Hassaniya*, an Arabic dialect), Arab-Islamic culture, and social organization. One of the most significant developments in Mauritania politics in recent years has been the emergence of the *Haratines* as a political and social force (though still atomized), and their still muted demand for a greater share of power.

Until his overthrow in a bloodless coup on July 10, 1978, Mokhtar Ould Daddah, the first president, had succeeded in contriving a Mauritanian national identity. Thanks to a consummate policy of ethnic and regional balancing, he deftly kept in check the underlying ethnic, cultural, and political tensions and successfully rebuffed aggressive territorial claims by the king of Morocco. He also made headways in establishing a viable, internationally respected state, and in launching a promising economic development program. Weary of an unpopular and losing war, the army whose top brass had enriched themselves looting the Western Sahara territory it was occupying took power in July 1978, and withdrew from the disastrous Western Sahara territorial conflict. Soon thereafter, dissension and personal ambitions within the military as well as foreign interferences led to a series of coups and countercoups. In the meantime, ethnic tensions worsened and degenerated into ethnic cleansing that made thousands of victims among Negro-Mauritanians, tens of thousands of whom were deported or forced into exile between 1986 and 1992.

On December 12, 1984, Colonel Maaouyia Ould Sid'Ahmed Taya, then Army Chief of Staff, staged the latest coup and remained in power until his overthrow on August 3, 2005. By then, the military and the security sector generally had been all but cleansed of its Negro-Mauritanian component, making it, certainly in its officer corps, almost exclusively Arab-Berber. In between, he had also "civilianized" and "democratized" the military regime starting in 1992, and firmly anchored Mauritania in the Arab world, by leaving ECOWAS and insisting that international institutions situate Mauritania in the North Africa geopolitical area. On August 3, 2005, Ould Taya was overthrown and the country was given a chance to turn the page on years of repressive military rule. The military junta that overthrew him handed power to a democratically elected civilian president in 2007, but he was in turn overthrown on August 3, 2008, leading to a serious crisis. This crisis ended with another election, which essentially legitimized the power of General Mohamed Ould Abdel Aziz, the instigator of Mauritania's two last coups d'état. "President" Ould Abel Aziz inherited thus all the challenges Mauritania has been facing since its independence from France on November 28, 1960.

Mauritania's security sector

Mauritania's security sector is comprised of the usual armed forces one typically finds in former French colonies. Its military's central pillar is the army, which was originally constituted by elements of the remnants of French colonial camel-back mounted troops, the *Goumiers*, and other colonial troops. In addition to the army, it is made up of the National Guard, the national navy, a tiny air force, military intelligence services, and the gendarmerie, a paramilitary corps. The Presidential Guard (the notorious BASEP that has its own commander, now also the personal chief of staff of the president who answers directly to the president) is part of the army. It has now become the central pillar of the security apparatus and has morphed, in essence, into a praetorian guard for regime security, certainly more so since its long-time commander first staged two coups, and became the internationally recognized head of state. There are no reserve forces. The various branches (army, navy, air force, and gendarmerie), are all managed by separate chiefs of staff and are under the responsibility of the Ministry of Defense. The National Guard is under the authority of the Ministry of Interior who also oversees the National Police at least nominally.

Until the mid-1970s, Mauritania's army was an inconsequential force of less than 3,000 men. The military emphatically burst on the political scene with the bloodless coup of July 10, 1978. Since, it never ceased to be a fixture on Mauritanian politics, with a pronounced sense of entitlement to be, more and more unabashedly, just that. Under Colonel Ould Taya, the police, which has become plethoric with no official figures, and intelligence services, have acquired a critical role due to the intensification of political (overt or covert) repression. A former military intelligence officer himself, President Ould Taya overly politicized intelligence and made it an important instrument of his regime[2] under the direction of a trusted army officer, Colonel Ely Ould Mohamed Vall, who, ironically, was to leverage his position to oust him in 2005 along with the commandant of the BASEP, his cousin.

Given the small size of its population, Mauritania now has one of the highest ratio of men in uniform to population in the sub-region. There are nearly 21,000 men in just the regular bodies of the military (including 5,000 paramilitary), compared for example to neighboring Senegal's 15,620, including 5,000 paramilitary, and Mali's 15,150, including 1,800 gendarmes and 4,800 other paramilitary bodies.[3] Arguably, until the recent surge in terrorist activities (see below), with ongoing armed rebellions, Mali and Senegal have more obvious security needs. Mauritania's defense and security budget as a percentage of GDP is far higher that that of its neighbors.[4]

Since it took power in 1978, the Mauritanian military has become, over the years, arguably one of the most dysfunctional security establishments in Africa. Up to then the military was a small unassuming cohesive institution largely spared the "racial," cultural/ethnic, regional, and ideological cleavages, which by then threatened the very fabric of the country. Soon, particularly after the 1984 coup, these lines of fracture found their way into the military establishments along with fierce personal rivalries. Similar to its African counterparts, Mauritania's officer corps rapidly became corrupted by the exercise of power, and the allure of material wealth accumulation. The security sector became gangrened by nepotism, clientelism, and endemic corruption, particularly in the police. These tendencies compounded and developed into the "de-professionalization" of the officer corps and troops alike and the development of an attitude of "everything goes." In the 1980s and 1990s, Colonel Ould Taya purposely exploited and exacerbated these tendencies and dysfunctions. By the time he was ousted, it was believed that many high-ranking officers in the entire security sector (army, navy, police, and customs), were deeply involved in, and owed their immense fortunes partly to, illegal traffic of all sorts, including drug and weapons.

After purging the military of non-Arab officers after their 1987 clumsy coup plot, Colonel Ould Taya sought to thoroughly "Arabize" all armed forces branches, by sending hundreds of select officers for training in military schools in Arab countries such as Iraq, Syria, Morocco, and Algeria. This further accentuated their politicization, disregard for military professionalism, and led to the proliferation of Arab nationalist (Nasserists and Ba'ath) and Islamist groups in the military and the security sector more generally. Anthony Pazzanita (1992) documents this situation.[5] The armed forces also fell victim to Colonel Ould Taya's calculations as he became more preoccupied with the survival of his regime when, after 2002, political and armed opposition grew. After the 2003, bloody coup attempt led by Nasserist officers from the Oulad Nacer and Laghlal ethnic groups from the southeast of the country, he beefed up the BASEP, promoted ultra loyal officers from his own and allied (northern) tribes and weakened other branches of the military. Some of these officers were typically positioned in strategic commands or made head of key parastatals and explicitly given a free hand to use public funds as they pleased. These moves weakened the military institution and increased the resentment of many junior officers left out of rapid promotions and the largesse of the regime. In turn, these divisions destabilized the regime/security apparatus relations as regime survival became dependent on the fealty of a few men, in particular the commander of the BASEP Colonel Ould Abdel Aziz. Colonel Ould Abdel Aziz used his position to easily take power on August 6, 2005, and made his cousin Colonel Ould Mohamed Vall the head of state as chairman of the military junta, the Military Committee for Justice and Democracy (CMJD).

After only 15 months of democratic civilian rule following a nearly botched transition, Colonel Ould Abdel Aziz took power again on August 3, 2008 and kept it, though the July 18, 2009 elections were denounced by the opposition as an electoral coup. He was sworn in as president on August 6, 2009, following the elections agreed to in the June 2, 2009 Dakar agreement sponsored by the international community. To complete this background, it is relevant to add that, as he scrambled to consolidate his regime, Colonel Ould Taya had sought to placate the United States government, after he supported Saddam Hussein in the first Gulf War, by establishing diplomatic relations with Israel in 1999. This decision was deeply resented on religious grounds by most Mauritanians regardless of political affiliation, and was exploited politically. Shortly after the United States launched the GWOT following the 9/11 attack, a much-contested President Ould Taya saw an opening and started using and exploiting domestically the language of anti-terrorism and anti-Islamic extremism. As discussed below, soon Mauritania, its political system, and its military became confronted with terrorism of its own. It is against this background that the role of the Mauritanian security sector's role in the GWOT must be appreciated.

Mauritania's terrorism woes

There is a discernible thread that runs throughout the evolution of the involvement of Mauritania's Military in the GWOT. However, four more or less discreet periods can be identified to analyze this involvement. These periods are not just chronological, as discussed below, they correspond also with attitudes and policies, and attempts of the country to play its role in the GWOT and face its own terrorism predicament. Often the approaches, policies, and behavior had more to do with Mauritania's domestic politics and social dynamics than with the objectives of the U.S. GWOT. The first of these periods was under President Ould Taya and ended with his overthrow in 2005, the same year when Mauritania experienced its first major terrorist attack. The second period corresponds with the military interlude that followed and ended in April 2007, when the military junta handed over power to a civilian democratic regime. The third period coincided with the democratic window that ended with the August 3, 2008 coup led by General Ould Abdel Aziz. The final period, which is still ongoing, started with the resulting military regime headed by Ould Abeld Aziz, now civilianized and legitimized by the July 18, 2009 elections.

Eagerly buying in the GWOT: The Ould Taya years, 2002–5

The U.S. GWOT came to Mauritania and to the rest of the Sahel region as a result of the September 11, 2001 attack on the U.S. homeland. One of its key underpinnings was the determination of the U.S. government not to allow ungoverned or poorly governed regions of the developing world to become havens for extremist groups and be used as staging grounds for future attacks against the United States and its allies. Because of its location and other attributes, and with a population 100 percent Muslim, Mauritania was therefore a prime candidate as a valued partner in the GWOT principles applied to the Sahel region. By 2001, Mauritania already had solid relations with the United States and benefited from continued military cooperation, particularly after the regime severed its military cooperation relations with France after the Captain Ely Ould Dah incident.[6]

It is therefore unsurprising that Mauritania should become a key country in the U.S.' anti-terrorist efforts starting with the State Department-funded Pan-Sahel Initiative (PSI) starting in 2002, with Special Operations Europe army special forces, marines, and air force. It concerned only Sahel countries proper, Mali, Niger, Chad, and Mauritania, and focused on building cross-border capabilities of the target states in fighting cross-border smuggling and terrorist activities. It entailed the training and equipment of one rapid-reaction company, in each of the military of these countries in anti-terrorist operations, by European Command special forces. In 2005, PSI became the Trans-Saharan Counter-Terrorism Initiative (TSCTI) with increased funding from $7 million in 2004, to $30 million in 2006 with the participation of the Department of Defense. It was also expanded to Senegal, Nigeria, Algeria, Morocco, and Tunisia. TSCTI became TSCTP (P for Partnership) with additional funding in 2008, with support from the DoD's Operation Enduring Freedom Sahara. That was before the creation of AFRICOM in 2007, now in charge of the counterterrorism strategy in Africa.

In accordance with President Ould Taya's wishes, Mauritania's military embraced and benefited from these GWOT-related programs through basic training, peacekeeping training, and the equipment of an especially trained unit in counter-terrorism, as well as in equipments such as desert adapted vehicles, surveillance, and transmissions. For such a vast country, clearly one of the weakest links among the Sahel states, this capacity building and the increased awareness of Mauritanians, their security forces in particular, of the terrorist threats and their implication on the side of the United States served the objectives of the GWOT, from the perspective of the U.S. Objectively, they did. However, this development was also very much to the liking of Mauritania's quasi-military regime. Considering the growth of his political opposition at the time, it served President Ould Taya's objectives of power perpetuation as well. This role in the U.S. GWOT allowed him to project himself as a strong leader allied to and backed by a superpower, singularly after the second Gulf War and the occupation of Iraq.

By 2002, President Ould Taya had been already in power for 18 years. His repressive policies steadily led to the radicalization of his opposition as was noted in 2001.[7] More crucially, his regime had succeeded in muzzling the political opposition through a series of clampdowns on the press and bans of major political parties. He also refused to allow a moderate Islamist political party, and repeatedly arrested and held high-profile trials for the main political leaders.[8] As a consequence some religious leaders became the only voices of opposition. They started to give voice to opposition positions and claims in Friday religious sermons and in widely circulated recorded tapes. They criticized the regime's diplomatic relations with Israel, and the presence of the Israeli Embassy in Nouakchott, and the occasional visits of Israeli officials. These tapped into the latent anti-Semitism in aspects of the Arab-Islamic culture in Mauritania and the deep and widespread resentment and hostility toward Israel's policy toward Palestinians. The criticisms only intensified and the rhetoric mounted during the Palestinian Intifadas. These developments are critical in understanding the role of the military, then a pillar to Ould Taya's regime, in the GWOT and the evolution of the latter in subsequent years. Nevertheless, independently of these domestic political dynamics, thanks to the vastness of the territory that escaped the control of the four states in the Sahel, there were traffics of all sorts and movements across the region of elements affiliated with the GSPC. In other words, the dangers U.S. strategists feared were starting to take shape. Indeed, soon enough, the GSPC, once a terrorist group indigenous to Algeria and without regional ambitions or agenda, became Al-Qaeda in the Islamic Maghreb (AQIM).

Meanwhile, domestic political dynamics asserted their precedence with the June 2003 bloody coup attempt that nearly toppled Ould Taya's regime. Indeed for 48 hours it had lost control of the country. Though rumor had it that the U.S. helped save the regime by jamming communications among coup makers, and giving Ould Taya shelter briefly, he owed his salvation only to the rally of loyal troops and the resistance organized by none other than Colonels Ould Mohamed Vall and Ould Abdel Aziz. However, for the first time in the history of Mauritania, following the failure of the coup, the officers who led it regrouped to set up an underground military resistance movement they called *Les Cavaliers du Changement* (Knights of Change), which vowed to keep fighting to overthrow the government. These military officers were all Arab-Berbers from Eastern ethnic groups, and were also, and maybe more importantly, Arab nationalists (of the Nasserist tendency) and Islamists, though not Salafists. This event complicated even more the whole issue of fighting terrorism, as many Mauritanians identified with their cause and applauded their daring. A relevant aspect of this coup attempt was that the leader of the coup was not even an active military personnel. He had been sent into early retirement for protesting certain policies. Ironically, at the time, fearing a possible coup,

Ould Taya had weakened the army, and starved it of the necessary equipment and appropriate training and professionalism, beefing up the BASEP instead.

When the coup occurred, all avenues seemed closed to a peaceful transfer of power. The regime's legitimacy had been severely eroded by not just its long tenure in power, but also the crushing social and economic living conditions of the overwhelming number of Mauritanians. Almost immediately, the Knights of Change were assimilated into a terrorist organization and Ould Taya's regime, with himself taking the lead, conflated fighting the opposition to the regime (part of which was now armed and still plotting to overthrow him) with fighting terrorism. Ould Taya made a concerted effort to impress on the U.S. and his other Western partners that he shared their views on the danger posed by the Islamist political movements, a move aimed explicitily at obtaining their political and military support.[9] Complicating the picture even further were the other activities of Mauritania's intelligence services in neighboring countries. Years later it appears that the Ould Taya regime was providing support in arms and funds to the Touareg rebellions in Mali and to the Casamance rebellion in Senegal. This was done apparently to weaken these regimes with which the Ould Taya regime had a history of contentious relations.

For this first period of the evolution of Mauritania's military involvement in the GWOT, the most consequential development was undoubtedly the attack allegedly carried out by the GSPC on the military outpost of Lemgheity on June 5, 2005. In a daring operation, a group of armed individuals overran the isolated army position, killing 15 soldiers, taking prisoners, and making away with military material and equipment. Many have raised questions as to whether or not the GSPC was responsible. Indeed it was alleged that this may have been the deed of elements controlled by Algerian intelligence through their control of segments of the terrorist movement in Algeria and throughout the region. For others, the attack may very well have been orchestrated by a segment of the military at the behest of Ould Taya to impress on its Western allies that the terrorist Islamist threat he has been warning against was indeed real.[10] According to keen observers of the Mauritanian political scene, many of those who took part in the attack appear to speak the Hassanya, the Arabic dialect spoken in Mauritania, and a hasty conclusion of the responsibility of the GSPC should be avoided.[11] The annual military maneuvers and training in anti-terrorism in the Sahel, led by European Command special operations forces code named "Flintock," happened to have been scheduled for most of the month of June 2005. It can hardly be argued that this was just a coincidence.

Whoever carried out the attack, it turned out to have been a most critical turning point that precipitated the end of the Ould Taya regime and opened up a new phase of the evolution of Mauritanian politics (and civil–military relations)—and involvement in the GWOT. This in turn was to affect U.S. efforts to fight terrorism in the Sahel. Ould Taya's reaction to the attack was to demand a more proactive, indeed aggressive, stand of the Mauritanian military in tracking the group responsible for the attack, without necessarily giving it the means to accomplish the mission. When in the first weeks of what appeared to be a badly improvised offensive against the presumed authors of the attack did not produce the expected outcome, he summoned military officers and was reported to have scolded, insulted, and humiliated them in July 2005. It was also rumored that assigning Colonel Mohamed Ould Abdel Aziz the responsibility of leading the regime's anti-terrorism offensive was a calculated move to prepare the ground for his subsequent sacking. Whatever underpinned Ould Taya's intention after the Lemgheity attack, the army and security forces, at the instigation of Colonels Ould Abdel Aziz and Ould Mohamed Vall, overthrew him on August 3, forcing him into exile.[12] That was exactly two months after the attack occurred. This set the stage for the second phase of the evolution of the Mauritania's security sector in the GWOT under a full-fledged military regime.

The GWOT and the Transitional Military Regime, 2005–7

The August 3, 2005 coup was evidently a direct result of the terrorist challenge Mauritania faced and was precipitated by the added pressure following the Lemgheity attack. This challenge had therefore tangible effects on the dynamics within the security apparatus and was decisive on the political system. As argued elsewhere, this coup was certainly not carried out to bring fundamental changes to any aspect of Mauritanian politics, security policies, or society, but to get rid of a head of state whose erratic behavior started to jeopardize a political arrangement and a spoils system that benefited the coup's masterminds and their allies.[13] Because the military Junta (the Military Committee for Justice and Democracy, CMJD) was at the helm, particularly its number one and number two were very much involved and indeed led Mauritania's efforts in the GWOT, it could be expected that the new military regime would not make a U-turn on Mauritania's commitment to the U.S. war on terror. After calling for the reinstatement of Ould Taya to no avail, of course, the U.S. government suspended its formal military assistance to and cooperation with the Mauritanian military, including antiterrorist training, during the 19 months the military regime interlude lasted. However, the same terrorist challenges that had an impact on Ould Taya's ouster were still very much present and AQIM elements were still eager to strike. The U.S. administration soon became reassured that the military leaders remained very much on the same wave length as the U.S. when it came to anti-terrorism and Mauritania's role in it. Indeed, according to Colonel Ould Mohamed Vall, the U.S. even requested, with insistence, that it be granted a military base in the north of the country to monitor areas of the Sahel, and generally well-informed sources alleged that the CIA had a detention location in the Mauritanian desert while the junta was in power.[14] The military authorities turned down this request.

While there were no terrorist attacks during the military interlude, the new military regime remained very much alarmed by the rise of Islamic radicalism and continued (unsurprisingly since they conceived and implemented them) the tough policies against them started under the regime they overthrew. For example, they refused to free most of the Islamists incarcerated, despite freeing the other political prisoners, including the members of the Knights of Change. Also unsurprisingly, the rhetoric of the Ould Taya regime continued as if to justify the military's continued and prominent role in the country's anti-terrorist efforts even after the end of the transition.

Before power was transferred to a civilian elected president, inaugurating the next phase of the evolution of the Mauritanian military's role in the GWOT, terrorists would strike again, reminding all that the challenge of terrorism was very much present. In December 2006, a group of armed men attacked an army desert patrol at El Ghallaouya, killing three soldiers, and injuring many more. Once again, the Algerian Salafist group was widely believed to be responsible, and efforts by the military to find those responsible remained vain. As Mauritanians geared up for its first democratic regime since independence, among the many challenges they faced, terrorism and certainly its political exploitation would remain a significant one for the new president.

The democratic window: 2007–8

That elected president was Sidi Ould Cheikh Abdallahi. While he was able to rally around his candidacy a large heteroclite coalition, he was considered, rightly, the candidate of the military. He benefited from the covert support of the number two of the junta, who also happened to be an in-law. An unassuming elderly man of the independence generation, he did not necessarily believe in the seriousness of the terrorist threat for Mauritania, certainly not in the threat that fundamentalist Islam was supposed to pose. A devout Muslim, he even had a Mosque built on the compound of the presidential palace, and returned the country to keeping Friday as the weekly holiday, reversing the decision previously made by Ould Taya to align the country on the typical Sunday weekly holiday. He also allowed a moderate Islamist party to be recognized and join the political landscape, reversing another Ould Taya policy. All these decisions apparently were made in good faith and were meant in his mind to appeal to a large segment of the Mauritanian public. They were seen, however, with alarm by some, including in the military, as overtures toward Islamists. They more accurately denoted a different analysis and approach to the terrorist and Islamist equation. Ould Cheikh Abdallahy seemed to adhere, contrary to most officers in the security establishment, to the "root causes" approach. He believed strongly Mauritania's brand of Islam could not cause terrorism or extremism and that any deviation was due to harmful foreign influences. Hence, in his view, fighting terrorism should start with understanding the socioeconomic misery and injustices that alienate young Mauritanians and make them easy prey, and addressing certain legitimate social and political concerns from non-violent Islamists.

Nevertheless, he also marked a certain continuity of the antiterrorist policies of previous regimes by appointing Colonel (later General) Ould Abdel Aziz to lead the anti-terrorist efforts, and providing him with substantial financial resources and very much unlimited discretion as personal military Chief of Staff to the president. With the restoration of constitutional order, the U.S. military cooperation, including its anti-terrorist aspect, resumed. In that respect too, there was a remarkable continuity. However, soon there were a few signs that indicated that there seemed to appear disagreement between the new president and the military establishment, certainly the man who was formally in charge of the antiterrorist policies of the country. The courts had ordered the release of a small group of alleged terrorists who had been in detention, to which the military objected to no avail. The president believed in and held to the separation of branches of governments and the independence of the judiciary and did not interfere with the decision. This marked also the differing philosophies between the democratically elected president and the military establishment over the priorities and methods of government. This divergence was to become public shortly before the August 6, 2008 coup that ended the democratic era phase. The terrorist threat for Mauritania would not subside during this democratic interlude.

Soon enough, the terrorist threat would become more evident with a series of activities that were to determine in large part the fate of the new democratic experiment. Less than a year after he became president, Ould Abdallahy was to face the repercussions of the assassination of four French tourists in the southeast of the country in December 2007. In February 2008, the Israeli Embassy was attacked along with a nightclub frequented by foreigners. These series of attacks were attributed to Mauritanian citizens, some of whom were arrested with the help of Western (mainly French) intelligence services and claimed affiliation with AQIM. What is significant in the increasing connection between antiterrorism and Mauritanian politics is that these attacks were later used to justify the August 6, 2008 military coup as a reaction to the president's weakness, even complicity, with Islamist terrorism. Again, as the increased frequency and boldness of terrorist activities after this coup would confirm, this was only a pretext to make the coup more acceptable to Westerners, particularly the U.S., presumed to be fixated on its GWOT. This argument did not sway the Bush administration then ending its term. It suspended all military assistance to the tune of $20 millions.[15] The French government was much more receptive to the argument, and certainly eager to take advantage of the coup to gain concession from a weak military regime contested at home and abroad. This maneuvering would be a sign of things to come, as Ould Abdel Aziz legitimized and consolidated his power, starting the last and still ongoing phase of Mauritania's military involvement in the GWOT on its own terms. Of course, the terrorist threat would not subside as attacks continued, the first one occurring roughly a month after the August 6, 2008 coup.

The post-democratic era

The coup that ended Mauritania's democratic experiment was due almost entirely to General Ould Abdel Aziz's ambition to become president. But it was certainly not unrelated to Mauritania's terrorist predicament. It was triggered by the elected president's clumsy sacking of all the chiefs of the security sector, after it became clear to him that at least two of its main leaders (Generals Ould Abdel Aziz and his long-time friend and hand-picked Chief of Army Staff Ould Gazouani) were engaged in political activities to undermine him with the help of his political enemies. General Ould Adbel Aziz had taken advantage of the president's trust to have him appoint trusted allies and friends to key command positions. This was justified in part by the necessity to fight the battle against terrorism more effectively. This move served him well to stage his coup, but it did not make a difference whatsoever in the fight against terrorism.

Since the coup, attacks seemed to intensify. On September 9, 2008, the Mauritanian army was, once again, attacked and ten were beheaded. The spectacular evasion of the main suspect in a terrorism trial and the subsequent shootout between the police and a cell in the heart of Nouakchott, the assassination in June 2009 of a U.S. citizen in the capital, and the suicide attack on the French Embassy in August 2009 captured the attention of the public. Later, there were a series of kidnappings of foreigners and battles between army patrols and AQIM affiliated groups engaged in drug trafficking. These events certainly weakened the antiterrorism argument of the coup, and made it plain that Mauritania was confronted with a serious terrorism problem and that a military regime may not be better equipped than a democratic one to address it effectively.

While the Ould Abdel Aziz regime made a turn about in engaging the group of Salafists imprisoned, adopting a softer approach to the fight against terrorism, it still carried the heavy badge of being perceived as allied to the West (more and more the French who helped in legitimizing his power), in a holy war against Islam. While the U.S. was just content to resume the military cooperation more and more focused on antiterrorism, the French took advantage of the coup to regain a foothold, including oil exploration contracts for TOTAL and the presence of an increasing number of French soldiers in the north of the country.

Mauritania's terrorism predicament and the environment it created also saw the emergence, since the latest coup of a major actor, the new national security director who seems to have been given free reign to develop and conduct a general antiterrorism strategy. General Ould Hadi, a shadowy character and Arab nationalist, is a relative of Ould Taya with whom he had a serious fall out. He seems to have emerged as a key actor. After the coup, in an effort to gain legitimacy for the new military regime, he had transparently politicized and recuperated for the benefit of the military junta any terrorist-related event, even manufacturing some for propaganda purposes. To a large extent, this has come to symbolize the attitude of Mauritania's now internationally recognized quasi-military regime's approach to its role in the fight against terrorism and extremism in the Sahel region.

Conclusion

In addition to its location in the heart of the Sahel, Mauritania is a particularly unstable country, as the two successful coups d'état in less than three years illustrate. It is also undermined by several factors of division exacerbated by increased poverty and the alienation of a growing unemployed youth population, easy prey to radicalism. In recent times, Mauritania has undergone far-reaching developments in its political system and, quite relatedly, in its security predicament. These developments have had or will have a direct impact on its posture in the GWOT and its national security generally.

This chapter makes evident that Mauritania was bound to be a key player in the U.S.-initiated GWOT. This is due to its geographical location, the political role its military has been playing ever since it took power in 1978, and its socio-cultural and political dynamics. The repressive nature of the quasi-military regime that was in power when the GWOT started and the rapid growth of Islamic radicalism it fueled in part, along with increased poverty due to economic mismanagement, made it all but certain that the GWOT would be exploited to serve the domestic and regional agendas of relevant actors. This was done to the hilt by Colonel Ould Taya and then to various extents and fortunes by the three (military or military-backed) regimes that followed his overthrow on August 3, 2005 in a military coup. The coup itself was directly related to the sudden challenge of the radicalization of the political opposition posed and by outright terrorist activities symbolized by the June 2005 Lemgheity attack. It is against this background that the role of the military in the GWOT has been analyzed.

The Lemgheity attack (and those that followed regardless of the regime of the moment) illustrated abundantly the threat terrorism objectively posed for Mauritania, notwithstanding the fact that the Ould Taya regime at the time was literally begging for manifestations and evidence of this threat to convince the West to accept it as a centerpiece in its counterterrorist strategy in the Sahel and consequently intensify its political and military support. Of the four periods this chapter has identified to analyze the evolution and involvement of the Mauritanian military in the U.S. GWOT, the period that started in 2002 and ended with the 2005 coup was certainly decisive in setting the stage for Mauritania's place and role in the efforts of the U.S. in the region. While the terrorist threat continued unabated thanks essentially to regional dynamics, the two following periods—the military regime interlude and the ephemeral democratic parenthesis—did not significantly affect the overall picture. The Mauritanian military leadership continued to see the threat as an opportunity to be in the good grace of the West (the U.S. certainly and increasingly France), but also, and more importantly, to score points in their overall strategy to keep the military as a major player in the domestic political game. Even during the democratic period, as the personal military chief of staff of the civilian president, it was still General Ould Abdel Aziz and his acolytes who called the shots. The democratically elected president appeared to (or was made to) downplay the threat. He certainly privileged dealing with the socioeconomic root causes of Islamic militancy, and providing a place in the democratic arena to moderate Islamists.

The last period that is still ongoing, is shaped by the return of the military to power in full force riding the tide of the now acknowledged dangers of domestic

Islamic radicalism. This radicalism of segments of Mauritania's youth is connected to the gathering threat of AQIM and related threats of narco-trafficking, kidnappings, and other illicit activities in the uncontrolled swathes of the Sahara desert. It did not help that many members of the security sector top brass has been implicated in some of these criminal activities. As he moved to take power and then consolidate it, General Ould Abdel Aziz cleverly leveraged the terrorist threat mainly with the French, accusing his predecessor of being soft on terrorism and vowing to be tougher. Again, the need to legitimize his power with France and the U.S. was the main consideration, although, it is now clear that regardless of its "instrumentalization," terrorism has become a major concern and needs to be dealt with, including by means other than military force.

The overriding concern of the U.S. side has remained the willingness of Mauritanian governments and military regimes to participate in the GWOT. As long as the GWOT (or its reincarnation) is needed, Mauritania will be called upon to play a major role. Given its lingering illegitimacy, it will willingly play that role, if only to send the message to its growing and impatient opposition that it has a powerful ally. This was already the scenario of the first stage inaugurated by Ould Taya. The United States must adjust its approach to take into consideration recent developments, including the increased role France has been playing since the August 6, 2008 coup. The U.S. will need in particular to pay more attention to what is called the "root causes" of terrorism in the area, and singularly dynamics in Mauritania's volatile political system.

Notes

1 http://ddpext.worldbank.org/ext/ddpreports/ViewSharedReport?REPORT_ID=9147 &REQUEST_TYPE=VIEWADVANCED& dimensions=140 (accessed February 17, 2010).

2 A clear indication of this trend was the illegally obtained wiretaps used to persecute leaders of the opposition in 1998 and in 2004.

3 See Center for International and Strategic Studies, *The Mauritanian Military* (Washington, D.C.: CISS, 2008).

4 According to CIA figures, in 2006, Mauritania has spent 3.6 percent of its GDP on defense, compared to 1.4 percent and 1.9 percent for Senegal and Mali respectively.

5 See Anthony Pazzanita, "Mauritania's Foreign Policy: The Search for Protection," *Journal of Modern African Studies* 30 (2), 1992, 288–300.

6 Captain Ould Dah was convicted in abstentia by a French court for torture after a group of black soldiers filed a lawsuit against him. He fled the country before his trial. In retaliation, Ould Taya expelled all French military assistants and moved even closer to the U.S. in terms of military cooperation.

7 See Boubacar N'Diaye, "Mauritania's Stalled Democratization," *Journal of Democracy*, 12(3), 2001, 88–95.

8 Ibid.

9 International Crisis Group, "L'Islamisme en Afrique du Nord IV: Contestation Islamist en Mauritanie: Menaces ou Bouc Emissaire," Brussels, Rapport Moyen-Orient/ Afrique du Nord No. 41, May 11, 2005.

10 See Abdoulaye Diagana, Aboubakr Ould Maroini, and Abdel Nasser Ould Yessa, "Impasse politique et réflexes sécuritaires en Mauritanie: Comment fabriquer du

terrorisme utile," Paris, July 2005. A Memorandum on the Situation in Mauritania sponsorerd by a number of civil society organizations and political parties.
11 See the commentary of a Radio France Internationale expert, Richard Laberivière, *Le Paradigme mauritanien, Radio France Internationale*, éditorial internationale on September 6, 2005.
12 For details on this coup, see Boubacar N'Diaye, "The August 3, 2005 Coup in Mauritania: Democracy Finally, or just another Coup?" *African Affairs*, 105(420), 2006, 421–41.
13 See ibid., 428–30.
14 See "La Mauritanie acceuillante de la CIA," http://ufpweb.org/fr/spip.php?article278 (accessed February 17, 2010).
15 www.nytimes.com/2008/09/16/world/africa/16mauritania.html (accessed February 20, 2010).

8 Good governance, West African regional security, and the U.S. war on terror

George Klay Kieh, Jr.

Introduction

Since the dawn of the post-September 11 era, the United States' counter-terrorism strategy has been anchored on the use of military means as the *deus ex machina* for "winning the war against terrorism." Accordingly, as part of its counter-terrorism strategy, the United States has sought to forge various bilateral and multilateral military–security relationships with various states and regional and sub-regional organizations in Africa, Asia, Europe, and the Americas. At the vortex of these relationships is the effort by the United States to help state actors at these various levels to develop national, sub-regional, and regional counter-terrorism infrastructures as integral parts of its overarching global counter-terrorism panoply. In this vein, in the case of the West African sub-region, the United States has established a military–security relationship with the Economic Community of West African States (ECOWAS), as well as bilateral ones with several countries. Additionally, outside of its military–security relationship with ECOWAS, the United States has established multilateral relationships with some West African states through its Trans-Sahara Counterterrorism Initiative/Partnership, one of its many counter-terrorism architectures on the African continent.

However, critics have observed that by relying primarily on the use of military means, the United States' counter-terrorism strategy in West Africa, Africa, and other sub-regions and regions, as well as at the bilateral level, fails to take cognizance of the complexity of terrorism.[1] Alternatively, they suggest that the U.S.' counter-terrorism strategy should be multidimensional, with the military approach as one component. In response, although the military approach remains the cornerstone of its counter-terrorism strategy, the United States has begun to add some non-military dimensions such as political liberalization and its attendant elements of good governance, multipartyism, the holding of regular elections, the rule of law, and the development of a vibrant civil society, among others. The emerging belief is that internal political liberalization and regional security can be used in tandem to help prevent, contain, and address terrorism. In the case of West Africa, as Kehinde Bolaji argues, "The promotion of good governance in West Africa can help prevent all forms of threats to security and provide avenues for contradictions and conflicts to be amicably resolved within the domestic/ national framework."[2]

Against this background, the purpose of this chapter is to examine the utility of good governance and regional security as counter-terrorism measures in the U.S.' war on terrorism in West Africa. In other words, can the combination of good governance and security at the domestic and subregional levels serve as useful instruments in helping to support the U.S.' global war on terror? In order to examine the research question, the chapter is divided into six major parts. In part one, the conceptual framework for the study is provided. This is followed by a review of the literature, and the articulation of the study's theoretical framework. Next, the chapter assesses the travails of the good governance project in the sub-region. The fourth part examines the African regional security architecture. Part five tackles the issue of the use of good governance and regional security as counter-terrorism methods. Sixth, the chapter transcends the good governance–regional security tandem, and offers an alternative approach to addressing the challenges of terrorism.

The conceptual framework

The conceptual framework of the study is anchored on two major terms: Good governance and regional security. Drawing from the United Nation's definition, good governance is conceptualized as a process of decision making and implementation based on the principles of participation, accountability, transparency, responsiveness, effectiveness, efficiency, equity and inclusion, and which follows the rule of law.[3]

Regional security is a web of cooperative relationships between and among states that is based on preventing, controlling, and addressing violent conflicts and other acts of violence that may cause death and destruction, and thus instability at the national, sub-regional, regional, and global levels.[4] The cooperative relationships may take many forms, including alliances (mutual defense usually against an external threat), and security regimes (norms of cooperation).[5]

Theoretical issues

The review of the literature

Background

In this section of the chapter, the scholarly literature is reviewed for the purpose of situating the study within the crucible of the scholarly works that have been done on good governance and regional security. This would provide the basis for deciphering the points of convergence and divergence between the study and the scholarly literature. In short, this part of the chapter revolves around the issue of the relationship of the study to the corpus of scholarly works on the two issues.

Good governance

Azeez (2009) observes that for the past two decades good governance has served as the "guiding principle" for newly established democracies in their quest to consolidate the democratization process.[6] Among others, the operationalization of good governance has revolved around the issues of adherences to proper administrative procedures, the institutionalization of reform, transparency, accountability, and popular participation.[7] In the specific case of Nigeria, he argues that there has been a deficit in good governance as evidenced by, *inter alia*, the burgeoning rate of mass poverty and deprivation.

Similarly, like Azeez (2009), Sharma (2007) delineates some of the other dimensions of good governance: "[R]esponsiveness, effectiveness, efficiency, equity, inclusiveness and the rule of law." In addition, emphasis is placed on the importance of the development of institutions that would serve the stake-holders fairly. As well, the link is drawn between good governance and the promotion of human rights.

In the same vein, Siddiqui (2001), drawing from the Pakistani experience, argues that the *sine qua non* for addressing the myriad of challenges facing the country is the establishment of good governance as the anchor of the planning and development processes. For example, the establishment of a good governance framework is particularly urgent at the local level. However, he takes cognizance of the fact that such a shift would require political will by public officials.

De Ferranti *et al.* (2009) posit that a comprehensive analytical framework is required, in order to gauge the progress or lack thereof of good governance in any country. Against this background, they suggest that four major variables—accountability, an anti-corruption regime, governance, and transparency—should constitute the foundational base of such a framework. Operationally, they suggest that the specific purpose of the framework should be to assess the obstacles to good governance in a country, and to proffer remedies.

In her study, Orlandini (2003) observes that good governance has joined the emergent parade of development paradigms and policies that are being trea-ted as "commodities" advertised by international development organizations and developed states and "consumed" in developing countries.[8] Drawing from the experience of Thailand, she contends that the political and intellectual elites of the country have commandeered the concept of good governance and are using it to advance their personal agendas. Furthermore, she argues that the "technocratic languages that accompany 'good governance' in policy docu-ments conceals an even more pervasive form of power. This is nevertheless discarded in its 'consumption' to assume a moral connotation, equating it with 'good leadership' or self-sufficient, harmonious society and resorting to culturally-embedded notions of self-discipline."[9]

Regional security

Tavares (2009) argues that regional organizations are becoming increasingly involved in the security domain, as evidenced by the development of capacities in areas such as conflict prevention, peacemaking, and peacekeeping. He attributes this phenomenon to the changing dynamics of the regional and global systems. Against this background, regional organizations have been catapulted into prominence in the post-Cold War international system.

Building on Tavare's premise, Kaunert (2010) examines the role of two of the European Union's supranational institutions—the European Commission and the Council Secretariat—in the formulation of the EU's counterterrorism policy. In the case of the Council Secretariat, Kaunert notes that it played a pivotal role in facilitating the transposition of the binding resolutions of the UN Security Council on funding of terrorism at the EU level.[10] As for the Commission, it played a key role in the development of the European Arrest Warrant as a counter-terrorism tool. Overall, Kaunert argues that the EU member states have used "pooled sovereignty" as the overarching framework of counterterrorism.

Ewi and Aning (2006) situate African regional security within the context of the evolving terrorism-driven international security agenda. Specifically, they argue that although terrorism has always been a threat to security on the African continent, the serious involvement of inter-governmental organizations in efforts to address the threat is a fairly recent development.[11] Using the African Union (AU) as a case study, they examine some of the measures the organization has taken to combat terrorism, including the adoption of the Declaration on the Code of Conduct for Inter-African Relations, and the Convention on the Prevention and Combating of Terrorism. However, they note that in order for the AU to play a constructive role in counter-terrorism, it must address some of its major internal problems, including financial and human resource capacities.

Acharya (2004) observes that September 11, 2001 ushered in the post-Cold War era in Asian security with terrorism as the premier issue.[12] According to her, the pre-September 11 regional security environment was shaped by four major issues: The changing regional "balance of power" due to the rise of China; the prospects of war in persisting regional flashpoints such as Korea, Taiwan, and Kashmir and the Spratly Islands disputes; the strategic and political fallout of the Asian economic crisis; and the emergence of regional multilateral cooperation with the establishment of ASEAN.[13] Acharya asserts that although the pre-September 11 regional security issues remain important, the tandem of terrorism and counter-terrorism has eclipsed them.

Obi (2006) focuses on the sub-regional level of the terrorism–counterterrorism dynamic. Using West Africa as the case study, he posits that the relevance of West African security arrangements to the U.S.' "war on terror" is due to the concern with internal security in West African states, as well as the emerging "globalization of security."[14] In terms of the U.S.–West Africa counter-terrorism strategy, he is critical of it for according primacy to what he calls "institutional and military approaches."[15] Under these strategies, he contends that both the United States and West African states have paid little attention to the exigency of the provision of national and international resources that are needed for addressing the harsh political and desperate socio-economic conditions that may provide the nourishment for dissent, violence, repression, proliferation of small arms and highly mobile youth fighters, and possibly terror. Alternatively, he suggests that addressing the historic, economic, and political roots of terrorism would be the most effective counter-terrorism strategy.

The theoretical framework

What are the linkages between the scholarly literature and this study? First, with regards to good governance, this study agrees with the literature that it is an important element. However, the literature portrays it as a technocratic and political decision-making and implementation framework that is delinked from the critical issues of human needs and the broader context of socioeconomic democracy. As Rita Kiki Edozie poignantly argues: "Good governance is not grounded in the structural contexts of economic, social and cultural power and institutional environment. [Hence], it is a transient framework for democratization."[16] Alternatively, in order to serve as an effective counter-terrorism strategy, good governance needs to be linked to the critical issues of addressing the material needs of people—what Mary Kaldor *et al.* aptly refer to as the "freedom from the fear of want."[17]

Similarly, the literature presents regional security in the traditional military–security context. Although, the military component is important to the formulation and implementation of a counter-terrorism strategy, it is limited by the fact that it does not address the undercurrents or the roots of terrorism. Understanding and dealing with the causes of terrorism is indispensable to effectively addressing the problem.

As its theoretical framework, the study builds on Obi's (2006) approach to the West African governance and regional security architectures as the most effective counter-terrorism strategy. Essentially, the theoretical framework is anchored on the premise that governance and sub-regional security, and their associated national dimensions in West Africa, should focus on the democratic reconstitution of the neo-colonial African states and the resultant addressing of the perennial multifaceted crises of underdevelopment, which have bedeviled the sub-region and its constituent states as the most effective counter-terrorism strategy. In other words, addressing the issues of "human security"—"the freedom from fear" and the "freedom from want"[18]—is the best and most effective counter-terrorism approach. This entails dealing with the issues of political rights, civil liberties, employment, poverty, education, and health care, among others.

The travails of good governance in West Africa: A background

The struggle for good governance in West Africa has evolved in two major phases: The bad or authoritarian governance (1960–90) and toward good governance (1990–present). The bad or authoritarian governance phase was incepted during the early post-independence era in the early 1960s. This stage commenced against the backdrop of the state of exhilaration that greeted the post-independence era. This was propelled by the hope entertained by Africans that the end of colonialism would have simultaneously terminated the vagaries of bad or authoritarian governance, which was a major hallmark of colonialism. As John Mukum Mbaku observes:

> Most Africans believed that independence would provide them the opportunity to rid themselves of the Europeans and their laws and institutions ... The new countries' leaders were expected to undertake state reconstruction through a democratic consultative process to create new governance structures based on African values, aspirations, traditions, customs, and view of the world, and resource allocation systems that enhanced indigenous entrepreneurship, maximized the creation of wealth, and ensured equitable allocation of resources.[19]

However, amid the celebration, West Africans grudgingly came to the realization that the end of colonialism simply represented the change of regime from a colonial one staffed by colonial agents, to indigenous ones with Africans at the helm. But, the governance architecture would remain the same. In this vein, in the context of an authoritarian neo-colonial state, the emergent post-colonial governance structure retained the features of its progenitor: The over-centralization of powers at the "center"; the lack of consultation, accountability, and transparency in decision making; the flaunting of rules; and the resultant emergence of a "culture of impunity." Additionally, the cult of the "hegemonic presidency" emerged as a reflection of the establishment of presidential suzerainty in the decision-making process.[20]

Exasperated by the persistence of poor or authoritarian governance, West Africans organized various civil society organizations as the vehicles for waging their struggles against the scourge. Regrettably, the various struggles were hamstrung by state-sponsored violence, the intrusion of military coups and the Cold War. In response to citizen-based actions against authoritarian governance, the various governments used repression as the premier vehicle for cowing citizens into submission.[21] To make matters worse, the military intervened and hijacked the democratic struggles in various states.[22] The resultant military rule, by and large, witnessed the exacerbation of the crisis of governance, evidenced by the increased lack of accountability, transparency, and consultation in decision making in the public sphere.[23] As for the Cold War, both the United States and the Soviet Union supported their various client regimes in the sub-region with economic aid and arms, thereby enhancing the capacities of these governments to rain terror on their citizens, and undermine the quest for good governance.[24]

By the late 1980s, three major developments occurred that helped the struggles for good and democratic governance. The cumulative effects of the "pro-good and democratic governance struggles" had taken their toll on the various authoritarian regimes in West Africa, despite state terror. Another major development was that the struggles for good and democratic governance and democratization by groups in various countries across the globe served as inspiration for the "democracy" movements in West Africa.[25] The end of the Cold War was the other important factor. This made the various American-cum-Western and Soviet client regimes disposable. That is, with the end of "superpower rivalry," the United States and the West were forced to rethink their blanket support for their authoritarian client regimes.[26] Ultimately, the United States and the other Western powers made the determination that they could no longer support "crude authoritarianism." Thus, they embraced the idea of political liberalization, including good governance, as the "new framework" for modulating the relations between them (the U.S. and the West) and their West African client states—the phenomenon Dennis Canterbury refers to as "neoliberal democratization" (the sanitizing of authoritarianism).[27]

At the sub-regional level, the Economic Community of West African States (ECOWAS) adopted a Protocol on Democracy and Good Governance in 2001. Among the document's major provisions are "The Constitutional Convergence Principles," which can be summarized thus:

- The separation of powers among the executive, legislative, and judicial branches.
- Every accession to power must be made through free, fair, and transparent elections.
- Zero tolerance for power obtained or maintained by unconstitutional means.
- Popular participation in decision making, strict adherence to democratic principles, and the decentralization of power at all levels of government.[28]

As well, Article 32 of the Protocol stipulates that "Good governance is the precondition for preserving social justice, preventing conflict, guaranteeing political stability and peace, and for strengthening democracy."[29]

Additionally, the West African states are parties to the continental African Union's Peer Review Mechanism. Established in 2003, the mechanism seeks assessment of nearly the entire range of state activity under four broad but interlinked themes: Democracy and political governance, economic governance and management, corporate governance, and socioeconomic development.[30] The mandate is to encourage conformity in regard to political, economic, and corporate governance values, codes, and standards among African countries and the objectives in socioeconomic development within the New Partnership for Africa's Development.[31] The evaluation of progress toward the establishment of good governance and democracy is based on a process of voluntary self-assessment.

Although good and democratic governance have not been widely established throughout West Africa, appreciable amounts of progress have been made since 1990. The remaining major challenges include making good governance a staple of the governance architecture of all of the states in the sub-region, ensuring that the states that have adopted it are consistent in their application, and designing the modalities for ensuring compliance with both sub-regional and continental standards on good governance. Overall, while good governance represents a major step forward, it needs to ultimately assume a democratic complexion in order to expand its utility in addressing the multi-faceted crises of underdevelopment plaguing the sub-region. The point is that while the prudent management of the affairs of the state is important, it must bear upon the improvement of human well-being as the critical condition for having salience and relevance to the lives of the subalterns in the sub-region. As Said Adejumobi argues: "The struggle for democratization in Africa has relevance not only in liberalizing the political arena and achieving civil and political liberties, but also to ensure better living standards and social welfare for the people."[32]

The West African regional security architecture

The West African regional security architecture is anchored on several pillars. The Protocol on Non-Aggression, which was adopted in 1978, seeks to prevent the occurrence of inter-state conflicts. Under Article 1 of the Protocol, "Member states shall, in their relations with one another, refrain from the threat or use of force or aggression or from employing other means inconsistent with the Charters of the United Nations and the Organization of African Unity [now the African Union] against the territorial integrity or political independence of the member states."[33]

Two years later, the Protocol on Mutual Assistance in Defense was added to the evolving regional security architecture. The Protocol delineated the situations that would call for joint sub-regional action on external aggression, as well as interventions in inter-state and intra-state conflicts.[34] In 1999, the Protocol was replaced by a broader arrangement. The impetus was provided by the lessons learned from ECOWAS' intervention in the first Liberian Civil War in 1990.

In this vein, the Mechanism for Conflict Prevention, Resolution, and Peacekeeping became the central pillar in the evolving sub-regional security multiplex. The foci of the "mechanism" are the provision of early warning, conflict prevention, peacekeeping, cross-border crime control, and the proliferation of small arms.[35] Operationally, the "mechanism" can be applied under the following conditions:

• Aggression against a member state or the threat of it.
• Conflict among several member states.
• Internal conflict that threatens to result in humanitarian disaster, or poses threat to peace and security in the sub-region.

- Serious violations of human rights and the rule of law, and in the event of the overthrow or attempted overthrow of a democratically elected government.[36]

In 2008, the ECOWAS Conflict Prevention Framework (ECPF) was adopted by the member states, in what Mohamed Chambas, the then President of the ECOWAS Commission, called "a systematic response to the new regional environment."[37] The ECPF's immediate purpose is to create space within the ECOWAS system and in member states for interaction and collaboration within the sub-region and with external partners to push conflict prevention and peacebuilding up the political agenda of member states.[38] Structurally, the ECPF has 14 components spanning from early warning to peace education.

The sub-regional security architecture is linked to the African Union's evolving "counter-terrorism regime" and the U.S.' "counter-terrorism initiatives" in Africa. In the case of the former, the member states of ECOWAS are parties to the African Union's Convention on the Prevention and Combating of Terrorism, and the supplementary protocol. Under the AU's anti-terrorism convention, member states are required to "review national laws and establish criminal offenses for terrorist acts as defined by the convention and make such acts punishable by appropriate penalties."[39] Correspondingly, the protocol calls on member states to "coordinate and harmonize continental efforts in the prevention and combating of terrorism in all its aspects, as well as the implementation of other relevant international instruments."[40] In terms of the American "counter-terrorism initiatives," several member states have participated, and continue to participate in them. For example, Niger and Mali participated in the Pan-Sahel Initiative (2002–4). The objective of the "Initiative" was to train and equip the troops of the participating countries so as to improve their border security, and ultimately deny the use of their sovereign territory to terrorists and criminals.[41]

As well, some West African states have supplemented the sub-regional and regional "counter-terrorism regimes" with national ones. The centerpiece of these evolving national anti-terrorism regimes revolves around the enactment and enforcement of various laws, pursuant to both the sub-regional and regional "counter-terrorism regimes." The laws cover issues such as the definition of terrorism and the delineation of terrorist acts. With American assistance, West African states are developing the military and law enforcement capacities. For examples, Ghana, Niger, and Nigeria have enacted national anti-terrorism regimes. In the case of Nigeria, its anti-terrorism regime has two major pivots: Laws and an anti-terrorism force. In the case of the former, in 2010, the Anti-Terrorism Act took effect. Its cornerstones are: (1) the delineation of acts of terrorism and terrorism offenses; (2) the funding of terrorism; (3) terrorist properties; (4) mutual assistance and extradition; and (5) investigation and prosecution.[42]

Good governance and regional security as the pillars of West Africa–United States' counter-terrorism strategy

Nature and dynamics

The emergent U.S.–ECOWAS partnership in combating terrorism in West Africa is anchored on two major pivots: The promotion of good governance in West African states, and the provision of assistance in various areas to strengthen ECOWAS' sub-regional security architecture so that it can help provide the requisite military, security, and legal means in combating terrorism. The good governance dimension is anchored on several assumptions. First, West African states should have representative governments, which are chosen through regular, free, and fair elections. The rationale is that elected governments will be legitimate, because they would be chosen by the electorate of the various countries. In short, in contractarian parlance, the governors of the various West African states would derive their authority to govern from the people.

Second, the governments should be accountable to their citizens for the ways in which they conduct public affairs. As the World Bank posits, "Accountability ensures actions and decisions taken by public officials are subject to oversight so as to guarantee that government initiatives meet their stated objectives and respond to the needs of the community they are meant to be benefiting."[43] Accountability can be pursued both horizontally and vertically. In the case of the former, the various agencies of the government serve as "checks" on one another.[44] For example, the courts would use the power of judicial review to keep the executive and legislative branches in check. Vertical accountability would be provided through several major channels, including the holding of regular free and fair elections, and other citizen-based actions, the media and other civil society organizations. Functionally, this genre of accountability would be provided by the private sphere that is outside of the purview of the government of an African state.

Third, public agencies and officials would be expected to conduct their affairs in a transparent manner. This would entail active disclosure by state officials at various levels about their activities and those of their respective agencies, so that the public can scrutinize these activities.[45] Several benefits are supposed to ensue. Broadly, this would help end the "culture of impunity," which has provided the foundation for the public sector in various African states. As well, it would help minimize corruption, because the openness would serve as a deterrent to public officials and agencies.

Fourth, the application of the "rule of law" would ensure the operation of an independent, efficient, and accessible judicial and legal system, with a government that applies fair and equitable laws equally, consistently, coherently, and prospectively to all people.[46]

Similarly, the regional security pillar is based on several contours. One major element is conflict management. And this entails managing inter-state and intra-state conflicts through the use of an array of methods—conflict prevention, peacemaking, peacekeeping, and preventive deployment, among others. One of the major ostensible goals is to prevent terrorists and terrorist organizations from taking advantage of the conflict environment, including the usual breakdown of state authority.

Another feature is the creation of a sub-regional legal regime consisting of treaties and protocols. The regime is supplemented by domestic and regional (African Union) legal anti-terrorist architectures. The sub-regional legal architecture has several major purposes: (1) to provide a common legal definition of terrorism; (2) to delineate various terrorist acts; and (3) to articulate the penalties for the commission of these terrorist acts. The overarching benefit is that it creates a shared legal approach that helps to minimize ambiguities and the potential conflicts between the sub-regional and domestic anti-terrorist legal regimes.

The enhancement of the military and security capacity of West African states is also a major plank. This has been and continues to be done through various American multilateral and bilateral military and security programs in the West African sub-region. For example, various West African states participated in the Pan-Sahel Anti-Terrorist Initiative—Mali and Niger. Currently, Mali, Niger, and Nigeria are participating in the Trans-Sahara Counterterrorism Partnership. These American-led efforts are designed to provide the militaries of these West African states with training in anti-terrorism, equipment, and supplies that are pivotal to engaging terrorist and terrorist organizations militarily. At the bilateral level, similar training is provided for the military of selected West African states. As well, the police and security units of various West African states have and continue to receive training from the United States in areas such as the monitoring of terrorists and terrorist organizations and the policing of borders, especially in countries like Mali and Niger that are in proximity to the vast Sahara Desert and its stretches of "ungoverned" and "ungovernable areas."[47]

Also, the establishment of a regional security architecture is designed to, among others, foster cooperation in various military and security related areas between and among the states in the sub-region, on the one hand, and the sub-region and the United States, on the other, in the latter's "global war on terror." The rationale is twofold. First, the sub-regional approach to combating terrorism is useful because it promotes the pooling of resources and the "economy of scale." Second, it makes it difficult for a country in the sub-region to help terrorists and terrorist organizations through the provision of "safe havens," training camps, launch pads for attacks, money, weapons, and other logistics.

Overall, the hope is that a representative government that practices "good governance" would deprive terrorist and terrorist organizations of the use of the veneer of "bad governance" as a vehicle for whipping up anti-government sentiments within the population, an avenue for recruitment, and the justification for engaging in terrorist acts. Particularly, the thinking is that the "dividends of good governance" would produce two major outcomes. The first one is that the citizens of the various West African states would become "stakeholders" in their various societies. Hence, these citizens would have vested interests in protecting their various "stakes." The other is that the government would acquire legitimacy and the associated trust and confidence of the citizens. In this context, West African governments would therefore be able to draw on the support of their citizens in the implementation of various anti-terrorist measures, including those enshrined in the domestic, sub-regional, and regional anti-terrorist regimes.

Assessment

The good governance–regional security–counter-terrorism approach has both strengths and weaknesses. In this section, we will discuss some of them. In terms of strengths, there is the recognition by ECOWAS and the United States that there is a crisis of governance in the West African sub-region. And the various sub-regional and regional regimes on good governance represent an important first step in addressing the crisis. As well, the emphasis on good governance contributes to the political democratization project in the sub-region by helping to articulate a roadmap for addressing the vagaries of authoritarianism. For example, the establishment of representative governments through the holding of competitive, free and fair elections, the critical role of accountability and transparency, and the rule of law, among others, are important features of a democratic order.

As for the sub-regional security architecture and its domestic and regional complements, they recognize the importance of preventing conflicts before they degenerate into violence, the effective management of violent conflicts so that they are resolved, and the development of a battery of legal, military, and security capabilities for addressing the threats of, and the commission of, acts of terrorism. The various conflict prevention methods, for example, that are outlined in the regional security architecture are useful for helping to minimize the degeneration of these conflicts into violence and its adverse consequences. The legal, military, and security instruments that are articulated in the sub-regional security multiplex and the complementary domestic and regional ones make invaluable contributions to capacity building both at the internal (within the respective West African states) and sub-regional levels.

On the other hand, the "good-governance regional security counter-terrorism" approach has some weaknesses. The thrust of good governance tends to be more managerial and technical in orientation. Hence, it privileges short-term stability over transformation. Alternatively, there needs to be the recognition that in order to establish long-term stability in the West African sub-region and its constituent states, the emphasis should be on the transformation of the economic, political, and social landscape. Another shortcoming that bedevils the governance regime is the implementation conundrum. West Africa and Africa in general have been known for the development of lofty regimes. But, there has usually been the disconnect between the lofty ideals that are enshrined in these documents and the implementation. Clearly, the sub-region would have to turn the proverbial "new leaf" by demonstrating a commitment to the scrupulous implementation of the planks of the sub-regional governance regime.

As for the sub-regional security architecture, it has several problems. It accords primacy to military means as the principal vehicles for tackling the scourge of terrorism. The fact is that the use of military force would have limited utility in dealing with a phenomenon that is deeply rooted in the vagaries of the domestic political economies of the various West African states, and the broader global political economy. That is, terrorists and terrorist organizations use the legitimate grievances of the subaltern classes in West Africa and the international system as the justifications for their actions. Hence, it is imperative that these issues be addressed, if terrorism is to be effectively countered.

Another lacuna is that some of the various domestic anti-terrorism regimes that are evolving in the subregion with American encouragement and support are undermining the formulation and implementation of an effective counter-terrorism strategy. This is because these anti-terrorism regimes are violating some basic political rights and civil liberties, thereby helping to maintain and expand the ambit of the legal, economic, political, security, and social conditions that propel terrorism. The Nigerian domestic anti-terrorism regime, for example, has been criticized for its provisions relating to investigation, detention, and trial.[48] As Amnesty International argues: "These [provisions] are imprecise and overboard. Others include due process, the deprivation of liberty and fair trial."[49] The related problem is that some governments in the sub-region are using the "war on terrorism" as a pretext for engaging in the violation of political human rights. For example, enforced disappearances, torture, and extrajudicial killings are being committed by military and security forces in the name of counter-terrorism.[50]

The failure to take cognizance of the role of American foreign policy in aiding and abetting of authoritarianism in the sub-region and the continent as a whole is a central weakness of the emergent U.S.–West African counter-terrorism partnership. By supporting authoritarian regimes, including acquiescing in the legitimation of fraudulent elections, the United States has and continues to contribute to the germination of the conditions that terrorist and terrorist organizations use as the justifications for their actions. One case in point was the decision by the Bush administration to acquiesce in the acceptance of the results of the fraudulent presidential election that was held in Nigeria in 2007. The United States justified its action on the basis of economic, strategic, and political considerations.[51] This action further exposed the underbelly of the hypocrisy that undergirds the United States' so-called "democracy promotion project" in West Africa, Africa, and in other parts of the world. In essence, the reality is that the United States only supports democracy if its serves American economic, political, and strategic interests.

Toward an alternative counter-terrorism strategy for the U.S.' "war on terrorism" in West Africa

Background

We suggest an alternative counter-terrorism strategy for the prosecution of the U.S. war on terrorism in West Africa based on the trilogy of human security, the democratization of American foreign policy toward West Africa, and the restructuring of the global political economy. Our proposal seeks to help fill the gaps in the emergent U.S.–West Africa counter-terrorism strategy in the sub-region.

Human security

Human security offers a new approach both to security and development.[52] As the United Nations Development Program aptly observes:

> The concept of security has far too long been interpreted narrowly: as security of territory from external aggression, or as protection of national interests in foreign policy or as global security from the threat of a nuclear holocaust. It has been related more to nation-states than to people.[53]

Certainly, this approach to security and development is different from the current U.S.–West Africa counter-terrorism strategy that emphasizes threats to states and traditional military capabilities.

Against this background, human security should therefore be the bedrock of the U.S.–West Africa counter-terrorism strategy, because it embodies the critical issues that are the internal root causes of terrorism in West Africa—unemployment, lack of income, poverty, food insecurity the lack of access to health care, threats from the state, and political repression, among others. Specifically, at the domestic level, West African states should make human well-being the centerpiece of their respective democratization, development, and national security projects. This would entail the establishment of a democratic developmental state that would invest in job creation; the reduction of poverty; food production and the required access and availability of food; access to health care; access to clean drinking water and sanitation; the provision of personal and community security; and the promotion of the respect for political rights and civil liberties of groups and individuals; accountability and transparency; the rule of law; mass participation in the political process; the holding of regular competitive free and fair elections, and "checks and balances" in the operation of the government, among others. In the final analysis, human security is a child who did not die, a disease that did not spread, a job that was not cut, an ethnic tension that did not explode into violence, a dissident who was not silenced.[54] Human security is not a concern with weapons—it is a concern with human life and dignity.[55] Concomitantly, American policy toward West African states both individually and regionally should seek to promote human security.

Such an approach would help address the conditions that constitute the kernels of terrorism. Particularly, when people's economic, political, social, and other needs have been addressed, they develop stakes in their polities. In turn, this would make it quite difficult for them to be amenable to engaging or supporting acts of terrorism, terrorists, and terrorist groups. This is because they would make the rational calculation that terrorist acts would adversely affect their stakes in their respective societies.

The democratization of American foreign policy

The crux of democratizing American foreign policy in West Africa is the imperative of resolving the dialectical tension between the "democracy promotion" rhetoric and the support for the praxis of authoritarianism. A major area concerns the need for the United States to only support democratic regimes in the subregion. These are regimes that are making laudable and consistent strides in the promotion of political democratization. The benefit is that these regimes are making efforts to address the political roots of terrorism— repression and the violation of political human rights, the lack of the rule of law, the lack of accountability and transparency, among others. In addition, with the legitimacy these regimes are acquiring, they would be well positioned to rally the support of their various citizenries in the formulation and implementation of an effective counter-terrorism strategy. On the other hand, the continual support for authoritarian regimes contributes to the festering of the conditions that promote terrorism.

A related issue is the importance of the United States supporting the holding of democratic elections. Concomitantly, the United States would need to be consistent in helping the efforts in denying fraudulent elections the aura of legitimacy. By doing this, the United States would be contributing to the development of a "culture of free and fair elections," and the broader democratization project in the sub-region. However, as has been argued, the perennial practice of the United States to acquiesce in the legitimation of fraudulent elections in the sub-region undermines the democratization project by making the citizens of the affected West African states to become demoralized and frustrated, and contributes to the crisis of legitimacy that is one of the major root causes of terrorism.

As well, the United States needs to encourage and assist West African states to develop domestic anti-terrorism regimes that do not violate political human rights. The United States' current practice of pressuring West African states to design and implement internal anti-terrorism architectures that foster an assault on basic political rights and civil liberties is counter-productive, and would ultimately undermine the "war on terror." This is because such an approach is helping to maintain the conditions that cause terrorism. Samuel Makinda provides a poignant analysis of the exigency of balancing the protection of fundamental political human rights and the need to combat the scourge of terrorism thus:

> Safeguarding the security of African states and peoples requires policies that undercut the base of terrorism and, at the same time, enhance norms, rules and institutions. In other words, the so-called war on terror should not be seen simply as a technical, management or military issue, but initiatives that minimize the conditions that give rise to terrorism while maximizing those that strengthen norms, rules and institutions.[56]

Restructuring the global political economy

The nature and dynamics of the current global political economy contributes to terrorism in several ways. In terms of its nature, the global political economy is based on gross asymmetries in power between the United States and other core states, on the one hand, and West African and other peripheral states, on the other hand. In this vein, West African states and other peripheral states are marginal actors who play nominal roles in the various international political and economic institutions such as the United Nations, the International Monetary Fund, the World Bank, and the World Trade Organization. All of these organizations are dominated by the United States and other core states. Accordingly, the United States and these core states wield tremendous power in the United Nations, and accrue a disproportionate amount of benefits from the International Monetary Fund, the World Bank, and the World Trade Organization. For example, the United States and the other cores states control the loan policies of the International Monetary Fund and the World Bank, and the rules of the World Trade Organization.

In terms of the dynamics of the system, its various modes of interactions between the United States and other core states, on the one hand, and West African and other peripheral states, on the other hand, reflect exploitation and injustice. A major example is the global trading regime, which is based on an "international division of labor" that has assigned West African and other peripheral states the role of producing raw materials to help feed the industrial–manufacturing complexes of the United States and other cores states. The related point is that the United States and the other core states produce the manufactured goods. This is then linked to the "system of unequal exchange" under which West African and other peripheral states are required to pay more for manufactured goods from the United States and other core states, but receive less for their raw materials. This situation often leads to "terms of trade" problems for these West African and other peripheral states, as well as the continuous fluctuation in their raw materials-dependent export earnings, which are the "lifeblood" of their respective economies.

The debt dimension of the dynamics of global economic interactions has adversely affected West African states in various ways. Under the Structural

Adjustment Programs (SAPs) that were fashioned by the International Monetary Fund (IMF), various West African states were pressured to accept loans from the IMF and the World Bank under very stringent conditions, such as the devaluation of their currencies, the removal of all barriers to trade and foreign investment, and the "rolling back of the state" through the privatization of public enterprises and the dismantling of the "public social safety net." Cumulatively, these conditions contributed to unemployment, the exacerbation of poverty and deprivation, and the undermining of the domestic entrepreneurship. Additionally, the servicing of the debt required that West African states shift much-needed resources from basic human needs such as education and health care to paying the interest on loans contracted from the United States and other cores states, the IMF, the World Bank, and Western commercial banks. Moreover, the payment of the interests on these loans represented the transfer of wealth from West African states to the United States and other core states.

Another unjust mode of interaction is foreign direct investment by multinational corporations and other businesses from the United States and other core states. Under American pressure, West African states have allowed these corporations to exploit the labor of workers by paying them very low wages, to exploit various West African states' natural resources and siphon off the profits to the United States and other core states, and to pollute the environment with impunity. On balance, private investments benefit the United States and other core states more in terms of the revenues generated and the access to various natural resources such as oil, diamonds, gold, and iron ore.

Cumulatively, the vagaries of the global political economy have contributed to the crises of socioeconomic underdevelopment in West Africa. Even if West African states were committed to, and desirous of, investing in the well-being of their respective citizens, the global political economy would constrain them from doing so. As the hegemonic power in the global political economy, the United States is therefore blamed for the deleterious effects that the global political economy has on the domestic political economies of West African states. The resultant shackles of mass poverty and deprivation fosters frustration and anger. With the subalterns having no stake in their respective political economies, they become vulnerable to the seduction of terrorism.

Against this background, as part of the U.S.–West African counter-terrorism strategy, the United States would need to play a pivotal role in restructuring the global political economy. In terms of the nature of the system, a new power arrangement needs to be devised that gives West African and other peripheral states meaningful roles in the United Nations and the international economic institutions in making the decisions that affect the lives of the citizens of West African and other peripheral states. Similarly, various "sea changes" need to be made in the various modes of interactions. The global trading system, for instance, needs to be made more equitable, especially in terms of the pricing structure for raw materials and manufactured goods. Another area is the formulation of more reasonable terms for the contraction of loans, especially official ones from the United States and other core states, as well as the IMF and the World Bank. Also, steps need to be taken to help West African states to hold metropolitan-based multinational corporations and businesses accountable for their investment activities in the constituent countries of the sub-region. This would include the fair and just treatment of workers, the reinvestment of significant amounts of the profits generated in the host West African states, increased royalties for host West African states, and environmental protection.

Conclusion

The U.S.–West Africa "good governance-regional security" approach to counter-terrorism is not sufficient to serve as an effective bulwark. That is, while the approach has some advantages, overall, it has several major gaps. Against this background, an alternative approach consisting of an emphasis on human security, the democratization of American foreign policy toward West Africa, and the restructuring of the global political economy would be more effective in addressing the menace of terrorism. The human security dimension focuses on the totality of issues related to human well-being—economics, food, the environment, personal matters, community issues, health, and politics. Moreover, it encompasses the elements of good governance. The pivot is human security not state or regime security is the most effective counter-terrorism strategy. This is because it seeks to address those issues that are the internal root causes of terrorism.

The other element is the imperative of democratizing American foreign policy toward West Africa. This would entail the United States' consistent support for regimes that are genuinely promoting democratization based on human development; the holding of regular, free, fair, and competitive elections, as well as the rejection of fraudulent elections; and the development of domestic anti-terrorism regimes that seek to strike a balance between the protection of people from violence and the respect for fundamental human rights.

At the global level, the international political economy needs to be restructured so that it can promote fairness and justice. Specifically, this would require American leadership in the efforts to democratize decision making in the United Nations and the various global economic organizations. Correspondingly, steps would need to be taken to reconstitute the various modes of interactions between the United States and other core states, on the one hand, and West African states and other peripheral states, on the other, in various areas, including trade, debt, and foreign investment.

Notes

1 For a sample of the critique of the United States' counter-terrorism strategy, see Martha Crenshaw, "Terrorism, Strategies, and Grand Strategies," in Audrey Kurth Cronin (ed.), *Attacking Terrorism: Elements of Grand Strategy* (Washington, D.C.:

Georgetown University Press, 2004), pp. 74–91; Kurt Campbell and Richard Weitz, *Non-Military Strategies for Countering Islamist Terrorism*, The Princeton Project on National Security Working Paper Series (Princeton, NJ: Princeton Project on National Security, 2006); and Jeremy Pressman, "Rethinking Transnational Counter-terrorism: Beyond a National Framework," *The Washington Quarterly*, 30(4), 2007, 63–77.

2 Kehinde Bolaji, "Preventing Terrorism in West Africa: Good Governance or Collective Security?" *Journal of Sustainable Development in Africa*, 12(1), 2010, p. 217.

3 See United Nations Economic and Social Commission for Asia and the Pacific, *What is Good Governance?*, www.unecap.org (accessed October 3, 2009).

4 See Alyson Bailee and Andrew Cottey, "Regional Security Cooperation in the Early 21st Century," in *SIPRI Yearbook, 2006: Armaments, Disarmament and International Security* (Solna: Stockholm International Peace Research Institute, 2006), pp. 195–98.

5 See ibid., pp. 195–222.

6 Ademola Azeez, "Contesting Good Governance in Nigeria: Legitimacy and Accountability Perspectives," *Journal of Social Sciences*, 21(3), 2009, p. 217.

7 Ibid.

8 Barbara Orlandini, "Consuming Good Governance in Thailand," *European Journal of Development Research*, 15, 2003, p. 16.

9 Ibid.

10 Christian Kaunert, "Towards Supranational Governance in EU Counter-Terrorism: The Role of the Commission and the Council Secretariat," *Central European Journal of International Security Studies*, 4(1), 2010, p. 10.

11 Martin Ewi and Kwesi Aning, "Assessing the Role of the African Union in Preventing and Combating Terrorism in Africa," *African Security Review*, 15(3), 2006, p. 32.

12 Amitav Acharya, *Terrorism and Security in Asia: Redefining Regional Order? IDSS Working Paper No. 113* (Singapore: Institute of Defense and Strategic Studies, Nanyang Technological University, 2004), p. 1.

13 Ibid.

14 Cyril Obi, "Terrorism in West Africa: Real, Emerging or Imagined Threats?" *African Security Review*, 15(3), 2006, p. 89.

15 Ibid.

16 Rita Kiki Edozie, *Reconstructing the Third Wave of Democracy: Comparative African Democratic Politics* (Lanham, MD: University Press of America, 2009), p. 20.

17 See Mary Kaldor, "Human Security: A New Strategic Narrative for Europe," *International Affairs*, 83(2), 2007, pp. 273–88.

18 Ibid.

19 John Mukum Mbaku, "Constitutionalism and Governance in Africa," *West Africa Review*, 6(2), 2004, www.westafricareview.com/isue6/kaluintro.html (accessed on May 15, 2010).

20 See H. Kwasi Prempeh, "Presidential Power in Comparative Perspectives: The Puzzling Persistence of the Imperial Presidency in Post-Authoritarian Africa," *Hastings Constitutional Law Quarterly*, 35(4), 2008, www.SSrn.com/abstract (accessed on June 10, 2010).

21 See Sahr John Kpundeh, *Democratization in Africa: African Views, African Voices* (Washington, D.C.: National Academies Press, 1992).

22 See George Klay Kieh, Jr. and Pita Ogaba Agbese (eds), *The Military and Politics in Africa: from Engagement to Democratic and Constitutional Control* (Aldershot: Ashgate Publishing, 2004).

23 See Pita Ogaba Agbese, "Soldiers as Rulers: Military Performance," in Kieh and Agbese (eds), *The Military and Politics in Africa*, op. cit, pp. 57–90.

24 See Odd Arne Westad, *The Global Cold War* (Cambridge: Cambridge University Press, 2006).

25 See Edozie, *Reconstructing the Third Wave of Democracy*, op. cit.
26 See George Klay Kieh, Jr., "United States Foreign Policy and Democratization in Africa," in Abdul Karim Bangura *et al.* (eds), *Stakes in Africa–U.S. Relations* (Lincoln, NE: iUniverse Press, 2007), pp. 61–84.
27 See Dennis Canterbury, *Neo-Liberal Democratization and New Authoritarianism* (Aldershot: Ashgate Publishing, 2004).
28 The Economic Community of West African States, *The ECOWAS Protocol on Democracy and Good Governance* (Abuja: ECOWAS Secretariat, 2001), pp. 5–6.
29 Ibid., p. 18.
30 See Ross Herbert and Steve Gruzd, *The African Peer Review Mechanism: Lessons from the Pioneers* (Johannesburg: South African Institute of International Affairs, 2008), p. 4.
31 The African Union, *The African Union's Peer Review Mechanism* (Addis Ababa: The AU Commission, 2003), p. 1.
32 Said Adejumobi, *Africa and the Challenges of Democracy and Good Governance in the 21st Century*, www.unpan1.un.org/intradoc/groups/public/document (accessed on January 27, 2010).
33 The Economic Community of West African States, *The Protocol on Non-Aggression* (Abuja: ECOWAS Secretariat, 1978), p. 1.
34 See Osita Agbu, *West Africa's Trouble Spots and the Imperative for Peacebuilding*, CODESRIA Monograph Series (Dakar: CODESRIA, 2006), p. 69.
35 See Nicole Ball and Kayode Fayemi (eds), *Security Sector Governance in Africa: A Handbook* (London: Center for Democracy and Development, 2004), www.ssronline.org/ssg_9/index.cfm (accessed on February 10, 2010).
36 Ibid.
37 Mohamed Chambas, "Foreword," in Alan Bryden, Boubacar N'Diaye, and Fumi Olonisakin (eds), *Challenges of Security Sector Governance in West Africa* (Geneva: Geneva Center for Democratic Control of Armed Forces, 2008), p. ix.
38 Ibid.
39 See the African Union's Convention on the Prevention and Combating of Terrorism (Addis Ababa: The AU Commission, 1999), p. 3.
40 See *The Protocol to the African Union's Convention for the Prevention and Combating of Terrorism* (Addis Ababa: The AU Commission, 2004).
41 See Jessica Piombo, *Terrorism and U.S. Counter-Terrorism Programs in Africa: An Overview, Working Paper* (Monterey: Center for Contemporary Conflict, 2007), p. 8.
42 See Emmanuel Ogala, "Senate Okays Nigeria's Terrorism Bill," *Next*, April 29, 2010, p. 1.
43 World Bank, *Accountability in Governance* (Washington, D.C.: The World Bank, 2008), p. 1.
44 For an excellent discussion of horizontal accountability, see Guillermo O'Donnell, "Horizontal Accountability in New Democracies," *Journal of Democracy*, 9(3), 1998, p. 112.
45 See Richard Oliver, *What is Transparency?* (New York: McGraw-Hill, 2004), p. 3.
46 See Sachiko Morita and Durwood Laelke, "Rule of Law, Good Governance, and Sustainable Development," *Proceedings of the 7th Conference on Environmental Compliance and Enforcement*, 1, 2005, p. 15.
47 See Angel Rabasa *et al.*, *Ungoverned Territories: Understanding and Reducing Terrorism Risks, Rand Corporation's Research Report* (Santa Monica, CA: Rand Corporation, 2007).
48 Amnesty International, *Nigerian Terrorism Bill Incompatible with Human Rights* May 30, 2010, p. 1.
49 Ibid.
50 See *Pambazuka News*, "Global Review of Anti-Terrorism Laws in the Commonwealth," September 14, 2007.

51 See Jendayi Frazer, Assistant Secretary of State for African Affairs, "Nigeria at a Crossroads: Elections, Legitimacy and a Way Forward," Testimony before the Subcommittee on Global Health and Africa, United States House of Representatives, June 7, 2007.
52 See Mary Kaldor, *Human Security: Reflections on Globalization and Intervention* (London: Polity, 2007), p. 182.
53 United Nations Development Program, *Human Development Report* (New York: Oxford University Press, 1994), p. 22.
54 Ibid., p. 22.
55 Ibid.
56 Samuel Makinda, "Terrorism, Counter-terrorism and Norms in Africa," *African Security Review*, 15(3), 2010, p. 20.

Part IV

The consequences of the U.S. war on terrorism for West Africa

9 The U.S. war on terrorism and civil–military relations in West Africa

Sylvester Odion-Akhaine

Introduction

The September 11, 2001 terrorist attacks on the United States signalled a new direction of military engagement in the twenty-first century. Indeed, the U.S. scholarly circle had substantially sketched the new fault lines of conflict in the twenty-first century. In his *The Clash of Civilization,* Huntington argued that the next global crisis would be between liberalism and Islamic fundamentalism.[1] Kaplan nuanced Huntington's prognosis by indicating the input of resource scarcity to general conflict in the new century.[2] As it were, the 9/11 events opened a new frontline for the U.S. in what its policy makers called the "war on terror." The three-word mantra, as Brzezinski[3] called it, has given vent to U.S. latent and manifest functions in the pursuit of the American century. It has given a powerful impetus to one of its foreign policy philosophical matrices—the Kantian philosophy of perpetual peace underpinned by the notion that democracies do not make war on each other. Farber and Gowa have differentiated between common interests and common polities and the superseding Cold War alliance dynamics that validated the philosophical standpoint at the time.[4] However, it has remained a useful foreign policy instrument as then U.S. President George W. Bush put it vividly in the 2006 National Security Strategy:

> America also has an unprecedented opportunity to lay the foundations for future peace. The ideals that have inspired our history—freedom, democracy, and human dignity—are increasingly inspiring individuals and nations throughout the world. And because free nations tend toward peace, the advance of liberty will make America more secure.[5]

This is the evident function and, second, it has provided the U.S. an unlimited avenue for rearmament for the realization of its global interest—especially access to global resources that are germane to U.S. survival. This finds almost a historical parallel in the post-Second World War foreign policy thrust of the U.S. According to Robinson, post-Second World War policy entailed two additional policies: To nurture a global environment for America's survival and to curtail the Soviet threat. The approach reflects the fact that even without the Soviet Union, there would be a problem of order and security for its worldwide interests.[6] This accounts for U.S. quests for deep involvement in African affairs—governance, economy, and security.

In terms of contribution to global resources, Africa has a lot to offer the rest of the world. A range of natural resources such as manganese, cobalt, chrome, vanadium, gold, antimony, fluorspar, and germanium abound. The Democratic Republic of the Congo and Zambia have 50 percent of world cobalt reserves, and 98 percent of the world's chrome reserves are in Zimbabwe and South Africa. South Africa also accounts for 90 percent of reserves of metals in the platinum group. The Gulf of Guinea countries such as Nigeria and Angola have proven oil reserves. Ghana has oil in its western province and Senegal harbors a great deal of potential in the Dome Flore Area, Casamance offshore. The United States needs these resources, and the war on terrorism has provided the needed pretext to boost its presence in Africa with the objective of securing its supply lines.[7] Walter Kansteiner, who was the Assistant Secretary of State for Africa during President Bush's first term, remarked during his visit to Nigeria in July 2002, "African oil is of strategic national interest to us ... it will increase and become more important as we go forward."[8]

It is important to note that part of the objective of the war on terror is to achieve the goal of freedom by "tailoring assistance and training of military forces to support civilian control of the military and military respect for human rights in a democratic society."[9] This is apt in the case of Africa, which has continued to labor under the specter of a backlash from its overdeveloped militaries in terms of their capacity for repression of the population and their changing role as moderators, guardians, and rulers in line with Nordlinger's typology.[10]

The war on terror provides the U.S. a useful pretext for securing its energy and other mineral resources interest through a web of military presence capped with the African Command (AFRICOM) in the Gulf of Guinea. As a militarization project, it does not enhance Africa's interest, but rather it will engender a security dilemma that ultimately undermines civil–military relations, an important post-transition project in the West African sub-region.

This chapter is organized into six sections. Section two deals with the conceptual component of the paper; section three illustrates patterns of civil–military relations in West Africa prior to the war on terror and the nagging concerns of the prevailing quasi-democratic regimes to prevent a military backlash. Section four focuses on the war on terror after 9/11 and the dimension of U.S. security inroad into the sub-region in the guise of training the armies for peacekeeping and re-professionalization. Section five underlines the strategic implication of U.S. military projects for Africa's sovereignty, a point that underlines the hidden and open opposition to AFRICOM. Section six concludes the chapter, arguing that the war on terror and its corresponding militarization, the divergence of interests, and unequal relations between the U.S. and the underdeveloped states of the sub-region will have a negative impact on civil–military relations.

Conceptual reflections

Civil–military relations refer to those complex patterns of relationship between the military establishment, political society as well as the civil society. Civil–military relations have over time been conceived in terms of civilian government's superintendence over the military institution both in its doctrinal direction and goal within the broad spectrum of societal interests. The trajectory of civil–military relations both as theory and practice has been shaped by concrete historical realities, in ways in which the structure and social fabrics of society are either determined or under-determined by the military institution. This notion flows from Andreski's polemity and biataxy in his *Military Organisation and Society*.[11] The one exists in situations in which the military swamps the rest of society—its social structure. The other circumstance occurs in situations in which force is the common determinant of social relations; or in Andreski's words, "a society in which the distribution of power and consequently wealth, prestige and other desirable things ... is settled by naked force."[12] Although the former presents a façade of Gramscian's war of position,[13] in the other, the rude triumph of the rule of force, there is a convergence in ways that they both shape society to the logic of "the man on horse back." It is to be noted that civil–military relations discourse has a certain ease of motion when the issues are debated on the soft fields of advanced democracy, because of a long historical socialization and habituation to certain roles in society of the military institutions. Needless to say that these societies have resolved basic problems of co-existence or in other words have settled the "rightfulness of the units."

In developing countries, especially in West Africa, ethnic and other national questions have remained fundamental in their destabilizing essentiality. Barely a decade ago, Cote D'Ivoire was torn apart by a new concept of citizenship—*Ivorite*—spurned by power-grabbing elites, while Nigeria is in the euphoria of a disarmament exercise it claimed has been successful in the Niger Delta. Ghana had its own share of violence in the Dagbon chieftaincy crisis in its Northern Province, while Senegal's Casamancais conflict, perhaps the oldest war in the sub-region, has yet to be resolved. Guinea Conakry was under renewed authoritarian rule, after the country's second military coup in 2008. In one case, the Camara-led regime murdered over 100 innocent citizens.

In a sub-region with such a profile, how relevant are civil–military relations theories? Does it call for new concepts to capture the seeming permutations? Kohn has reflected on threats to civil control of the military and pondered on how transition would come about without provoking more crises that would endanger the democratic process. His answer was simple: "On the answer to this problem, undoubtedly worked out slowly and painfully, will rest much of the future of democracy in human society."[14]

The non-resolution of what I have called first-tier democratic conditionality in nation-building seems to make superfluous the overweighed discourse of civil–military relations. It inclines the debate towards civilian control of the military with its corresponding table of contents, namely democratic control of the military with civil supremacy over issues of domestic politics, defence, and foreign policy. Truly, civil–military control should pay attention to those issues that have kept most society anomic in the developing world. Or what the minders of the Trans-Saharan Security Initiative have called the triangle of stability—the economic, socio-political, and security interface.[15] Without their resolution, those societies will remain militarized along what Hutchful and Aning have called "old and new militarism," a complex mix of state and non-state violence.[16] In what follows, I examine the patterns of civil–military relations in West Africa before the launch of the U.S.' war on terrorism. My focus is on Ghana, Nigeria, and Senegal.

The patterns of civil–military relations before 9/11

Ghana: in the shadow of a "revolution"

Chairman Jerry Rawlings dominated the Ghanaian political architecture for over two decades. He was head of the Armed Forces Ruling Council (AFRC), which seized power in 1979. After a bout of civil interregnum, he seized the reins of power again on December 31, 1981, and by self-transmutation he became the elected president of Ghana for two consecutive terms, 1993–2000. While in power, he built an authoritarian complex with an outcome that the opposition qualified as a "culture of silence" in Ghanaian society. It was in this socio-political milieu that power alternation took place in 2000. The civil–military relations in a society that somewhat approximated Andreski's polemity and biataxy was predictable. A preoccupation with authoritarian back-lash became the norm of the new administration of John Kufuor who began to talk about securing the state. He explained: "What I mean by securing the state is ensuring that the security agencies of the state are firmly in place and are loyal to the new government and to the state as a whole, so there is no untoward upset in the state machinery."[17]

For democratic consolidation, Luckham has argued in the case of Ghana that constitutional sanctions or sheer legalese cannot achieve it but an active civil society and a strong economy that provides the dividends of democracy can.[18] However, there was demonstrable bias on the part of the administration in favor of civilian and not democratic control of the military. First, President Kufuor appointed his brother Dr. Kwame Addo Kufuor as his defense minister, changed the service chiefs including the Inspector-General of Police, and appointed a former Defense Chief, General Mohammed Hamidu, as the National Security Adviser. He disbanded the 64th Battalion believed to be made up of elements loyal to Rawlings and reorganized the Bureau of National Investigation (BNI), where Captain Kojo Tsikata held sway for a long while. Above all, Kufuor ran his government from his own home, possibly to ensure his security. He also set up a post-transition National Reconciliation Commission, a move that had as its covert purpose the stigmatization of the

Rawlings administration. These moves in the reckoning of some analysts amounted to an anti-coup strategy devoid of institutional logic:

> While it is possible to capture all these presidential efforts within an institutional framework that approximates the thematic focus of the government strategy as: a) subordination of the military to civilian authority by placing civilians in key military decision-making organs and through the retirement of "politicized" officers; b) addressing past human rights violations; and c) promoting an anti-corruption crusade in the security sector, it is very difficult to really capture whatever reform that is going on in any institutional sense.[19]

They further argued that a broad definition of security that transcends the traditional sector to human security and factors in the legislature and civil society would best achieve the goal of democratic control.[20]

As the new administration came to power after the 2000 general elections, a complementary if fundamental security need had arisen with the oil find in the Western Province (Tanor Basin). Maximizing the country's interest in respect of the new resources had become imperative, and it meant above all securing oil through a new security complex and the Ghanaian Maritime Authority lacked the capacity to achieve that. Reengineering the Ghanaian Navy and the maritime authority became important. The navy needed sufficient power to enforce the regulations. The question became whether to create a coast guard institution or retrain the navy to carry out coast guard duties? This security awareness exists among Ghanaian state actors and civil society. As early as 2000 the U.S. had begun talk about the Gulf of Guinea (in the African press) as an "ungoverned area" in terms of maritime domain awareness (MDA), which Admiral Henry G. Ulrich underlined as follows: "[S]ecurity means that there's governance. And, where there's security and governance is not where people who we describe as terrorists like to go. We're trying to eliminate voids [of law and order]."[21]

The Gulf of Guinea initiative converges with the Ghanaian authority's notion of how to go about the maritime security imperatives unlike the civil society conception of it. On the way forward, retired General N. C. Coleman, Director of Programs at the Africa Security Dialogue and Research (ASDR), quipped: "Thank you for telling us what we required, but it must be home grown."[22] The state response was to embrace it. Beyond the two reasons we have accounted for above, Ghana's perpetual vulnerability in terms of the outward orientation of its economy underlines its neo-colonial propensities. I will explain this in subsequent sections of this chapter.

Nigeria's reverse curve

Before the 1966 military coup in Nigeria, Omoigui paints a picture of harmonious civil–military relations, which took on the classical model: Soldiers rarely seen in public, segregated from civilian housing areas, and barred from public debate in the press. Besides the absence of external threat, British officers' supervision relegated the army command to an insignificant role. Both foreign policy and army internal security roles rested on the laps of the political class.[23] In this idyllic picture of civil–military relations, a point that is assumed but never emphasized in the Nigerian case, is the "Glover syndrome"— a situation in which a handful of revolting slaves were converted into the nucleus of what is today's Nigerian Army. These elements, ethnically based, were used in the pacification of the peoples of Nigeria by the British. The point here is that *ab initio*, the military was indoctrinated to see the people as the enemy (there is less information on the extent to which the original doctrinal supposition was transformed in the decolonization period). Although short-lived, in the post-independence era, a top civilian echelon of the political authorities supervised the military institution.

However, when the army took over the control of government, civil–military control was naturally dealt a mortal blow in the classical sense of that institution being subordinated to civilian authorities. Incrementally, the military became the hegemonic institution directing the socio-political and economic levers of society. Indeed, Andreski's polemity and biataxy combined. By the sheer fact of control of society, the military as an institution entrenched itself in the accumulation process of the political economy. The contradictory dynamics of that process produced outcomes that were a realization of Finer's pessimism of the fate of military coups in developing countries—a relief in which one successful coup produces another with spells of short-lived civil regimes.[24] By 1999, the military institution in Nigeria had so immolated itself to the point of destruction of the *esprit de corps* that had existed in the institution. Its content and complexion was captured by one of the institution's most respected officers, General Salihu Ibrahim, alias "army job," who observed:

> We became an army of "ANYTHING IS POSSIBLE." It became the norm for subordinate officers to sit and not only discuss their superiors, but to pass judgment in absentia. We became an army whereby subordinate officers would not only be contemptuous to their superiors but would exhibit total disregard to legitimate instructions by such superiors. We threw overboard, the bond of esprit de corps and created divisions, particularly within the officers corps with various allegiance and loyalty to the different groups so created. Then we went ahead to make a complete turn about from our established traditions. We created such a situation whereby we were operating mini-armies within the larger Nigerian Army, to such a ridiculous extent that some commanders had the audacity to kit their troops without any recourse to existing regulations or Army Headquarters.[25]

That was the state of the military. The rest of the society was under siege, press freedom receded, arbitrary arrest and detention were the order of the day, and extra-judicial execution was rampant, as the civil society fought the military in a variety of ways. To be sure, those who could not endure the atmosphere of siege went into exile. As a result of the annulment of the 1993 presidential elections and the subsequent execution of nine environmental activists in a renewed wave of authoritarianism, the state became a pariah. It was under this condition for self-survival that the military implemented a transition to civilian rule and handed over power to General Olusegun Obasanjo, a former military head of state, in May 1999.

Senegal: Between Scylla and Charybdis

Civil–military relations in Senegal, West Africa's oldest liberal democracy, are somewhat dodgy to the extent that it elicits different conclusions on the part of observers and participants alike. The reason is that Senegal has not experienced an overly state militarism, or coup d'etat, apart from the Senghor-Dia power struggle in 1962. Also, its state actors have managed a measured expansion of the democratic space in ways no other African country has done in the post-colonial era. In 1974, President Senghor legalized opposition parties along ideological lines in response to agitation from the civil society. He voluntarily handed over power to Abdul Diouf in 1981. And through the instrumentality of co-optation, opposition forces were often mollified. The gendarmerie and the army were used to pacify political opponents and the press,[26] while the pacification of the Movement of Democratic Forces of Casamance (MFDC) had resulted in large-scale human rights abuses in the country's Casamance province. In 1976, rights abuses, especially torture, caught the attention of the UN Committee Against Torture.

Other factors that have influenced civil–military relations are the presence of French troops in Senegal. Their presence coupled with the close relationship that Senghor and subsequently Diouf had with Paris helped to keep the military out of the political turf as a dominant actor. The military often acted in a ministerial capacity, especially the ministry of interior. Diop summed up this point by noting that the likelihood of a coup is reduced by the fact that:

> The ruling class has boosted the army's professional status. The Top officer classes work in a system of power sharing between branches of the armed forces. The top brass have outstandingly cushy salaries, emoluments and perks. Beyond that there is French control over the military establishment. All these factors have helped to maintain military loyalty. Further, state oversight of the officer class is ensured through the creation of an extravagantly equipped proto-militia known as an operation field force unit (legion de Gendarmerie d'Intervention).[27]

There is what may be called the "Mouride veto" in moderating the authoritarian propensities of government in ways that are positive. The mouride enclave of Touba and their marabouts constitute a government within government that the Parti Socialist (PS) while in power cultivated this social group for legitimacy and control of the peasantry. This utility, as it were, was a moderating factor.

How has the emergence of Abdoulaye Wade in 2000 changed this pattern of civil–military relations? Three important areas call for scrutiny. These are the regime's response to the Casamancais conflict, steps taken for democratic consolidation, and cooperation with its erstwhile colonial master—France. The Casamancais conflict has been referred to by many scholars as West Africa's oldest low-intensity civil war. Ideologically, the Casamancais demand is self-determination beyond greater autonomy within the Senegalese state. In a bid to fulfill pre-election campaign promises to resolve the Casamancais crisis, President Wade took steps to resolve the conflict through direct talks with the marquis. He appointed General Abdoulaye Fall to move the peace process forward, ably assisted by his civilian emissary, Latif Aidara. Between 2002 and 2004 a couple of peace meetings were brokered by the Senegalese government, the height of which was the historic Bnadjikaky meeting involving Senegalese army brass, Aidara and factions of the MFDC. In response to the May 2004 meeting called by Abbe Diamacoune, in which the government was asked to remove soldiers from the Bignon–Diouloulou highway, it responded positively.[28]

Despite these measures, there are indications that Wade might adopt the same attitude of the previous PS administration by regarding the conflict as a "law and order" problem, and in turn opt for a military solution. In 2000, barely a few months in office, he ordered an air raid on the rebels operating on the Guinea–Bissauan border, as a consequence of the separatist attack on military patrol in the region, in pursuit of his public affirmation that the conflict in the province would end in matter of weeks.[29] To be sure, the Senegalese state has yet to meet the critical demand of the peoples of Casamance. As Zounmenou has rightly noted:

> In Senegal itself, the Casamance conflict remains a security concern. Despite the 2004 agreement signed between the government and a separatist rebel called the Movement of the Democratic Forces of Casamance (*Movuvement des forces democratiques de Casamance*) (MFDC) to end the long-running conflict, peace has not yet been consolidated in the region and proposed negotiations have been postponed many times. Sporadic and localized armed fighting and banditry continue to obstruct a sustainable settlement of conflict, which is already compromised by divergent approaches between the political and military factions of the rebel movement.[30]

The *alternance* of 2000 was a milestone in the political history of Senegal. It marked the end of PS hegemony with the ascension to power by Abdoulaye Wade's Democratic Party of Senegal (PDS), a long-time opposition party through the coalition for change (SOPI). Rather than permit the routinization of electoral turnover, indications are that the country's democratic process is being deconsolidated. In 2001, Wade altered the constitution: He shifted the parliamentary elections due in 2006 to merge with the presidential elections of February 2007. This action did not only elicit widespread protest, but also sullied the electoral process as the regime was accused of creating conditions for electoral fraud.[31] In 2008, Wade arbitrarily postponed local polls. While his incessant sacking of his prime ministers, from Moustapha Niasse, Mame Madior Boye to Iddrisa Seck is indicative of a crisis of confidence, the increasing prominence of his son, Karim Wade, in state affairs, points to a possible dynastic succession. For example, he headed the Preparatory Committee for the Organization of Islamic Conference held in Dakar in 2008. All of these have engendered tension with the polity, undermining the point that democratic consolidation is a long-term affair, requiring selfless commitment of contending forces in society and respect for national institutions.[32]

West Africa and the war on terror from 9/11

Ghana

In the wake of the war on terror, two important developments demonstrated the Ghanaian government's readiness to embrace the American government. The first was the base agreement with the U.S. under which Ghana has become one of its "lily pad" facilities with access to Kotoka Airport and the strategic Tamale airfield in the Northern Region, as well as the Exercise Reception Facility in Bundase and Achiase to facilitate troop deployments for exercises or crisis response within the region. The second is the American Service Members Protection Act otherwise known as the "no-surrender treaty," which it signed with the U.S. in clear contravention of the Rome Treaty to which the country is a signatory. Its national parliament ratified the treaty by a vote of 101 to and 53 against for pecuniary reasons and a vague national interest. Of course, Second Deputy Speaker Ken Dzirasah made the point that to "sign this Agreement we shall be turned into defenseless beggars in perpetuity, and this must not be allowed to happen in this House, since any decision taken today binds the country forever to other people's aprons."[33]

For those miffed by Africa's black star behavior, the truth is that with the exception of Nkrumah's conscious engagement with the U.S. and Rawling's testy relationship, several successive governments in Ghana had always behaved slavishly towards the U.S. General Ankrah proved a pawn in the diplomatic chessboard of the U.S. in the 1960s. He shipped Soviet anti-aircraft guns and ammunition, the type that was being used by the Vietnamese against the U.S., as a gift to President Johnson. The U.S. reciprocated by a $35m aid loan to Ghana.[34]

Nevertheless, the Ghanaian government appeared to be reaping the benefit of its alliance with the U.S. For example, U.S. development assistance to Ghana in the fiscal year 2007 totaled more than $55.1 million. Ghana's $547 million compact with the Millennium Challenge Corporation is perhaps the icing on the cake of the U.S.–Ghanaian development partnership. Since the war on terror, Ghana has been engaged with the U.S. in areas of military cooperation beyond the aforementioned base agreement. It was one of the first African militaries to benefit from the Africa Contingency Operations Training Assistance (ACOTA) in 2003. The country is also a bilateral partner to the U.S. on its International Military Education Training (IMET) program. It participated in the USS Gunston Hall exercises in 2005, and was host to USS Fort McHenry calls in 2007. In the run-up to the December 2008 election, its police and army units had training exercises with the U.S. military as part of a re-professionalization program.[35]

Nigeria

The Obasanjo administration made two moves. One of which was controversial. The first was the prompt retirement of 93 so-called "political military officers" who had been part of the military dictatorship. There were 53 from the army, 20 from the navy, 16 from the air force, and four from the police. And two years after another 234 officers were also retired, and they included three Major-Generals, four Brigadier-Generals, 15 Colonels, 54 Majors, and 116 Captains. The rationale, which was provided by then Chief of Army Staff General Victor Malu, was to restore professionalism to the army and prevent subversion of the democratic order.[36]

The second step was the invitation to the Military Professional Resource Incorporated (MPRI), a private security firm, whose directors include former U.S. officers, to help re-professionalize the military. The sore point was the remit of foreign minders in the re-professionalization of the army such as defense policy and peacekeeping, a turf on which the Nigerian army considers itself as one of the best in the world. The public viewed the in-road of the MPRI as the acquisition of Nigerian strategic defence information for the advancement of U.S. interest. While disagreeing with the expressional autonomy of General Malu as a violation of the professional ethos of the military, Ofeimun[37] approbated the principle that foreign experts have no place in our national army; were they to play a role, it must be through the minders of the army, the Generals. Even General Abacha way back in 1996 resented the idea of an African crisis response force, which was sold to some African leaders by the Clinton administration, which was why the project could not really fly and was soon replaced by the African Crisis Response Initiative (ACRI).

General Victor Malu was replaced by an acknowledged professional, General Martin Lurther Agwai. This period also coincided with the U.S.' declaration of the war on terror. Nigeria's relationship with the U.S. in the security sector reform blossomed, and the MPRI continued its work of re-professionalization. In my private encounter with a staff of MPRI, my perception was that those who hired the outfit were concerned about the overhaul of the Nigerian army to make it a national military organization rather than an instrument of ethnic hegemons. It is doubtful if this goal had been achieved, given the renewed ethnicization of the army under the current leadership in Nigeria.[38] But the point needs to be made that the civil–military dilemmas of the civilian government in Nigeria found a vent in the U.S. security design for the continent, a role that ACRI was out to play through the provision of both training for peacekeeping and humanitarian aid, as well as the modernization of local armed forces to be able to combat terrorism in Africa in line with the design of the U.S.

Beyond MPRI, Nigeria has had more specific cooperation with the U.S. Under the ACRI successor program, ACOTA, the Joint Combined Arms Training System (JCATS) training center was opened in Abuja, in Nigeria, on November 25, 2003. The JCATS, run by MPRI, is based on the use of sophisticated simulation software that mimics battlefield conditions. Nigeria and Canada are the only countries with JCATS software. It involves bringing people together for a couple of weeks for war exercises under limited duration. Nigeria is among 44 African countries that took part in a program specifically for officers, the International Military Education and Training Program (IMET), which provided training for more than 1,500 officers in 2002. In 2006, the country's share of the training budget was $800,000.[39] In March 2004, U.S.-Eucom Deputy Commander General Charles Wald visited Nigeria. The country has been a beneficiary of Foreign Military Sales (FMS) and Foreign Military Sales Financing (FMF) programs, which involve sale of military equipment by the Department of Defense (DOD) to friendly countries by means of U.S. credit often routed through the FMF. Nigeria has continued to purchase arms and equipment directly from U.S. defense contractors through the Commercial Sales Program overseen by the Department of State. The country participated alongside units of the U.S. Army Special Forces and Rangers in the Flintlock 2007 exercise, which was held in Mali in August of that year. It benefited from the U.S.' Excess Defense Articles Program (EDA) under which the country received some refurbished coaster patrol vessels to combat the Niger Delta militants. Nigeria, among other countries, benefited from the Section 1206 Fund, Pentagon's privilege fund, providing training and equipment to foreign forces to "combat terrorism and enhance stability."[40]

Senegal

Upon ascension to power, President Wade was loud in soliciting for weapons to cushion his defense needs. This was nudged by its fragile relations with its southern and northern neighbors, Guinea-Bissau and Mauritania respectively. Wade was ready to cultivate other powers and looked up to the U.S., a country that has since 1965 trained more than 1,000 Senegalese military officers. The Office of Defence Cooperation (ODC) has handled most of the country's relationship with the U.S. Based in the U.S. Embassy in Dakar is the ODC, a four-person team, headed by an American military officer. It manages all traditional and non-traditional security assistance activities in Senegal, as well as coordinating host nation support, conducting joint planning and acting as liaison for other defense matters of mutual concern. Senegal partners with the U.S. IMET program, which provides military education and training to Senegalese military and civilian personnel. Like Ghana and Nigeria, Senegal has also benefited from ACRI (Senegal is the first African country to have completed training under this program). Under the program, 400 Senegalese soldiers were trained in psychological warfare including socialization to NATO doctrines. The country is involved in the West African Training Cruise (WATC), a multinational naval training program for West African countries, and the Joint Combined Exchange Training (JCET) programs involving bilateral exercises by Special Forces with units of the Senegalese Armed Forces. The objective is to socialize them to Pentagon norms, and to install U.S. equipment over the long term.

Indeed, Senegal had been involved in several military exercises with the U.S. military. In 2005, the country was part of the exercise conducted by the duck landing ship USS Gunston Hall and the catamaran HSV-2 Swift.[41] Senegal was also part of the Flintlock 2005 and 2007 counter-terrorism exercises. Like Nigeria, Senegal has been a beneficiary of the section 1206 privilege fund FY2008. Above all, the U.S. has secured an airfield in Dakar, as part of its "lily pad" facilities instead of a permanent base, where U.S. forces could dash in and out during crisis. Obviously, the U.S. presence in Senegal seemed to have relegated the French, the country's erstwhile colonial master, to a second fiddle. The former U.S.-Eucom Deputy Commander General Charles Ward, now AFRICOM Commander, lent credence to this point: "They're Francophile countries that obviously have strong lineage and history with France. The French would be involved in that respect."[42]

Strategic interest, elite preference, and the future of civil–military relations

In the foregoing, I have shown the patterns of civil–military relations in West Africa, especially in Ghana, Nigeria, and Senegal prior to the advent of the war on terror. Similarly, I have shown the nature and character of the relationship post 9/11. However, in 2008, the overall U.S. military activities in the continent coalesced into a full military command known as African Command (AFRICOM). According to Theresa Whelan, Deputy Assistant Secretary of Defence for African Affairs, AFRICOM will:

> [E]ncourage and support African leadership initiative, not to compete with it or discourage it. U.S. security is enhanced when African nations themselves endeavor to successfully address and resolve emergent security issues before they become serious that they require considerable international resources and intervention to resolve.[43]

This is perhaps the salesman's message, but the latent function is to protect its access to the sources of energy and strategic mineral resources that it requires, and to acquire them by force if necessary—a twenty-first-century application of the "Carter Doctrine."

The militarization of U.S. foreign policy in Africa is driven by a "Robinson Crusoe complex," and Africa is "no man's land," and its resources are available for plunder by the master warrior. It will have the following consequences for the continent. First, it will lead to the proliferation of arms in the continent. Second, it will lead to overdependence of African armies on U.S. weapon systems and the consequent aggrandizement of the Military Industrial Complex. This agrees with the report of the PwC's global aerospace and defense leader Richard Hooke to the extent that "the US is in the driving seat" and could "dominate the supply of the world's arms completely."[44] Third, it will provide the U.S. troops opportunity to master the African terrain for future combat operations.[45] Fourth, it leads to the imposition of pliant regimes subservient to the U.S. interest with a long-time impact on democratic consolidation in the continent. These scenarios approximate the "grand area plan" implemented by the U.S. in the Middle East, which unhinged at the turn of the last century. The "grand area plan" was the area strategically necessary for world control, especially the "stupendous strategic resources" of the Middle East, and it was to be insured by the imposition of surrogate regimes.[46] Nicol Lee of TransAfrica, a leading African-American organization focusing on Africa, is right to conclude that "AFRICOM is about sovereignty and resource grab."[47] In Africa, this can lead to a resurgence of nationalism where even at this inchoate stage of militarization of the continent, it is seen by the African public as an imperial project par excellence: Exploit the resources of the continent through the MNCs/TNCs backed by the armor of the U.S. This explains why former Ghanaian President Kufuor, for example, publicly asked George Bush what AFRICOM was all about during the latter's visit to Ghana in 2007. And similarly, Nigerians also subjected the late President Umaru Musa Yar'Adua to explaining to the public the content of his meeting with Bush in December 2007, because they feared that he might have ceded the country's territory to the U.S. for a military base. The president explained that he told President Bush to support Africa's security formula instead of direct U.S. involvement.[48]

The *Nigerian Tribune* in its editorial approximated the public sentiments: "America's overseas military bases are countries within countries. Indeed, the soldiers behave like an army of occupation. They commit crimes outside their bases but go scot-free. The military base authorities do not recognize local laws." In a note of finality, it said, "AMERICAN troops under AFRICOM program should be kept out of Nigeria. American interests, whatever they are, cannot be more important than the good health and peace of Nigerians."[49] Nigerians' concern is understandable. The U.S. regards Nigeria's oil as strategic. According to a Senior Pentagon Official, "a key mission for U.S. forces [in Africa] would be to ensure that Nigeria's oil fields, which in the future could account for as much as 25 per cent of all U.S. oil imports, are secure."[50] Between May 31 and June 2, 2000, the National Army War College's Center for Strategic Leadership organized a war game session concerning the delta with participation from security agencies and oil companies.[51] In 2006, NATO troops war gamed a civil war involving crisis over energy resources on the shores of Cape Verde.[52] And in May 2008, the U.S. Army War College war gamed Nigeria in a scenario set in 2013.[53]

Nevertheless, an interim balance sheet of the various military cooperation programs reveals anti-democratic tendencies, as well as militarization of conflicts. In Ghana, there is perception of a culture of impunity by the military in violating civil codes such as obeying of traffic rules and extortion of the civil populace by the police force.[54] Between 1999 and to date, Nigeria has been militarized. There was the Odi massacre in November, 1999, Zaki-Biam, 2000, and several incursions into the Niger Delta by federal forces. The latest in this regard was the May 2009 carnage in Gbaramatu Kingdom in Niger Delta. In Senegal, President Wade had dithered in terms of addressing the Casamancais autonomy question, and had also evinced anti-democratic behavior in his conduct to opposition forces and tinkered with the rules and regulations of the democratic process. These pose a great deal of challenges to civil–military relations in the sub-region. An overt militarization project, which AFRICOM represents, can hardly nurture it.

Conclusion

I have attempted in this chapter to present the complex mix of geopolitics, militarization, and energy interests in the U.S. global war on terror, especially in the West Africa sub-region. Essentially, governance in Africa has been authoritarian with a consequent strain on civil–military relations. Therefore, viewed from its benign purpose, the war on terrorism has presented to some extent opportunity for re-professionalizing African militaries, and to put them under civilian control. But as an imperial project, the dynamics can only accent militarization of the continent. This is underlined by the present scope of U.S. engagement: Large-scale training/exercises, port calls, base agreements and huge investment in the energy sector.

Importantly, because of a conflict of interest between the rulers and the ruled, and the extent to which external factors shape those interests, civil–military relations will more likely be testy. And also a conflict of interest lurks between the U.S. and African countries. Given the former's superpower status, African interests can easily be subverted. This can engender a continent-wide nationalist response similar to those in the Middle East. As is well known, conflicts can hardly nurture democratic civil–military relations nor serve the larger goal of democratic consolidation.

Notes

1 Samuel P. Huntington, *The Clash of Civilization*. Foreign Affairs, (Summer), 1993, available at <*http://sixtessurvivor.org/docs/huntington1993.html*>. Accessed August 20, 2010.
2 Robert D. Kaplan, "The Coming Anarchy," *Atlantic Monthly*, February 1, 1994, www.theatlantic.com (accessed August 20, 2010).

3 Zbigniew Brzezinski, "Terrorized by 'War on Terror': How a Three-Word Mantra Has Undermined America," *Washington Post*, March 25, 2007.
4 Henry S. Farber and Joanne Gowa, "Common Interests or Common Polities? Reinterpreting the Democratic Peace," *The Journal of Politics*, 59(2), 1997, pp. 393–417.
5 National Security Strategy of the United States (Washington, D.C.: The White House, 2006).
6 Williams Robinson, "Globalization, the World System, and 'Democracy Promotion' in U.S. Foreign Policy," *Theory and Society*, 25(5), 1996, p. 621.
7 Pierre Abrahamovici, "United States: The New Scramble for Africa," *Le Monde Diplomatique*, July 2004, mondiplom.com (accessed August 20, 2010).
8 Michael Klare and Daniel Volman, "The African 'Oil Rush' and American National Security," May 2006, http://concernafricanscholars.org (accessed August 20, 2010).
9 National Security Strategy of the United States, op. cit., p. 6.
10 Eric A. Nordlinger, *Soldiers in Politics* (Englewood Cliffs, NJ: Prentice Hall, 1977).
11 Stanislav Andreski, *Military Organization and Society* (London: Routledge and Kegan Paul, 1954).
12 Ibid.
13 Antonio Gramsci, *Selection from the Prison Notebooks*, (London: Lawrence and Wishart 1998).
14 Richard H. Kohn, "An Essay on Civilian Control of the Military," *American Diplomacy*, 2007, www.unc.edu/depts./diplomat/ (accessed August 20, 2010).
15 Trans-Saharan Symposium, Abuja, Nigeria, June 22–26, 2009.
16 Eboe Hutchful and Kwesi Aning, "Militarization and State Reconstruction in Africa: The West African Case," in Sylvester Odion-Akhaine (ed.), *Path to Demilitarization in West Africa* (Lagos: Center for Constitutionalism and Demilitarisation, 2001), pp. 24–45.
17 Kayode Fayemi, Thomas Jaye, and Zaya Yeebo, "Democracy, Security and Poverty in Ghana: A Mid-Term Review of the Kufuor Administration," *Democracy and Development: Journal of West African Affairs*, 3(2), 2003, p. 65.
18 Robin Luckham, "Transition to Democracy and Control over Ghana's Military and Security establishments," in Kwame Ninsin (ed.), *Ghana: Transition to Democracy* (Accra: Freedom Publications, 1998), p. 123.
19 Fayemi *et al.*, "Democracy, Security and Poverty in Ghana," op. cit., p. 65.
20 Ibid., p. 66.
21 J. Peter Pham, "Strategic Interests: Securing the New Strategic Gulf," *World Defense Review*, June 7, 2007, http://worlddefensereview.com/pham060707.shtm (accessed August 20, 2010).
22 General N. C. Coleman, Interview, Accra, October 20, 2009.
23 Nowa Omoigui, *History of Civil–Military Relations in Nigeria*, www.dawodu.com/omogui10/htm (accessed August 20, 2010).
24 S. E. Finer, *The Man on Horseback* (New York: Praeger, 1972).
25 General Salihu Ibrahim, Valedictory Speech, 1993.
26 Moussa Paye, "The Regime and the Press," in Momar Couba Diop (ed.), *Senegal: Essays in Statecraft* (Dakar: CODESRIA, 1993), pp. 324–69.
27 Momar Coumba Diop, "Introduction: From 'Socialism' to 'Liberalism': The Many Phases of State Legitimacy," in Momar Couba Diop (ed.), *Senegal: Essays in Statecraft* (Dakar: CODESRIA, 1993), p. 6.
28 Martin Evans, *Senegal: Movement des Forces Democratiques de la Casamance (MFDC)*, Briefing Paper (London: Royal Institute of International Affairs, 2004), pp. 12–13.
29 "Armed Conflict Report," *Ploughshares*, www.Ploughshares.ca/ACRText/libraries/ACR-Senegal.html (accessed August 20, 2010).

30 David Zounmenou, "Senegal's Democracy: Has Wade Lost His Edge?" *African Security Review*, 17(3), 2008, pp. 75–79.
31 Ibid., p. 77.
32 Ibid., p. 79.
33 *Ghana News Agency*, October 31, 2003.
34 See The Socialist Forum of Ghana, *The Great Deception*, 2007, pp. 42–44.
35 General William Ward, "Written Testimony: Annual Posture Statement to Congress on U.S. Africa Command," March 17, 2009.
36 Odia Ofeimun, "Collateral Functions, Military Disengagement, and the Democratization Process," in Sylvester Odion-Akhaine (ed.), *Path to Demilitarization in West Africa* (Lagos: Center for Constitutionalism and Demilitarization, 2001), p. 121.
37 Ibid., p. 123.
38 *Insider Weekly*, 2009.
39 Klare and Volman, "The African 'Oil Rush,'" op. cit.
40 Daniel Volman, "AFRICOM: The New U.S. Military Command for Africa," June 27, 2008, http://concernedafricascholars.org (accessed August 20, 2010).
41 Pham, "Strategic Interests," op. cit.
42 Cited in Pierre Abrahamvici, "United States: The New Scramble for Africa," *Le Monde Diplomatique*, July 2004. www.mondiplom.com. Accessed August 20, 2010.
43 Volman, "AFRICOM," op. cit.
44 Guy Anderson, "US Defense Budget will equal ROW combined 'within 12 Months,'" *Jane's Defense Industry*, May 4, 2005, *www.janes.com* (accessed August 20, 2010).
45 Volman, "AFRICOM," op. cit.
46 Noam Chomsky, "U.S. Aid and Torture," *Journal of Palestine Studies*, 13(2), 1984, pp. 186–88.
47 Conn Hallinan, "Into Africa: The Militarization of U.S. Foreign Policy," *Berkeley Daily Planet*, March 30, 2007.
48 See *The Independent on Sunday*, December 16, 2007.
49 See the editorial of *Nigerian Tribune*, November 20, 2007.
50 Quoted in Klare and Volman, "The African 'Oil Rush,'" op. cit.
51 Ken Silverstein, "Private Warriors: Clinton's Trip to Nigeria," *Democracy Now!*, August 25, 2000.
52 Hallinan, "Into Africa," op. cit.
53 Daniel Volman, "Full Report on U.S. Army War Games for Future Military Intervention in Nigeria and Somalia," August 17, 2009, http://concernedafricanscholars.org (accessed August 20, 2010).
54 Yao Graham, Interview, Accra, Ghana, October 21, 2009.

Part V

The prospects and lessons

10 The West African stability architecture and the U.S. war on terror

A new vision

Zakaria Ousman

Introduction

The European colonial legacy left West Africa, in the early days of the post-independence era, with a plethora of problems. Despite the pretentions about establishing the foundations for liberal democracy, the colonial powers left West Africa with an authoritarian state construct that was anchored on one-party rule.[1] Within this framework, the post-colonial African state, like its colonial progenitor, visited repression on the population, as evidenced by the violation of human rights. According to Freedom House, by the end of the second decade of the post-independence era, the West African landscape was primarily adorned with authoritarian regimes consisting of both the civilian and military variants.[2] On the social and economic fronts, by the end of the 1980s, the sub-region was enveloped in a crisis. For example, only about 30 percent of the population had access to health care.[3] Also, the illiteracy rate stood at a troubling 60 percent.[4] Overall, the majority of the people of the sub-region were living perilously on the margins. The "Structural Adjustment Programs" (SAPs) that were designed and implemented by the International Monetary Fund (IMF) exacerbated the social and economic problems by, among others, decimating the "social safety net," and "rolling back the state."[5]

The crises of governance and development plunged countries like Liberia and Sierra Leone into civil wars in 1989 and 1991 respectively. These wars terrorized the people, occasioned the injuries and deaths of thousands of civilians, and forced scores of others to be displaced internally, as well as to become refugees in various countries in the sub-region, Africa, and the world.[6] In other cases like Niger, the military, through a coup, intervened and aborted the process of democratization that was set into motion in 1991, as part of the broader "third wave of democratization" that began sweeping through the West African sub-region and the African region.

Clearly, the crises that have rocked West Africa over the past five decades have profound implications for terrorism. One of the major effects is that the crises provide terrorists and terrorist organizations with the opportunity to capitalize on the mass disaffection that undemocratic governance and socio-economic underdevelopment engender. That is, amid mass poverty and deprivation, the citizens of the various affected West African states view the state as irrelevant and distant from them. Hence, portions of them would perceive terrorism as an instrument for pressing their claims against often negligent ruling elites and the state apparatus.

In this vein, the central argument of this chapter is that the United States needs to support the construction of a stability architecture in West Africa as the critical element of its counter-terrorism strategy in the region. Specifically, this would entail working with West African states in addressing the governance, development, and security challenges that have bedeviled the sub-region since the post-independence era. In order to explicate the argument, the chapter begins with a survey of the West African governance, development, and security landscape. This is followed by linking the environment to terrorism. Next, the chapter suggests the major elements of the new stability architecture that would serve as an effective counter-terrorism strategy in the U.S. war on terrorism.

The West African governance and development landscape

The governance landscape

Several studies have attempted to show a correlation between democracy and the viability of the economy. Thus, while it is difficult to agree with Richard Joseph (1996) that West Africa is an unfinished state,[7] it is tempting to succumb to the popular view of George Ayittey, who succinctly described West Africa as a truculent African tragedy,[8] which may be akin to Wole Soyinka's analysis that Africa has had a wasted generation.[9] Our leaders have squandered too many opportunities for development and nation-building. There are rising banditry, kidnappings, and economic crimes. The current spate of violence is triggered more by social problems such as unemployment and poverty than by religious or ethnic considerations. Even seemingly religious fanatics such as members of the Boko Haram sect in Nigeria are essentially anti-establishment people, who are more interested in attacking the instruments of power, such as police stations and public buildings, than places of worship and members of other religions.

We have, within the past 50 years, witnessed a cruel circle of domination by a tiny clique of over-recycled and opportunistic cabal wearing the toga of democracy. The crude circle of self-perpetuation and domination over the years has led to entrenched corruption and misrule. In 2007, the World Bank, for example, listed Nigeria as a fragile state with a "soft economy." Nigeria shared this distinction with Burundi, Cambodia, the Comoros, the Democratic Republic of Congo, Guinea-Bissau, and Laos. Fragile states as defined by the World Bank are countries characterized by weak institutions, poor governance, high mortality rates, low life expectancy, with mortality rates 20 percent higher than other developing countries.[10] While it may not be patriotic to add to these negative indices, Nigeria's case is compounded by the fact that the nation does not fit into any of the economic systems such as monopoly capitalism of the West or the command economies of the East. Rather, the nation is running a highly corrupt economy, where the essence of governance is the self-enrichment of the leaders. Now, Nigeria ranks fifteenth among the failed states of the world.[11] It is perhaps the only oil producing nation in this category of failed states.

One crucial but recurring lesson is the failure of governance across time and space (although there have been some occasional benevolent leaders). Good governance has constantly been stifled by self-interest, greed, short-sightedness, and the lust to obtain and retain power. It is not surprising that the history of West Africa is littered with corruption, socioeconomic violence, failed attempts at ensuring peaceful co-existence, and misrule. The political economy of the West African sub-region has been distorted by the deeds of dictators, some of them using wretched ideological underpinnings to justify tyranny. Sekou Toure, Dadis Camara, Samuel Doe, Charles Taylor, Gnassingbe Eyadema, Sani Abacha, and other dictators in the sub-region set their nations back for several decades, because of corruption and misrule. Outright coercion and the privatization of public resources were the hallmarks of their leadership. Many of these dictators first appeared in the political firmament as patriots; but having grabbed power, they used it for their own selfish interests; and those who opposed them were either killed, jailed, or exiled.

Several specific cases are necessary to illustrate the crisis of governance across the sub-region. For example, Liberia had a harrowing experience because of Samuel Doe's attempt to perpetuate himself in power.[12] Not only did he engage in mindless persecution, he destroyed all the political institutions and privatized governance.[13] By the time of his demise, he had virtually looted the nation. Charles Taylor, who was thrust into power because of the vacuum that was created in the wake of Doe's ouster, followed the Doe pattern of corruption, dictatorship, and the privatization of public resources.[14] More than any country in Africa, Nigerian leaders seem to have learnt nothing from history. President Ibrahim Babangida's bid for self-perpetuation was the hidden agenda behind the annulment of the June 12, 1993 elections.[15] Abacha who came to power in the wake of the 1993 electoral crisis turned out to be the most brutish of all Nigeria's military dictators.[16] Olusegun Obasanjo, who had ruled Nigeria as a military dictator and was twice democratically elected the country's president, was not satisfied with ruling Nigeria for 11 years. Instead, he wanted the constitutional restriction on two terms lifted so he could run for a third term.[17]

In West Africa, the era of military and other forms of dictatorship seem over. We have democratic governments; however, the legacy of the privatization of the sub-region's wealth and political power has become an albatross. Some presidents are the richest men in their countries. Public offices at all levels of government are dominated by powerful mandarins who use their positions to cultivate personal militias to secure their estates acquired with public resources. This trend has characterized governance and has largely yielded stagnation, regression, and instabilities. The tragic consequences of this are increasingly clear: A rising tide of poverty, decaying public utilities and infrastructures, social tensions and political turmoil, and now, a premonition of inevitable drive into more conflicts and violence.

Fraudulent elections represent a major dimension of the crisis of governance in West Africa. Elections are designed to produce a leadership that represents the will of the people and commands their respect, but as the Nigerian example clearly shows, the 2003 and 2007 elections were merely endorsements of pre-selected candidates at both the state and the local levels. This clearly reflects the absence of democracy within political parties. Also, the elections were poorly organized and massively rigged. Overall, these fraudulent elections have diminished citizens' confidence in the electoral process and institutions, and may contribute to undermining West Africa's capacity to manage its internal conflicts. Elections, when badly rigged, may fuel violent tensions and other separatist tendencies.

The primary legal constraints on better governance in the region include incompatible legal regimes, outdated statutes, and the absence of sufficient domestic application and implementation of existing laws. In some countries, the penal code does not recognize corruption as a crime. Other problems of poor governance include interference with oversight bodies, corruption, and despotism.

The development landscape

The sub-region's economy is highly uncompetitive and characterized by, among others, a large informal sector (the only viable sector of the economy, for the most part), high levels of unemployment, high cost of doing business, and significant idle capacity. Despite its rich mineral and natural resources base, West Africa hosts the third-largest concentration of the poor in the world.[18] Decades of brutal military dictatorships and poor governance have created a legacy of instabilities, ethnic tensions, and corruption.

Also, the sub-region is one of extreme paradoxes, with widespread and endemic poverty in the midst of plenty. Abundant fresh water, arable land, pastures, fisheries (inland and marine), forestry, mineral resources, including iron-ore, diamonds, petroleum, and natural gas have not been properly utilized to create wealth and development for the people. Instead, kleptocratic rulers, in collusion with unscrupulous foreign investors, have illegally appropriated much of the wealth. Overall, the region has the potential to build a prosperous economy, reduce poverty significantly, and provide the basic social and economic services that their populations need.

In the sub-region, capitalism is only interpreted to mean primitive accumulation, which does not enhance the forces of production. The war against West Africa's brand of capitalism is a battle against the privatization of leadership. The sub-region has the worst legacy of young people with no education or skills except the art of killing. Even those countries generously endowed with natural resources have had to wrestle with leadership problems.

Governments do not provide social services to cushion people against the ravages of capitalism. For example, high unemployment rates among the youth is causing frustration and anger, with many of them feeling they were used by some leaders to cause chaos and not rewarded for it. More than 70 percent of the youth in many parts of West Africa are unemployed, and many of them often idle about at trading posts or take up occasional day jobs exposing themselves to manipulation by politicians.[19] We spend public monies to organize series of workshops and conferences, yet we pay lip service to sustainable development. It is very clear that the Millennium Development Goals (MDG) are not attainable, but our economic sorcerers and prophets engage in the intellectual deception of brandishing figures to bamboozle the masses. For instance, if the Nigerian economy is developed to rank twentieth in the world, the chances are that most of our deceased nationalists would resurrect and rejoice. But, when the criminal economy thrives on primitive accumulation, executive lawlessness, then our national development can only be postponed. The mind-boggling question is why is kleptocracy thriving in spite of loud public pronouncements that the rule of law is being implemented? Our democracy has become a cruelly manipulated chess game; it has indeed become an unending tale of squandered opportunities as a mindless bourgeois class has laid siege of the nation, and they have one consuming aim in mind, that of privatizing the leadership of the nation.

Another development challenge concerns the marginalization of women, especially in the economic arena. Women contribute to the domestic economy as farmers, petty traders, domestic workers, and homemakers. However, their work is grossly undervalued and poorly rewarded, and to worsen their conditions, they have no direct access to credit facilities because of low income and lack of collateral. Their lack of formal training means that they are not able to access other opportunities available in the better paying employment sectors of the economy.

Furthermore, in the sub-region, there is real hunger in the land. Amid the rising tide of unemployment, the average worker has been reduced to a mere creature. The civil servant is now a real servant. West Africa does not need Yuri Gagarin in space to feed her people. All that government is required to do is to deploy our production resources to create wealth and opportunities for the population. It is pertinent to highlight how much difference good governance can make. Take Senegal, for example. It is one of the countries in West Africa that has shunned military rule (the other is Cape Verde). It has been able to achieve a measure of economic development and political stability that is the envy of its neighbors. Surprisingly, Senegal attained this success with little or no natural resources.

The security landscape

Background

The security landscape in the sub-region is littered with several challenges. Among them are civil wars, communal violence, and human trafficking, which are driven by ethnic and religious factors. These conflicts have exacted heavy tolls on the affected states, including deaths, injuries, internal displacement, refugee crises, and the exacerbation of the crises of socioeconomic underdevelopment.

Civil wars

West Africa has witnessed a number of civil conflicts since independence. Among them are the Nigerian Civil War (1966–70), the First and Second Liberian Civil War (1989–97 and 1999–2003), the Sierra Leone Civil War (1991–2002), the Guinea-Bissau Civil War (1998–9), and the Ivorian Civil War (2002–10). The general causes of these conflicts include pervasive social and economic inequality and wealth distribution (especially regarding the petroleum resources), religious intolerance, and political manipulation and representation. Issues of identity and ethnicity have their own dynamics that contribute to such conflicts. Overconcentration of power is another factor that instigates conflicts. The principle of separation of powers with its inherent checks and balances is also problematic, largely because of the excessive powers of the executive *vis-à-vis* the legislature and judiciary, a legacy of the long period of military rule.

The Nigerian Civil War, for example, which was the result of a secessionist bid by leaders of the southern part of the country, remains a landmark political event and a yardstick that reminds all Nigerians of the fragility of the polity, and the need to continue at nation-building. More than a decade of violence in Liberia, Sierra Leone, and Cote d'Ivoire in the 1990s and early 2000s led to over one million deaths, due directly to conflict-related casualties, as well as to diseases and malnutrition that were exacerbated by the conflict.[20] In a few short years, the civil war in Cote d'Ivoire, for example, displaced 750,000 people internally, and triggered refugee outflows of half a million people.[21] Overall, the number of internally displaced persons and refugees in the sub-region has grown at an alarming rate. For example, in 2011, there were 520,000 internally displaced persons, and 149,000 refugees in the sub-region.[22] In the case of refugees, for example, it has created considerable strain. Agriculture is disrupted in the area from which the refugees flee. In addition, refugees can put severe burdens on economic and administrative structures in the countries that provide refuge.

Overall, the economic and political consequences of violent conflict are enormous. As well, the legacy of conflict includes substantial loss of livelihoods, employment, and incomes, debilitated infrastructure, the collapse of state institutions and the rule of law, continuing insecurity, and fractured social networks. After a quarter of a century of protracted conflict, Sierra Leone, for example, stands as one of the most impoverished, conflict-prone states in the world, and ranks near the bottom of all human development indicators.[23]

Ethno-religious violence

The pattern of intra-state conflicts in the last two decades or so has created areas that have become flash points of conflict and violence. Nigeria, which accounts for 50 percent of the ethnic groups and population in the region, has experienced the most protracted and recurrent ethno-religious conflicts, which appear to have peaked since the return to civil rule in 1999. The recurrent sectarian conflicts that pit the Muslim majority against the Christian minority have partly resulted from the fear and anxiety that attended the adoption of the Islamic legal code – Sharia – by states in the northern parts of the country in the aftermath of the return to civilian rule. The majority of conflicts in West Africa come from such communal ethno-religious sources.

In the case of the Niger Delta, which accounts for Nigeria's oil and gas deposits from which about 80 percent of the country's foreign exchange is derived annually, it has experienced one of the most protracted and deadly conflicts since the 1990s. The conflict in the Niger Delta is largely a product of poverty in the midst of plenty and worsening environmental consequences of oil production, which is destroying the livelihood opportunities of the communities. The Niger Delta crisis has pitted the local communities against the oil companies, against the state, or against one another. The inter-communal conflicts have resulted in massive loss of lives and property, while also disrupting economic activities, particularly oil prospecting, extraction, and distribution. Hostage abductions for ransom from oil companies and gang warfare among rival youth cults have led to severe cutbacks in oil production, estimated at about 500,000 barrels/day, about a quarter of Nigeria's estimated daily production of two million barrels.[24]

Many instances of ethno-religious conflicts are reactions to a collective memory of domination by the various ethnic minorities, and the legacy of colonialism in reversing the previous pattern of autonomy of small communities. The post-colonial state inherited a system of government from the British, French, Portuguese, and other European colonialists that the ruling elites have repeatedly manipulated to promote sectional or regional interest rather than national ones.

West Africa has a sharp dichotomy between ethnic as opposed to civic citizenship, in which a pan-West African notion of citizenship exists at the national level, while indigeneity operates at the local level. The dichotomy between an indigene and a settler has hardened into a theory of clan and ethnic exclusiveness and often provides the basis of inclusion or exclusion. This distinction frequently frames access to state power and resources. Resistance to rather than passive acceptance of exclusion has been the basis of much of the intra-state and communal violence plaguing West Africa.

Human trafficking

Human trafficking has become one of the major security conundrums in the sub-region. Trafficking in West Africa of the young started around the second half of the 1980s, following the economic difficulties caused by the Structural Adjustment Programs (SAPs). Young people started leaving their countries in the hopes of getting better job opportunities in Europe and North America.

Huge financial gains accrued to human traffickers. The apparent wealth of the traffickers serves an incentive to others to join the train. Those at the apex of the trade are said to be rich and influential West Africans in the society who employ the services of others. Extreme poverty and hopelessness are the driving force. Improvement of the economy, the provision of jobs, skill acquisition, and basic amenities will stem the tide.

Sustained efforts need to be made to combat human trafficking. Some of the major steps needed are the organization of greater awareness campaigns, the provision of economic alternatives for families, rehabilitation, the awarding of scholarships to those who wish to study in higher institutions, and the provision of free education. In other words, states in the sub-region will have to address the needs of their citizens if human trafficking is to be effectively addressed.

The challenge of terrorism

The sub-region is plagued by the scourge of terrorism. The perpetrators are both domestic terrorist groups and Al-Qaeda and its affiliates. For example, Mauritania and Nigeria are faced with the challenge of dealing with domestic terrorist groups. In Mauritania, domestic terrorist groups continue to wreak havoc by attacking various military installations. Also, recently, domestic terrorist groups in Nigeria launched bomb attacks in Abuja, the capital city.

At the external level, Al-Qaeda in the Islamic Maghreb (AQIM), an affiliate of Al-Qaeda, is positing threats to the security and stability of Niger. Moreover, AQIM is making sustained efforts to establish its foothold in other West African states. One of the major strategies that is being used by AQIM in this vein is the building of collaborative relationships with various domestic terrorist organizations throughout the sub-region.

Furthermore, the uncontrolled areas of the Saharan region of West Africa offer sanctuary to terrorist groups like AQIM. The fact that these vast expanses of territory are not governed provides *carte blanche* for these terrorist groups to operate in them without hindrance. In this vein, the United States has undertaken various initiatives at both the bilateral and multilateral levels to West African states to help deal with issues such as border monitoring and patrol that are central to combating terrorism.

Toward the stability architecture

Background

As has been discussed, the crises of instability bedeviling the sub-region involve a complex set of interrelated problems, and in many aspects, have deep roots in attitudes and structures. Accordingly, solutions need to be similarly profound in their scope. But often they are opposed by a formidable array of entrenched political and economic interests.

The requirement is a new vision in which priority is turned to peace, security, and sustainable development. To do this, there is a need for sustained efforts on many fronts on a long-term basis. It will require courageous political decisions, because the relationships between and among the political, socio-economic, and security landscapes are not simple ones. For example, a political crisis exists only in relation to the socio-economic and political environment. Africa is suffering a political crisis that is intimately linked to its politically troubled landscape. Political strife has disrupted peace, and poor governance has also contributed to political instability. When troubles arise, economic life stagnates, including employment prospects. An exodus of rural unemployed to the cities or to neighboring countries is a potent source of civil friction. Civil wars, border disputes, and other forms of strife affect a significant number of countries. They disrupt government services, decrease farmers' security and willingness to invest for the future, and necessarily result in higher military expenditures. A stark indicator of the extent of the crisis is provided by the number of refugees and displaced persons in West Africa.

The elements

Fundamentally, the stability architecture in West Africa should be designed to address the governance, development, and security crises in the sub-region. In the area of governance, the most critical needs include the establishment of political stability. First, countries need to implement changes within an overall strategy aimed at enhancing democracy and democratic principles. Hence, such a strategy needs to comprise policies that balance and resolve some of the conflicts that have arisen and will continue to arise. Importantly, the ballot box should and must replace the bullet. However, the resulting state legitimacy should clearly go beyond elections. Its real substance should be anchored on installing representative institutions, which foster inclusive politics, and mitigate the risk of conflict or its recurrence through paying attention to, among others, the continuing socioeconomic and political inequalities between and among groups. Moreover, the ultimate measure of the authority of a legitimate and effective state is based on whether there is an established social contract between the governors and the governed, the reciprocity between state provision of security, justice, and economic opportunities, and citizen acceptance of the authority of the state. Furthermore, some key institutional challenges need to be addressed in order to establish such a state. These include the promotion of security and the rule of law, the control of corruption and rent seeking, the establishment of an effective civil service with respectable fiscal institutions and revenue mobilization capacity.

Also, transparency and accountability are essential to attract such support. In addition, sustainable economic development requires an environment that assures citizens' security, supports inclusive development, provides adequate infrastructure, protects property and investment from predation, ensures predictable and fair taxes and incentives, and reduces the cost of doing business.

Moreover, the leaders must be accountable to the citizens for their actions. Leadership is the key in determining the parameters of reform and the institutional transformation underpinning them.

Another important requirement in the area of governance is the effective management of ethnic, regional, and religious cleavages. In essence, managing diversity is the identification, acceptance, and understanding of those differences and similarities that allow individuals or groups within countries to appreciate others, to become aware of and fully use their talents and abilities to make unique contributions to groups and organizations. Diversity management, for example, is about good people management (creating an environment where individuals feel valued, and promote nation-building, social harmony, and economic growth). In this direction, for example, tribalism that connotes unhealthy rivalry among ethnic groups within a country must be confronted with sound public policies.

In order to establish socioeconomic stability, the overarching development strategy should be a long-term task that is framed by the imperative of good and effective management. In turn, such a framework should take advantage of the sub-region's vast economic potentials. With its huge population and a rich stock of natural and human resources, it has the potential to experience rapid economic growth, if the governance architecture is right. The region is currently one of the largest oil and gas producers. Thus, a growing and stable economy is part and parcel of the solution. Specifically, the dividends from economic growth should be used to tackle the vexing problem of mass abject poverty, unemployment, including for the disaffected youth, and the addressing of basic human needs—education, health care, housing, transportation, and the provision of clean drinking water and acceptable sanitation. Also, efforts should be made to address the negative consequences of private investments through multinational corporations from the developed states, and the structural adjustment programs that have been imposed by the International Monetary Fund and the World Bank as part of neo-liberal orthodoxy.

On the security front, the roots of civil conflicts need to be addressed. One way to do so is through the construction of schools and the enrollment of children. This is one of the most effective ways to bring a peace dividend to the local population, and help the government rebuild the social contract. Redressing historical inequalities can only be achieved on the basis of a sound and clear analysis of local realities. Beyond meeting the needs of those who have been directly active in conflict, reintegration should also address the war-induced vulnerability of others groups. Fostering local governance and supporting civil society organizations can empower people and local organizations to accelerate economic recovery and to claim and exercise their rights, including carrying out human rights advocacy.

Lowering the probability of conflict relapse and consolidating peace have to be fundamental priorities in macroeconomic policy. Inclusive recovery requires that we focus on those sectors that employ the bulk of the population. Government commitment to restore credibility, confidence and competiveness is paramount for improving the business and investment environment climate. There is no example of long-term development without a sustained increase in output per capita. Strong development programs are also those that pay more attention to social inclusion and equity.

Similarly, countries emerging from violent conflict face extraordinary constraints in mobilizing the human and financial resources that are urgently needed, first for humanitarian relief, and subsequently for economic recovery. The lack of economic opportunities due to the underlying socioeconomic and political barriers that young people, in particular, face raises the risk of violence. War, exacerbated diseases, and malnutrition kill by far more people than missiles, bombs, and bullets.

The implications for the U.S. war on terrorism

As has been argued, continual instability in West Africa as a consequence of the crises of underdevelopment would provide fertile grounds for terrorist groups to win the sympathy of the population, and to especially recruit disaffected youth, who do not have stakes in their respective countries. Accordingly, in order to successfully combat terrorism in West Africa, the United States should invest in helping to address the governance, development, and security challenges facing the sub-region. In the governance area, the U.S. would need to match its pro-democracy rhetoric with concrete actions. That is, the U.S. recurrent claim that it supports the establishment of democracy in West Africa and elsewhere on the African continent should not simply be a rhetorical expression that is designed to impress Americans at home and placate West Africans. Instead, the U.S. needs to consistently and persistently support the forces of democracy in the sub-region. In short, condoning the excesses of client regimes, while condemning those of adversarial regimes, is the type of hypocritical stance that would help undermine the moral authority of the United States.

On the development front, the U.S. needs to invest in concrete projects such as the construction of schools, hospitals, and health care centers, and the infrastructure of the states in the sub-region. Instead of spending billions of dollars on an assortment of military programs, the U.S. could invest the money in helping to improve the material conditions of the citizens of the various constituent states of the subregion. Such an approach would help to empower people economically and improve their standard of living. In turn, this would make it quite difficult then for these citizens to develop empathy for terrorist groups. This would be because these citizens would have developed stakes in their various societies.

Conclusion

The central finding of this chapter is that the building of a stability multiplex in the West African sub-region is the *sine qua non* for the success of the U.S. war on terrorism. As has been discussed, the crises of underdevelopment that have plagued the sub-region for the past five decades provide the roots for the resort to terrorism and the empathy for it. For example, in the governance area, the sub-region has been plagued with various autocratic civilian and military regimes that have, amongst others things, violated fundamental human rights, undermined the development of democratic institutions and a democratic political culture based on political pluralism, the rule of law, transparency, accountability, and a vibrant civil society. Even the "third wave of democratization" that began sweeping across the sub-region in the early 1990s has not led to democratic transition and consolidation in several of the countries. In fact, in some cases like Niger, there has been a reversal, as the military has intervened and seized power.

In the development arena, the constituent states of the sub-region are still faced with the challenges of abject poverty, mass unemployment, underemployment, overall deteriorating standards of living, inadequate educational opportunities, the lack of access to health care, clean drinking water, and acceptable sanitation. Even in states like Benin, which have made laudable strides in terms of political democratization, the social and economic conditions of the majority of the people are horrendous. In other words, political democratization is not leading to socioeconomic democratization. Accordingly, sustained efforts need to be made concerning the crafting of the democratic project in a comprehensive way that embodies the various facets of the society, including the political, economic, environmental, political, and social.

In the security arena, the civil wars in Cote d'Ivoire, Liberia, and Sierra Leone have ended. However, these states are faced with the daunting challenges that attend post-conflict peacebuilding. In the case of Cote d'Ivoire, the task is made even more difficult by the leadership crisis that was occasioned by the 2010 disputed presidential election. On the one hand, the election commission ruled that the opposition candidate Alasanee Quattara won the presidential contest. On the other hand, the Supreme Court ruled that the incumbent Laurent Gbagbo won the election. The resultant state of confusion then plunged Cote d'Ivoire into a state of continuing crisis. Although the leadership stalemate has been resolved, the security situation is still tenuous. Also, while the civil wars in the sub-region have ended, Nigeria, nevertheless, continues to be plagued with recurrent ethno-religious violence. Additionally, the conflict in the country's Niger Delta region continues to fester. Human trafficking, counterfeiting, money laundering, and drug trafficking remain major security challenges in the sub-region.

Finally, the U.S. war on terrorism in the sub-region will not succeed if the crises of underdevelopment, which are the major sources of underdevelopment in the sub-region, are not addressed. Hence, instead of according primacy to the military aspects of counter-terrorism, the U.S. should invest the help to address the governance and human security challenges in the sub-region as part of the effort to construct a stability architecture. In the long term, this is the most effective counter-terrorism strategy, because it would help attack the roots of terrorism.

Notes

1 See Peter Schraeder, *African Politics and Society: A Mosaic in Transformation*, 2nd ed., (Florence, KY: Wadsworth Publishing, 2003).
2 See Freedom House, *Freedom in the World: Comparative and Historical Data, 1973–2011* (Washington, D.C.: Freedom House, 2011).
3 United Nations Development Program, *Human Development Report* (New York: Oxford University Press, 1992), pp. 130–33.
4 Ibid.
5 See John Mukum Mbaku, "The African Debt Crisis and the New Globalization," in George Klay Kieh, Jr. (ed.), *Africa and the New Globalization* (Aldershot: Ashgate Publishing, 2008), pp. 29–50.
6 See United Nations Office for the Coordination of Humanitarian Affairs, IDPs, Refugees, Returnees, West Africa, October 16 (New York: OCHA, 2003).
7 Richard Joseph, "Nigeria: Inside the Dismal Tunnel," *Current History*, 95(601), 1996, pp. 193–200.
8 George Ayittey, *Africa Betrayed* (New York: Palgrave Macmillan, 1993).
9 See Maya Jaggi, "Ousting Monsters," *Guardian*, November 2, 2002.
10 World Bank, *Fragile and Conflict Afflicted Countries* (Washington, D.C.: The World Bank, 2005).
11 Fund for Peace, *Failed State Index* (Washington, D.C.: Fund for Peace, 2009).
12 See J. Gus Liebenow, *Liberia: The Quest for Democracy* (Bloomington, IN: Indiana University Press, 1987).
13 See George Klay Kieh, Jr., *The First Liberian Civil War: The Crises of Under-development* (New York: Peter Lang Publishing, 2008).
14 See Adekeye Adebajo, *Building Peace in West Africa: Liberia, Sierra Leone, and Guinea-Bissau* (Boulder, CO: Lynne Rienner Publishers, 2002).
15 See Kayode Samuel, *Political Transition in Nigeria, 1993–2003: Commentaries on Selected Themes* (Lagos: Malthouse Press, 2010).
16 See Ebenezer Babatope, *The Abacha Years: What Went Wrong* (Ibadan: Heinemann Educational Books, 2004).
17 Siddque Mohammed, "The Masquerade Unmasked: Obasanjo and the Third Term," in Said Ademujobi (ed.), *Governance and Politics in Post-Military Nigeria* (New York: Palgrave Macmillan, 2010), pp. 173–206.
18 See Fund for Agricultural Development, *Rural Poverty: Western and Central Africa* (Rome: IFAD, 2001).
19 See United Nations Economic Commission for Africa, *Strategies to Promote Youth Self-Employment in West Africa* (Addis Ababa: UNECA, 2010), p. 4.
20 See Ploughshares, *Armed Conflicts Report* (Boston: Ploughshares, 2002).
21 See ibid.; and Internal Displacement Monitoring Center, *Cote D'Ivoire: Country Report* (Geneva: IDMC, 2011).
22 See United Nations Office of the High Commissioner for Refugees, *Regional Operations Profile: West Africa* (Geneva: UNCHR, 2011).
23 United Nations Development Program, *Human Development Report* (New York: Oxford University Press, 2008).
24 See Sopuruchi Onwuka, "Nigeria's May Oil Exports Average 2.1 Million Barrels Daily," allAfrica.Com, June 16, 2010.

11 West Africa and the U.S. war on terrorism

The lessons

Kelechi Kalu

Introduction

In pursuit of its national security interests across the globe, but especially in Sub-Saharan Africa, it is a major advantage that the United States was not officially involved in the European colonizing projects in Africa. Indeed, the United States is often remembered through the Atlantic Charter and the consequent rearrangement of the international political and economic institutions at the end of the Second World War as the defender of individual liberty and self-determination for all. And, while the U.S. liberally promoted the values of individual rights and free market economy across the globe in ideological competition against the Soviet Union, it is also remembered for playing a significant role in maintaining illiberal regimes in power in Africa. Indeed, rather than using political and economic freedoms to gauge the values that anchor the United States' actions and interests in Africa, security and stability best explain its behavior in Africa and elsewhere in the international system.

Consequently, the ideologically informed U.S.–Cold War politics did not bode well for American values of democracy and free markets for Africa and Africans. Under autocratic leaders, the middle class and the masses suffered political, economic, cultural, religious, and other forms of marginalization in their own countries; and, in many instances, those that challenged the autocrats paid the ultimate prize without the benefit of judicial trial. The result for various states in Africa was the lack of effective nation-building projects, the irrelevance of the state to the masses that resulted in general citizens' alienation from the geopolitical spaces that were expected to serve as sources of economic, political, cultural, and religious security. Instead, guns manufactured in American and European factories were readily available to soldiers across Africa, whose penchants for coups, counter-coups, and outrageous violations of human rights were remarkably ignored by local and official Western policy makers and media. Thus, public policy and governance—the peoples' health, economic, and educational welfare—were in decay across the continent. Subsequently, the schools of thought on state failure characterized most of the states in Africa as lacking the institutional capacity for good governance, legitimacy, and the ability to control excessive corruption by the beginning of the new millennium. Indeed, with the end of the Cold War, the absence of the Soviet Union as an ideological and strategic competitor for the United States and her Western allies led to eruptions of built-up and stored anger due to the resentment of a Western presence in the Middle East and North Africa, culminating in the unfortunate attacks on the U.S. on September 11, 2001.

Prior to 9/11, conditions of anomie that existed in Africa were largely ignored. This raises some questions on the renewed interests in African security following 9/11. For example, to what extent is poverty-induced purposelessness a source of terrorism? If poverty is a source of terrorism, why did Africans not terrorize their societies before 9/11? What are the connections between ungoverned spaces, poverty, and peoples' vulnerability to recruitment as terrorists? More specifically, what features of West Africa's geopolitical, religious, and cultural spaces make it easier or more difficult as a terrorist platform against the United States? Since we only touch on these questions in concluding this volume, suffice it to say that to the extent international terrorism was not an issue in Sub-Saharan Africa prior to 9/11, the actions and behaviors of the U.S. in collaboration with various governments in the region, especially in pursuing Islamic fundamentalists, will either truly create and fester international terrorism or lead to improving the peoples' welfare to forestall the possibility of homegrown or imported terrorist ideation in West Africa.

Economic conditions in Sub-Saharan Africa prior to 9/11

States that are assumed to be effective are those that are characterized by their capacity for ensuring the security of their people and territory, able to provide basic services—education, health, road, energy—and other infrastructures that make life worth living. And, such states have to be able to protect and guarantee the political and civil liberties of their citizens to enable them pursue their interests with as few uncertainties as possible.[1] Since the 1980s, various states in Sub-Saharan Africa have not been able to execute the functions of security, providing basic services and ensuring the citizens' liberties.

As long as the indicators for international socioeconomic data have been kept, Sub-Saharan Africa has been at the lowest rung of comparable sub-regions globally. For example, most of the countries in the Sub-Saharan Africa (SSA) region are listed in the low income bracket of both *World Development Report* and *Human Development Report* published by the World Bank and the United Nations Development Program (UNDP) respectively. From the 2002 *Human Development Report*,[2] average life expectancy in 2000 for SSA, for example, was 48.7 years. And, with the adult literacy rate at 61.5 percent, PPP at $1,690, the SSA region with an overall Human Development Index of 0.471 was the only region that was collectively declining compared to regions like Latin America with an overall index of 0.726, and South Asia at 0.570—both listed in the low income bracket of the 2002 report. Similarly, with 34 percent of the population in SSA undernourished between 1997 and 1999, and 9 percent of adults living with HIV/AIDS (by 2001, 15 million women and 2.6 million children were living with the disease), coupled with 121 cases of tuberculosis per 100,000 people in 1999,[3] the region was more focused on dealing with problems of food, shelter, and health rather than terrorism.

Indeed, evidence from the socioeconomic data shows that the region is the least technologically diffused with limited access to phones or internet for most of the citizens. For example, except for South Asia with seven persons per 1,000 people with access to telephone mainlines in 1990, SSA was the least region with access to mainline telephone access. However, by 2000, while 33 persons per 1,000 had access to telephones in the South Asian region, the number for SSA was 15. But for the Arab states, the indisputable source of the resentment and anger that resulted in the 9/11 attacks, 35 persons per 1,000 had access to telephone in 1990, which drastically increased to 77 persons per 1,000 by 2000. Indeed, access to cellular mobile phones in Arab states was 38, South Asia four, and SSA region with 19 subscribers per 1,000 in 2000.[4] Access to the infrastructure of communication is highlighted here because of its central role in the capacity of the 9/11 attackers to plot and execute their projects. Thus, with poor economic and social conditions, poor information communication infrastructure, the Sub-Saharan Africa region is also a poor candidate as an incubator of global terrorism. Indeed, from 1990–8, the number of Sub-Saharan Africans who owned personal computers were so negligible that there was no data to report. Also, those with access to public telephones per 1,000 persons were approximately 0.5 percent between 1990 and 1998.[5] This was a period in which other demographic and economic data were also gloomy for Sub-Saharan Africa. For example, while the total population stood at 628 million with an average annual growth rate of 3.0 percent in 1998, the total gross national product was a mere $304.2 billion with an average annual growth rate at 2.2 percent, compared to France with a total population of 59 million in 1998 but with an average annual growth rate of 0.5 percent for 1990–8 and a total gross national product of $1.5 trillion, and an average annual growth rate of 3.2 percent for 1997–8.[6]

Politically, and as a result of illiberal regimes governing within platforms of insecurity and instability, high levels of political crises across the SSA region resulted in a series of intrastate conflicts ranging from Sierra Leone, Liberia, DRC, Rwanda, and Burundi to Sudan. And, based on the poor economic conditions already discussed above, one can conclude that on the eve of 9/11, the SSA was a neglected region first by the various governments that failed in the development of their various states; and second, by the United States, France, and others that previously supported such illiberal regimes, and supplied the resources that most of the governments in the SSA used to terrorize their people. Such profound neglect, manifested in various regimes' failures in post-independence nation-building projects, created conditions of anomie and the existence of ungoverned spaces across Sub-Saharan Africa. Some scholars and policy makers have misrepresented such spaces, which are occupied by resources-agitating rebels, gangs, and criminals, especially in West Africa, as potential sources of international terrorism. Indeed, as Stewart Patrick[7] argues, while weak states tend to provide the ideal environment for illicit activities by non-state actors:

> [T]he relationship between transnational organized crime and weak states is parasitic. All things being equal, criminal networks are drawn to environments where the rule of law is absent or imperfectly applied, law enforcement and border controls are lax, regulatory systems are weak, contracts go unenforced, public services are unreliable, corruption is rife, and the state itself may be subject to capture.[8]

However, while poorly governed and therefore weak states tend to attract illicit activities by non-state actors like Al-Qaeda, narcotic traffickers and other criminal gangs, under globalization such weakness is not sufficient reason to assume that ungoverned spaces will necessarily fall into the hands of international terrorists. As argued above, it is the poorly developed infrastructure in many Sub-Saharan African states, especially in West Africa, that has actually insulated the ungoverned spaces from international terrorist cells largely because "[i]n a global economy, realizing high returns depends on tapping into a worldwide market to sell illicit commodities and launder the proceeds, which in turn depends on access to financial services, modern telecommunications and transportation infrastructure."[9] But then, there still is the vexing issue of the connections of ungoverned spaces, poverty, and peoples' vulnerability to recruitment for reasons that are not necessarily honorable. The problem is that the conditions in these ungoverned spaces make them conducive as recruiting grounds for potential domestic and international terrorists. The question then is how to preemptively forestall connections between ungoverned spaces as sources of future illicit activities and their potential as terrorist incubators.

Ungoverned spaces as sources of terrorism

One of the most globally relevant revolutions of all time is information technology, specifically the internet, which has created a borderless world as a framework for information exchange in advancement of both good and evil agendas. Today, the real ungoverned and perhaps ungovernable space is the information superhighway; not the Sahel or the remote areas that various governments in SSA have failed to develop. It is these ungoverned spaces, partly as a result of globalization-induced "interdependence of open society, open economy, and open technology infrastructure,"[10] that illegitimate non-state actors like Al-Qaeda, drug and human traffickers, and criminal gangs occupy to foment troubles for states and their citizens across borders.

While the United States can and does expend resources to, for example, Chad, Mali, and Mauritania for purposes of "tracking and neutralizing" suspected terrorists in the Sahel, it is the kind of efforts embedded in the Trans-Saharan Counterterrorism Partnership (TSCTP)[11] that is likely to prevent both the physically ungoverned and information superhighway spaces in SSA from becoming incubators for global terrorism. The TSCTP, according to William Bellamy, is

> ... a five-year, $500 million initiative, whose focus expanded from training host nation militaries to include a range of governance and public diplomacy programs. These were designed, among other things, to "deny terrorists safe havens, operational bases and recruitment opportunities, and to enable African governments to resist attempts by Al Qaeda and others to impose their radical ideology on traditionally moderate and tolerant Muslim populations in the region."[12]

Thus, while the conditions that characterize Sub-Saharan African states prior to 9/11 were also present in places like Afghanistan and part of Pakistan where the terrorists found safe havens for carrying out their plots, there are two key differences with SSA. First is religion. While a significant proportion of the citizens in Sub-Saharan Africa, but especially in West Africa, are Muslims, the brand of Islam in SSA is more tolerant of diversity, because of the cultural, linguistic, and religious diversity that compels individuals and groups to be sensitive to other views in public spaces. Indeed, it is not uncommon to observe people of different religions interacting on the basis of common cultures and languages in the region. Such fluidity is in contrast to the cultural and linguistic unity enhanced by the tools of globalization that provided opportunities for Al-Qaeda and the 9/11 terrorists to use ungoverned spaces in Afghanistan, Yemen, and elsewhere to carry out their attacks against the United States in 2001.

Since religious, cultural, and linguistic diversity within a framework of poverty, poor infrastructure, and illiberal regimes ensured that SSA citizens are less connected to the global information infrastructure, they are, by extension, more likely to use globalization tools like open societies, open economies, and borders for economic purposes rather than for ideologically based terrorism. However, as evident in the chapter on the crisis in the Niger Delta region of Nigeria, how the United States and non-governmental actors like Shell Petroleum and Chevron collaborate with Nigeria to resolve the poor development-induced anomie and violence in the region will determine the extent to which global actors like Al-Qaeda and issues like terrorism, which defy sovereign state boundaries, are stopped before they metamorphose into instability. Required collaborations must also extend to policy-defined approaches to institution building, fair and equitable access to markets, and investment opportunities that will increase the capacity of sovereign states in the region to engage their citizens in viable economic and civic activities. If the United States, non-state actors, and states in the region continue the past tendency for contradictions in principle and practice, it is likely to retard efforts that come out of mere collaborations with the military and executive arms of governments in SSA.

If there is a clear lesson from the terrorist attacks on Tanzania, Kenya, the United States, Britain, Spain, and elsewhere, it is that while global information infrastructure provides opportunities for increasing economic opportunities for the wealthy countries, firms and individuals, the costs of neglect to the issues that affect ordinary citizens in poorer societies can be used by the ideologically smart-but-concerned as a galvanizing framework within the context of globalization to settle scores that have nothing to do with the causes of the poor and angry. Consequently, if the United States is serious about combating terrorism, especially in SSA, the foregoing lesson suggests that the pre-9/11 practice of giving logistical and financial support to authoritarian African governments be revisited to include openly consistent moral leadership in support of fairness and transparency in the region when the governments fail to meet their obligations to their people. For example, the electoral impasse in Ivory Coast in 2010 teetered toward a civil war with consequences for internally displaced persons and massive migrations across bordering states such as Liberia, Guinea, Sierra Leone, Burkina Faso, and Mali. The pressures such unplanned migrations brought in neighboring states, especially in fragile states like Liberia, Mali, Niger, and Guinea, offered opportunities for criminal gangs, non-state actors like drug and human traffickers, and rag-tag Al-Qaeda "want to be noticed" to play the hero's part for citizens in distress. Ultimately, if enhanced with good governance, economic productivity, and physical security, human security offers tremendous opportunity to closing the vacuum through which non-state actors undermine sovereign states' capacity to control their physical territory through reliance on their citizens.

The political economy of West Africa

While the "war on terror" was declared by President George W. Bush following the attacks on the United States on 9/11, the concept of *war on* was usually deployed in non-military contexts. According to Geoffrey Nunberg:

> The "war on" pattern dates from the turn of the century, when people adapted epidemiological metaphors like "the war on typhus" to describe campaigns against social evils like alcohol, crime and poverty—endemic conditions that could be mitigated but not eradicated. Society may declare a war on drugs or drunken driving, but no one expects total victory. "The war on terror," too, suggests a campaign aimed not at human adversaries but at a pervasive social plague.[13]

Indeed, and serendipitously, the "war on terror" arguably is the most plausible phrase that captures what is needed in the context of U.S. relations with Sub-Saharan African countries in order to deny potential safe havens for Al-Qaeda in the region. The *war on* concept presupposes a need for preemptive action to disperse gathering storms of weak state infrastructure, illegal trade in small arms, joblessness, disease, and financial frauds committed in and around ungoverned spaces near porous borders. Such preemptive action would involve enhancing the capacity of West African states to develop the institutional capacities—police, judiciary, investigative, and correctional institutions[14]—that will enable individual states to unilaterally, and when necessary collectively, confront the menace that is part of globalization-driven borderless crimes against states, but especially, crimes against soft targets as was the case on 9/11 in the United States. Accomplishing this requires attention to nation-building efforts in the SSA region that have largely been unproductive since the 1960s, especially in the areas of political stability, education, and economic growth.

The *war on* concept in West Africa requires the rebuilding and/or strengthening of existing socioeconomic structures of states in the region, which requires the "reconstruction of the enabling conditions for a functioning peacetime society to include the framework of governance and rule of law."[15] As previously argued, most states in West Africa have poor institutional capacities for law enforcement, necessary for maintaining physical human security and confidence of investors and other entrepreneurs. The result is government incapacity in most instances to adequately govern all of its sovereign territories. Thus, in addition to strengthening the capacities of government to make and enforce laws within its territorial boundaries, the existence of ungoverned territories should equally be denied to potential non-state actors with extremist agendas that are likely to use such spaces for dishonorable activities like training terrorists or religious extremists.

Logically, when governments have capacities for making and enforcing laws, it creates a conducive and safe atmosphere for local citizens to engage in various social functions that help enhance economic activities that create employment and wealth, which together enhance citizens' pride of belonging to the state. In turn, such feelings of belonging based on concrete economic and social interests legitimize the government and its institutions, such that external or internal non-state actors with destructive agendas will find it difficult to operate within the borders. Therefore, enhanced state–society relationships that are based on enabling frameworks of economic activities, respect for law and order, and protection for citizens' political and civil rights are necessary preconditions for thwarting terrorism in West Africa. Economic and electoral frustrations combine to intensify actions that lend themselves to insecurity in the region.

Curbing such insecurity requires that citizens' lives be protected through effective enforcement of the laws such that political issues, for example disputed electoral outcomes, are dealt with within political/judicial institutions to prevent the use of identity differences like ethnicity, religion, and region as a pretense for intensifying insecurity that can become adjudged as instances of terrorism. As a number of states in West Africa have not had effectively functioning political and judicial institutions, collaboration on the basis of "the war on terrorism" should take the form of helping states with weak political and judicial institutions to construct, reconstruct, and strengthen the police, courts, and other civil conflict management/resolution mechanisms that enhance the physical security, as well as the political and civil liberties, of the citizens. Perceptions of regional, ethnic, religious, and gender inequities are often instrumentalized when citizens do not have adequate access to redress their grievances in courts of law. Where such access results in blatant decisions that undermine constitutional provisions, they deepen perceived and real instances of injustice and inequity.

Similarly, as we have argued above, government incapacity or unwillingness to carry out its sovereign responsibilities on behalf of all its citizens is more likely to render such neglected citizens vulnerable to economic frustrations, making them targets for recruitment into illegal activities. Bringing such citizens back into the fold of effective and active citizenry requires strategic attention by government officials to issues of socioeconomic well-being of the citizens. This is especially cogent for those citizens on the margins of urban centers who, without employment, shelter, or access to health care are geographically more accessible to either politically disaffected individuals or itinerant radical groups seeking to recruit anomic individuals into their folds. Bringing these and other individuals back into effective and active citizenry will require the provisions of measurable policies that help to transform lives. Specific projects such as constructing or rehabilitating dilapidated schools, community health care facilities, a welfare program that links access to food with work programs, and the provision of shelters are likely to begin the process of rehabilitating "forgotten or lost citizens". And, if left un-retrieved, these "forgotten citizens" will remain vulnerable to recruitment into destructive activities that might challenge state sovereignty and threaten security of persons and properties as evidenced across the bordering spaces between Nigeria, Niger, and Chad as well as in the Niger Delta region of Nigeria.

Thus, recalibrating the strategies for fighting the "war on terror" to include *war on* anomie, poverty, hopelessness, and human rights violations and political/economic marginalization across the region are likely to yield outcomes that will forestall the region as an incubator for terrorism and other forms of international criminal activities. The United States' interests in West Africa should remain multidimensional and include access to such minerals as crude petroleum, gas, and uranium, denial of the region to Al-Qaeda and its sympathizers as a safe haven for training, recruitment, and use as a platform to threaten the U.S. However, U.S. interest should also include access to markets for U.S. goods and services, which consequently require strengthening state institutions and their capacities to function independent of other states and non-state actors. Accomplishing such tasks requires going beyond providing money as the Bush administration did for good governance without actual provisions for measurable and sustainable benchmarks—protecting the physical security of the citizens, their political and civil rights, and reducing instances of electoral malpractice and ensuring that citizens effectively participate in making decisions that affect their lives—for evaluating what constitutes good governance. Indeed, without such measurable indicators as mechanisms for accountability, many of the states in the region—Nigeria, Chad, Niger, Liberia,

Cote d'Ivoire, Guinea, and Gambia—have used their "war on terror" relationships with the United States as excuses and platforms to undermine human rights protections, marginalize their citizens, especially those identified as "political radicals," who in most instances are merely agitators for political change. The region can be secured against Al-Qaeda, as well as international criminal gangs, if the United States becomes a neutral and honest broker on matters of elections and leadership transitions in the region.

Conclusion

Ultimately, securing the region requires that the U.S. works with states in West Africa to strengthen their capacities for executing their sovereign functions and collaborate with them to ensure enhanced economic activities that create sustainable employment and other socioeconomic structures. Such long-term collaboration will build trust between the United States and various states in West Africa—the kind of trust that currently does not exist between West African states and citizens and their former colonizers—which is necessary for multilateral and bilateral engagements for solving transnational and transborder problems such as financial crimes, narcotics trafficking, and international terrorism.

Finally, consistently urging the governments in this sub-region to protect the rights of their citizens against repressive state institutions and structures will ensure that the citizens will become active civic participants in their own economic and political welfare as well as in the security of their states: Potent weapons against criminal gangs and international terrorists and terrorisms. However, the current U.S. counter-terrorism strategy, which focuses on building the military–security capacities of West African states, is not enough. This is because it only seeks to address the physical aspects of human security.

Notes

1 See Stuart E. Eizenstat, John Edward Porter, and Jeremy M. Weinstein, "Rebuilding Weak States," *Foreign Affairs*, January/February 2005, pp. 134–46.
2 UNDP, *Human Development Report: Deepening Democracy in a Fragmented World* (New York: Oxford University Press, 2002), p. 152.
3 Ibid., p. 173.
4 Ibid., p. 189.
5 UNDP, *Human Development Report Human Rights and Human Development 2000*, (New York: Oxford University Press, 2000), p. 201.
6 Ibid, pp. 230–34.
7 Stewart Patrick, "Weak States and Global Threats: Fact or Fiction," *The Washington Quarterly*, 29(2), 2006, pp. 27–53.
8 Ibid., pp. 38–39.
9 Ibid.
10 Maryann Cusimano Love, *Beyond Sovereignty: Issues for a Global Agenda*, 3rd ed. (Belmont, CA: Thomson Wadsworth, 2007), p. 3.
11 William Mark Bellamy, "Making Better Sense of U.S. Security Engagement in Africa," in Jennifer G. Cooke and J. Stephen Morrison (eds), *U.S. Africa Policy*

Beyond the Bush Years: Critical Challenges for the Obama Administration (Washington, D.C.: Center for Strategic and International Studies, 2009), pp. 9–33.

12 Ibid., p. 22.
13 Quoted in Brigitte L. Nacos, *Terrorism and Counterterrorism: Understanding Threats and Responses in the Post-9/11 World* (New York: Pearson Longman, 2006), p. 178.
14 Bellamy, "Making Better Sense of U.S. Security Engagement in Africa," op. cit, p. 17.
15 John J. Hamre and Gordon R. Sullivan, "Toward Postconflict Reconstruction," in Alexander T. J. Lennon (ed.), *The Battle for Hearts and Minds: Using Soft Power to Undermine Terrorist Networks* (Cambridge, MA: The MIT Press, 2003), p. 174.

Bibliography

Abrahamovici, Pierre. 2004. "United States: The New Scramble for Africa." *Le Monde Diplomatique.* July. mondiplom.com. Accessed August 20, 2010.

Acharya, Amitav. 2004. *Terrorism and Security in Asia: Redefining Regional Order?* IDSS Working Paper No. 113. City of Singapore: Institute of Defense and Strategic Studies, Nanyang Technological University.

Addo, Prosper. 2006. *Cross-Border Criminal Activities in West Africa: Options for Effective Responses.* KAIPTC Paper No. 12. Accra: Kofi Annan International Peacekeeping Training Center.

Addy, David Nii. 2007. *The Challenges of Developing a Policy Agenda for Security Sector Reform and Governance in West Africa.* Accra: Kofi Annan International Peacekeeping and Training Center.

Adebajo, Adekeye. 2002. *Building Peace in West Africa: Liberia, Sierra Leone, and Guinea-Bissau.* Boulder, CO: Lynne Rienner Publishers.

Ademujobi, Said. (n.d.) *Africa and the Challenges of Democracy and Good Governance in the 21st Century.* www.upan1.un.org/intradoc/groups/public/document. Accessed January 27, 2010.

Africa Network for Environmental and Economic Justice. 2004. *Oil and Poverty in the Niger Delta.* Abuja: ANEEJ.

Agbese, Pita Ogaba. 2004. "Soldiers as Rulers: Military Performance." In George Klay Kieh, Jr. and Pita Ogaba Agbese (eds) *The Military and Politics in Africa: From Intervention to Democratic and Constitutional Control.* Aldershot: Ashgate, pp. 57–90.

Agbu, Osita. 2006. *West Africa's Trouble Spots and the Imperative for Peacebuilding.* CODESRIA Monograph Series. Dakar: CODESRIA.

Air Force Association. 2004. *2005 Statement of Policy.* www.afa.org/AboutUs/Policyis sueo5.asp. Accessed November 28, 2009.

Amanze-Nwachukwu, Chikeze. 2009. "Nigeria: Niger Delta Country Loses U.S. $24 Billion in Nine Months." *This Day.* April 9.

Amnesty International. 2010. *Nigerian Terrorism Bill Incompatible with Human Rights.* May 30.

Amoa, Baffour Dokyi. 2006. "Small Arms and Conflict in Africa." *The Patriotic Vanguard* (Sierra Leone). September 26.

Anderson, Guy. 2005. "U.S. Budget Will Equal ROW Combined Within 12 Months." *Jane's Defense Industry.* www.janes.com. Accessed August 20, 2010.

Andreski, Stanislav. 1954. *Military Organization and Society.* London: Routledge and Kegan Paul.

Associated Press. 2004. "Madrid Massacre Death Toll Revised." June 9. www.breakin gnews.ie/archives/2004/0609/world/kfojkfojidkf. Accessed on December 2, 2010.

Auty, Richard M. 1993. *Sustaining Development in Mineral Economies: The Resource Curse Thesis*. London: Routledge.

Ayittey, George. 1993. *Africa Betrayed*. New York: Palgrave Macmillan.

Azeez, Ademola. 2009. "Contesting Good Governance in Nigeria: Legitimacy and Accountability Perspectives." *Journal of Social Sciences*, 21(3), pp. 217–24.

Babatope, Ebenezer. 2004. *The Abacha Years: What Went Wrong*. Ibadan: Heinemann Educational Books.

Bailee, Alyson and Cottey, Andrew. 2006. "Regional Security Cooperation in the Early 21st Century." *SIPRI Yearbook, 2006: Armaments, Disarmament and International Security*. Solna: Stockholm International Peace Research Institute, pp. 195–98.

Bailey, Tomas A. 1970. *A Diplomatic History of the American People*. 10th ed. Englewood Cliffs, NJ: Prentice Hall.

Ball, Nicole and Kayode Fayemi (eds.) 2004. *Security Sector Governance in Africa: A Handbook*. London: Center for Democracy and Development.

BBC News. 2007. "Benn Criticizes 'War on Terror.'" April 16. http://news.bbc.co.uk/2/ hi/6558569.stm. Accessed November 28, 2009.

Bellamy, William Mark. 2009. "Making Better Sense of U.S. Security Engagement in Africa." In Jennifer G. Cooke and J. Stephen Morrison (eds) *U.S. Africa Policy Beyond the Bush Years: Critical Challenges for the Obama Administration*. Washington, D.C.: Center for Strategic and International Studies, pp. 9–33.

Berschinski, Robert. 2007. *AFRICOM's Dilemma: The "Global War on Terrorism," Capacity Building, Humanitarianism, and the Future of U.S. Security Policy in Africa*. Strategic Studies Institute, U.S. Army War College. www.strategicstudiesinst itute. army.mil/pubs/display.cfm?PubID=827. Accessed September 6, 2010.

Birdsall, Nancy and Subramanian, Arvind. 2004. "The Resource Curse." *Australian Financial Review*. September 10.

Bolaji, Kehinde. 2010. "Preventing Terrorism in West Africa: Good Governance or Collective Security?" *Journal of Sustainable Development in Africa*, 12(1), pp. 207–22.

Bowman, Karlyn. 2005. "U.S. Public Opinion and the Terrorist Threat." In *One Issue, Two Voices*. Washington, D.C. and Ottawa: Woodrow Wilson International Center for Scholars and the Canada Institute, pp. 2–9.

Bright, Martin, Harris, Paul, Bouzerda, Ali, and Daly, Emma 2003. "Horror in Casablanca as al Qaeda toll hits 41." *Observer*. May 18. www.guardian.co.uk/world/ 2003/may/18/alqaida.terrorism2. Accessed December 2, 2009.

Brown, John. 2007. "Out to Pasture." *Guardian*. November 2.

Brzezinski, Zbigniew. 2007. "Terrorized by 'War on Terror': How a Three-Word Mantra Has Undermined America." *Washington Post*. March 25.

Campbell, Kurt and Richard Weitz. 2006. *Non-Military Strategies for Countering Islamist Terrorism*. The Princeton Project on National Security Working Paper Series. Princeton, NJ: Princeton Project on National Security.

Canterbury, Dennis. 2004. *Neo-Liberal Democratization and New Authoritarianism*. Aldershot: Ashgate Publishing.

Center for International and Strategic Studies. 2008. *The Mauritanian Military*. Washington, D.C.: CISS.

Chambas, Mohamed. 2008. "Foreword," in Alan Bryden, Boubacar N'Diaye, and Funmi Olonisakin (eds) *Challenges of Security Sector Governance in West Africa*. Geneva: Geneva Center for Democratic Control of Armed Forces, pp. ix–x.

Chomsky, Noam. 1984. "U.S. Aid and Torture." *Journal of Palestine Studies*, 13(2), pp. 184–92.

CNN-USA. 2003. "World Trade Center: New York Reduces 9/11 Death Toll by 40." October 29.

Cilliers, Jakkie. 1996. "Africa, Root Causes and the War on Terror." *African Security Review*, 15(3), pp. 58–71.

Collier, Paul and Anke Hoeffler. 2002. "Greed and Grievance in Africa's Civil Wars." *Quarterly Journal of Economics*, 115, pp. 755–89.

Crenshaw, Martha. 2004. "Terrorism, Strategies, and Grand Strategies." In Audrey Kurth Cronin (ed) *Attacking Terrorism: Elements of Grand Strategy*. Washington, D.C.: Georgetown University Press, pp. 74–91.

Dagne, Ted. 2002. *Africa and the War on Terror*. CRS Report RL 31247. January 17.

Davis, John. 2007. "The Bush Model: US Special Forces, Africa, and the War on Terror." In John Davis (ed.) *Africa and the War on Terrorism*. Aldershot: Ashgate Publishing, pp. 143–62.

——2007. "Introduction: Africa's Road to the War on Terror." In John Davis (ed.) *Africa and the War on Terrorism*. Aldershot: Ashgate Publishing, pp. 1–16.

Dawar, Rasool and Dozier, Kimberly. 2010. "Record Level of U.S. Drone Attacks Hit Afghan Militants." *The Huffington Post*. September 15.

De Ferranti, David, Jacinto, Justin, Ody, Anthony, and Ramshaw, Graeme. 2009. *How to Improve Governance: A New Framework for Analysis and Action*. Washington, D.C.: Brookings Institution Press.

Diagana, Abdoulaye, Maroini, Aboubakr Ould, and Yessa, Abdel Nasser Ould. 2005. "Impasse politique et réflexes sécuritaires en Mauritanie: Comment fabriquer du terrorisme utile." *A Memorandum on the Situation in Mauritania*, sponsored by a number of civil society organizations and political parties.

Diop, Momar Coumba (ed.). 1993. *Senegal: Essays in Statecraft*. Dakar: CODESRIA.

Doherty, Ben. 2011. "80 Die As Pakistan Bombing Launches 'Wave' of Bin Laden Revenge Strikes." *Reuters*. May 14.

Douglas, Oronto, Okonta, Ike, Kemedi, Imieari Von, and Watts, Michael. 2004. *Oil and Militancy in the Niger Delta: Terrorist Threat or another Columbia*. Niger Delta Economics of Violence Working Paper No. 4. Berkeley, CA: Institute of International Studies, University of California at Berkeley.

Dziewanowski, Marian Kamil. 2003. *Russia in the Twentieth Century*. 6th ed. Upper Saddle River, NJ: Prentice Hall.

Editor. 2005. "Islamist Terrorism in the Sahel: Fact or Fiction?" *International Crisis Group's Africa Report*. No. 92, March 31.

Edozie, Rita Kiki. 2009. *Reconstructing the Third Wave of Democracy: Comparative African Democratic Politics*. Lanham, MD: University Press of America.

Echevarria, Antulio J. II. 2007. *2007 Key Strategic Issues List (KSIL)*. Strategic Studies Institute, U.S. Army War College. www.strategicstudiesinstitute.army.mil/pubs/display.cfm?pubID=796;

——2008. "Key Strategic Issues List, July 2008." Strategic Studies Institute, U.S. Army War College. www.strategicstudiesinstitute.army.mil/pubs/display.cfm?pubID=860. Accessed September 6, 2010.

Eizenstat, Stuart E., John Edward Porter, and Jeremy M. Weinstein. 2005. "Rebuilding Weak States." *Foreign Affairs*, January/February, pp. 134–46.

Emmanuel, Ajiboye Olanrewaju, Olayiwola, Jawando Jubril, and Babatunde, Adisa Waziri. 2009. "Poverty, Oil Exploration and Niger Delta Crisis: The Response of the Youth," *African Journal of Political Science and International Relations*, 3(5), pp. 224–32.

Evans, Martin. 2004. *Senegal: Movement des Forces Democratiques de la Casamance (MFDC)*. Briefing Paper. London: Royal Institute of International Affairs.

Ewi, Martin and Aning, Emmanuel Kwesi. 2006. "Assessing the Role of the African Union in Preventing and Combating Terrorism in Africa." *African Security Review*, 15(3), pp. 32–46.

Farah, Douglas. 2009. "Nigeria and al Qaeda." *DouglasFarah.com*. September 7. www. douglasfarah.com/article/490/nigeria-and-al-qaeda. Accessed December 5, 2009.

Farah, Douglas and Richard Shultz. 2004. "Al Qaeda's Growing Sanctuary." *Washington Post*. July 14, p. A19.

Farber, Henry S. and Joanne Gowa. 1997. "Common Interests or Common Polities? Reinterpreting the Democratic Peace." *The Journal of Politics*, 59(2), pp. 393–417.

Fayemi, Kayode, Jaye, Thomas, and Yeebo, Zaya. 2003. "Democracy, Security and Poverty in Ghana: A Mid-Term Review of the Kufuor Administration." *Democracy & Development: Journal of West African Affairs*, 3(2), pp. 53–87.

Feickert, Andrew. 2005. *U.S. Military Operations in the Global War on Terrorism: Afghanistan, Africa, the Philippines, and Colombia*. CRS Report for Congress. Washington, D.C.: Congressional Research Service.

Finer, Samuel E. 1972. *The Man on Horseback*. New York: Praeger.

Fleshman, Michael. 2001. "Counting the Costs of Gun Violence." *Africa Recovery.*,15 (4), pp. 1–4.

Florquin, Nicolas and Eric G. Berman (eds). 2005. *Armed and Aimless: Armed Groups and Human Security in the ECOWAS Region*. Geneva: Geneva Small Arms Survey.

Flynn, Stephen. 2004. *America the Vulnerable*. New York: Harper Collins, 2004.

Folarin, Teslim. 2008. "Resolving the Niger Delta Crisis." www.allafrica.comstories/200807040994.html. Accessed November 17, 2010.

Forest, James J. and Matthew Sousa. 2006. *Oil and Terrorism in the New Gulf: Framing U. S. Energy and Security Policies for the Gulf of Guinea*. Lanham, MD: Lexington Books.

Forrest, Joshua. 1998. "State Inversion and Non-State Politics." In Leornardo Villalon and Phillip Huxtable (eds). *The African State at a Critical Juncture*. Boulder, CO: Lynne Rienner Publishers, pp. 45–56.

Frazer, Jendayi. 2007. *Nigeria at a Crossroads: Elections, Legitimacy and a Way Forward*. Testimony of the Assistant Secretary of State for African Affairs before the Sub-committee on Global Health and Africa, United States House of Representatives. June 7.

Freedom House. 2011. *Freedom in the World: Comparative and Historical Data, 1973–2011*. Washington, D.C.: Freedom House.

Fund for Agricultural Development. 2011. *Rural Poverty: Western and Central Africa*. Rome: IFAD.

Fund for Peace. 2009. *Failed State Index, 2009*. Washington, D.C.: Fund for Peace.

General James Jones. 2006. *Statement Before the U.S. Senate Armed Services Committee*. March 7.

General N. C. Coleman. 2009. Interview. Accra, Ghana. October 20.

General Salihu Ibrahim. 1993. *Valedictory Speech*. Abuja, Nigeria.

General William E. Ward, Commander, United States Africa Command. 2009a. *Statement Before the U.S. Senate Armed Services Committee*. March 17.

——2009b. *Written Testimony: Annual Posture Statement to U.S. Congress on U.S. Africa Command*. March 17.

Global Witness. 2003. *For a Few Dollars More: How Al-Qaeda Moved into the Diamond Trade, A Report*. London: Global Witness.

Graebner, Norman A. 1961. *An Uncertain Tradition: American Secretaries of State in the Twentieth Century*. New York: McGraw-Hill.

Gramsci, Antonio. 1998. *Selection from the Prison Notebooks*. London: Lawrence and Wishart.

Halberstam, David. 2001. *War in a Time of Peace: Bush, Clinton, and The Generals*. New York: Scribner.

Hallinan, Conn. 2007. "Into Africa: The Militarization of U.S. Foreign Policy." *Berkeley Daily Planet*. March 30.

Hamre, John J. and Gordon R. Sullivan. 2003. "Toward Postconflict Reconstruction." In Alexander T. J. Lennon (ed.) *The Battle for Hearts and Minds: Using Soft Power to Undermine Terrorist Networks*. Cambridge, MA: The MIT Press, pp. 169–83.

Harsch, Ernest. 2009. "Africa Looks Beyond 'War on Terror.'" *Africa Renewal*. October, pp. 16–19.

Herbert, Ross and Steve Gruzd. 2008. *The African Peer Review Mechanism: Lessons from the Pioneers*. Johannesburg: South African Institute of International Affairs.

Hindustantimes. 2010. "Al-Qaeda Leaders Who Have Been Killed and Arrested." June 1.

Holly Fletcher. 2008. *Egyptian Islamic Jihad. Briefing Paper*. New York: Council on Foreign Relations.

Huntington, Samuel. 1993. "The Clash of Civilizations." *Foreign Affairs*, 73(2), pp. 22–49.

Ihonvbere, Julius. 2000a. *Africa and the New World Order*. New York: Peter Lang Publishing.

——2000b. *Recipe for Perpetual Crisis: The Nigerian State and the Niger Delta Question, Boiling Point: The Crisis in the Oil Producing Communities in Nigeria*. Lagos: Committee for the Defense of Human Rights.

International Crisis Group. 2005. *"L'Islamisme en Afrique du Nord IV: Contestation Islamist en Mauritanie: Menaces ou Bouc Emissaire." Rapport Moyen-Orient/Afrique du Nord*. No. 41. May 11.

Jaggi, Maya. 2002. "Ousting Monsters." *Guardian*. November 2.

Johnson, Scott. 2009. "Money Talks: The Islamists' Rebellion in Nigeria Isn't the Latest Front in the Global War on Terror." *Newsweek*. August 3.

Jones, Abeodu Bowen. 1973. "The Republic of Liberia." In J. F. A. Ajayi and Michael Crowder (eds). *History of West Africa*. Vol. II. New York: Columbia University Press, pp. 310–12.

Joseph, Richard. 1996. "Nigeria: Inside the Dismal Tunnel." *Current History*, 95(601), pp. 193–200.

July, Robert W. 1970. *A History of the African People*. 2nd ed. New York: Charles Scribner's Sons.

Kaldor, Mary. 2007. "Human Security: A New Strategic Narrative for Europe." *International Affairs*, 83(2), pp. 273–88.

——2007. *Human Security: Reflections on Globalization and Intervention*. London: Polity.

Kaplan, Robert D. 1994. "The Coming Anarchy." *Atlantic Monthly*. February, pp. 1–10.

Kaunert, Christian. 2010. "Towards Supranational Governance in EU Counter-Terrorism: The Role of the Commission and the Council Secretariat." *Central European Journal of International Security Studies*, 4(1), pp. 8–31.

Kegley, Charles W. Jr. and Wittkopf, Eugene R. 1979. *American Foreign Policy*. New York: St. Martin's Press.

Keili, Francis Langumba. 2008. "Small Arms and Light Weapons Transfer in West Africa: A Stock-taking." *Disarmament Forum*, 4, pp. 5–11.

Khan, Amil. 2009. "Al Qaeda's Spreading Tentacles in West Africa Opposed by Traditional Leaders." *Telegraph*. March 28.

Khouri, Rami. 2007. "Karen Hughes' Two-year Halloween." *The Daily Star*. November 3.

Kieh, George Klay, Jr. n.d. "United States Foreign Policy and Democratization in Africa." In Abdul Karim Bangura et al. *Stakes in Africa–U.S. Relations*. Lincoln, NE: iUniverse Press, pp. 61–84.

——2008. *The First Liberian Civil War: The Crises of Underdevelopment*. New York: Peter Lang Publishing.

Kieh, George Klay, Jr. and Agbese, Pita Ogaba (eds) 2004. *The Military and Politics in Africa: From Engagement to Democratic and Constitutional Control*. Aldershot: Ashgate Publishing.

Kilcullen, David. 2004. "Countering Global Insurgency." *Small Wars Journal*. November 30. htttp://smallwarsjournal.com/documents/kilcullen.pdf. Accessed November 28, 2009.

Klare, Michael and Volman, Daniel. 2006. *The African "Oil Rush" and American National Security*. May. http://concernafricanscholars.org. Accessed August 20, 2010.

Koch, Andrew. 2005. "U.S. Seeks Security in African Waters." *Jane's Defense Weekly*. February 16.

Kohn, Richard H. 2007. "An Essay on Civilian Control of the Military." *American Diplomacy*. www.unc.edu/depts./diplomat/. Accessed August 20, 2010.

Laberivière, Richard. 2005. "Le Paradigme mauritanien." *Radio France Internationale*, éditorial international. September 6.

Lawrence, Cline. 2007. "Counterterrorism Strategy in the Sahel." *Studies in Conflict & Terrorism*, 30(10), pp. 889–99.

Le Sage, Andre. 2007. *African Counterterrorism Cooperation: Assessing Regional and Sub-regional Initiatives*. Washington, D.C.: Africa Center for Strategic Studies.

Lerory, Christopher J. 2005. "Threat Perceptions in the United States and Canada: Assessing the Public's Attitudes toward Security and Risk in North America." *One Issue, Two Voices: Issue Four*. Washington, D.C. and Ottawa: Woodrow Wilson International Center for Scholars and Canada Institute.

Liebenow, J. Gus. 1987. *Liberia: The Quest for Democracy*. Bloomington, IN: Indiana University Press.

Love, Maryann Cusimano. 2007. *Beyond Sovereignty: Issues for a Global Agenda*. 3rd ed. Belmont, CA: Thomson Wadsworth.

Makinda, Samuel. 2010. "Terrorism, Counter-terrorism and Norms in Africa." *African Security Review*, 15(3), pp. 1–14.

Malan, Mark. 2008. "US Civil–Military Imbalance for Global Engagement: Lessons from the Operational Level in Africa." *Refugees International*. July.

Mariner, Joanne. 2009. "The Global Impact of the U.S.' War on Terror Abuses." *FindLaw*. March 11.

Martinez, Luiz. 2010. "For the First Time, More U.S. Troops in Afghanistan than Iraq." *ABC News*. May 24.

Mbaku, John Mukum. 2008. "The African Debt Crisis and the New Globalization." In George Klay Kieh, Jr. (ed.) *Africa and the New Globalization*. Aldershot: Ashgate Publishing, pp. 29–50.

——2004. "Constitutionalism and Governance in Africa." *West Africa Review*, 6(2), www.westafricareview.com/isue6/kaluintro.html. Accessed May 15, 2010.

Midgal, Joel. 2006. "Mental Maps and Virtual Checkpoints: Struggles to Construct and Maintain State and Social Boundaries." In Joel Midgal (ed.) *Boundaries and Belonging: States and Societies in the Struggle to Shape Identity.* Cambridge: Cambridge University Press, pp. 3–26.

Misol, Lisa. 2004. "Testimony on Small Arms and Conflict in West Africa." *US Congressional Human Rights Caucus.* May 20.

Mohdavy, Hossein. 1970. "The Patterns and Problems of Economic Development in Rentier States: The Case of Iran." In Michael A. Cook (ed.) *Studies in the Economic History of the Middle East.* Oxford: Oxford University Press, pp. 37–61.

Morita, Sachiko and Laelke, Durwood. 2005. "Rule of Law, Good Governance, and Sustainable Development." *Proceedings of the 7th Conference on Environmental Compliance and Enforcement.* Washington, D.C.: INECE, pp. 15–21.

Morrison, Stephen J. and Hicks, Kathleen. 2008. "Integrating 21st Century Development and Security Assistance." Washington, D.C.: Center for Strategic and International Studies.

Motlagh, Jason. 2005. "U.S. Takes Terror Fight to Africa's 'Wild West': Critics Say Saharan Plan Backs Despots, is Magnet for Trouble." *Chronicle Foreign Service.* December 27, pp. 1–2.

MSNBC News. 2011. "U.S. Forces Kill Osama bin Laden in Pakistan." May 2.

N'Diaye, Boubacar. 2006. "The August 3, 2005 Coup in Mauritania: Democracy Finally, or Just Another Coup?" *African Affairs,* 105(420), pp. 421–41.

Nacos, Brigitte L. 2006. *Terrorism and Counterterrorism: Understanding Threats and Responses in the Post-9/11 World.* New York: Pearson Longman.

N'Diaye, Boubacar. 2001. "Mauritania's Stalled Democratization." *Journal of Democracy* 12(3), pp. 88–95.

Nichols, Michelle. 2007. "Muslims Believe U.S. Goal to Weaken Islam: Poll." *Reuters.* April 24. www.reuters.com/article/politicsNews/idUSN2332112320070424?feedType=RSS. Accessed November 28, 2009.

Nordlinger, Eric A. 1977. *Soldiers in Politics.* Englewood Cliffs, NJ: Prentice Hall.

Obi, Cyril. 2006. "Terrorism in West Africa: Real, Emerging or Imagined Threats?" *African Security Review,* 15(3), pp. 87–101.

O'Brien, Kevin and Karasik, Theodore. n.d. "Case Study: West Africa." In Angela Rabasa, Steven Boraz, Peter Chalk, Kim Cragin, and Theodore W. Karasik (eds). *Ungoverned Territories: Understanding and Reducing Terrorism Risks.* Santa Monica, CA: The Rand Corporation, pp. 173–206.

Odion-Akhaine, Sylvester (ed.) 2001. *Path to Demilitarization in West Africa.* Lagos: Center for Constitutionalism and Demilitarization.

O'Donnell, Guillermo. 1998. "Horizontal Accountability in New Democracies." *Journal of Democracy,* 9(3), pp. 112–26.

Ofem, Nneoyi I., and Ajayi, A.R. 2008. "Effects of Youth Empowerment Strategies on Conflict Resolutions in the Niger-Delta Region of Nigeria: Evidence from Cross River State." *Calabar Journal of Agriculture and Rural Development,* 6(1–2), pp. 139–46.

Office of the Coordinator for Counterterrorism, U. S. State Department. 2011. *The Terrorist Enemy.* Washington, D.C.: U.S. State Department.

Office of the President of the United States. 2006a. *National Strategy for Combating Terrorism.* Washington, D.C.: The White House.

——2006b. *National Security Strategy of the United States.* Washington, D.C.: The White House.

——2010. *National Security Strategy of the United States*. Washington, D.C.: The White House.

Ogwu, Joy and Olaniyan, Ray. 2005. *Nigeria's International Economic Relations: Dimensions of Dependence and Change*. 2nd ed. Lagos: Nigerian Institute of International Affairs.

Okereke, C. Nna-Emeke. 2010. "Al-Qaeda in the Islamic Maghreb (AQIM) and the Question of Security in West Africa." *African Journal for the Prevention and Combating of Terrorism*, 1(1), pp. 65–67.

Oliver, Richard. 2004. *What is Transparency?* New York: McGraw-Hill.

Omeje, K. 2008. *Extractive Economies and Conflicts in the Global South. Multi-Regional Perspectives on Rentier Politics*. Aldershot: Ashgate Publishing.

Onuoha, Freedom. 2011. "Nigeria's Vulnerability to Terrorism: The Imperative of Countering Religious Extremism and Terrorism (CONREST) Strategy." *Peace and Conflict Monitor*. February 2.

Onwuka, Sopuruchi. 2010. "Nigeria's May Oil Exports Average 2.1 Million Barrels Daily." allAfrica.com, June 16.

Opoku, John Mark. 2007. *The Challenges of Developing a Policy Agenda for Security Sector Reform and Governance in West Africa*. Accra: Kofi Annan International Peacekeeping and Training Center.

Orlandini, Barbara. 2003. "Consuming Good Governance in Thailand." *European Journal of Development Research*, 15(2), pp. 16–43.

Osuntokun, Akinjide. 2002. *Environmental Problems of the Niger Delta*. Lagos: Ebert Foundation.

Ottens, Nick. 2010. "America's Shadow War on Terror." *Atlantic Sentinel*, August 17.

Owens, John and Dumbrell, John. 2008. "Introduction: America's 'War on Terrorism:' New Dimensions in U.S. Government and National Security." In John Owens and John Dumbrell (eds.) *America's "War on Terrorism."* Lanham, MD: Lexington Books, pp. 1–24.

Palmer, Ronald. 2007. "Political Terrorism in West Africa." In John Davis (ed.) *Africa and the War on Terrorism*. Aldershot: Ashgate Publishing, pp. 103–12.

Pambazuka News. 2007. "Global Review of Anti-Terrorism Laws in the Commonwealth." September 14.

Paterson, Thomas G. (ed.) 1978. *Major Problems in American Foreign Politics*. Vol. II. Lexington, MA: D. C. Heath.

Paterson, Thomas G., Clifford, J. Garry, and Hagan, Kenneth J. 1977. *American Foreign Policy*. Vols. I & II. Lexington, MA: D. C. Heath.

Patrick, Stewart. 2006. "Weak States and Global Threats: Fact or Fiction?" *The Washington Quarterly*, 29(2), pp. 27–53.

Paye, Moussa. 1993. "The Regime and the Press." In Momar Couba Diop (ed.) *Senegal: Essays in Statecraft*. Dakar: CODESRIA, 1993, pp. 324–69.

Pazzanita, Anthony. 1992. "Mauritania's Foreign Policy: The Search for Protection." *Journal of Modern African Studies*, 30(2), 288–300.

Petrou, Michael. 2009. "Al Qaeda in North Africa." *Macleans*. May 6. www2.macleans.ca/2009/05/06/al-qaeda-in-north-africa. Accessed December 2, 2009.

Pham, J. Peter. 2007. "Strategic Interests: Securing the New Strategic Gulf." *World Defense Review*. June 7. http://worlddefensereview.com/pham060707.shtm. Accessed August 20, 2010.

Piombo, Jessica. 2007. *Terrorism and U.S. Counter-Terrorism Programs in Africa: An Overview*. Working Paper. Monterey, CA: Center for Contemporary Conflict.

Ploch, Lauren. 2009. "Africa Command: US Strategic Interests and the Role of the US Military in Africa." Washington, D.C.: Congressional Research Service, RL 34003. January 5.

Plougshares. 2002. *Armed Conflicts Report*. Boston: Ploughshares.

Post, Jerrold M. 2002. "Killing in the Name of God: Osama Bin Laden and al Qaeda." In Barry R. Schneider and Jerrold M. Post (eds) *Know Thy Enemy: Profiles of Adversary Leaders and Their Strategic Cultures*. Maxwell Air Force Base, AL: USAF Counter-Proliferation Center.

Prempeh, H. Kwasi. 2008. "Presidential Power in Comparative Perspectives: The Puzzling Persistence of the Imperial Presidency in Post-Authoritarian Africa." *Hastings Constitutional Law Quarterly*, 35(4). www.SSrn.com/abstract. Accessed on June 10, 2010.

President Barrack Obama. 2009a. *Inaugural Address*. January 20.

——2009b. *Text of Speech in Cairo*. June 4.

President George W. Bush. 2001b. *Speech to Joint Session of Congress After the World Trade Center and Pentagon Bombings*. September 20.

——2001b. *Text of Speech at the National Cathedral*. Washington, D.C. September 14.

——2002. *The State of the Union Address*. CNN.com. January 29. http://transcripts.cnn.com/2002/ALLPOLITICS/01/29/bush.speech.txt/. Accessed December 12, 2009.

Pressman, Jeremy. 2007. "Rethinking Transnational Counter-terrorism: Beyond a National Framework." *The Washington Quarterly*, 30(4), pp. 63–77.

Rabasa, Angel and Peters, John. 2007. "The Dimensions of Ungovernability." In Angela Rabasa *et al.* (eds) *Ungoverned Territories: Understanding and Reducing Terrorism Risks*. Santa Monica, CA: The Rand Corporation, pp. 7–14.

Rashid, Ismail. 2004. "West Africa's Post-Cold War Security Challenges." In Adekeye Adebajo and Ismail Rashid (ed.) *West Africa's Security Challenges: Building Peace in a Troubled Region*. Boulder, CO: Lynne Rienner Publishers, pp. 383–94.

Risk Management Solutions. 2009. "Global Terrorism Trends 2009." *Terrorism Risk Briefing*. August. www.rms.com/Publications/RMS_Terrorism_Risk_Briefing_August_2009.pdf. Accessed November 30, 2009.

Sala-I-Martin, Xavier. 2004. *How Oil Demon Captured Nigeria's Soul*. Washington, D.C.: The International Monetary Fund.

SAMAA. 2011. "About 200 'Launch Cross-border Attack' on Pakistan Post." June 1.

Samuel, Kayode. 2010. *Political Transition in Nigeria, 1993–2003: Commentaries on Selected Themes*. Lagos: Malthouse Press.

Schmitt, Eric and Mekhennet, Souad. 2009. "Al Qaeda Branch Steps up Raids in North Africa." *New York Times*. July 9. www.nytimes.com/2009/07/10/world/africa/10terror.html. Accessed December 2, 2009.

Schraeder, Peter. 2003. *African Politics and Society: A Mosaic in Transformation*, 2nd ed. Florence, KY: Wadsworth Publishing.

Siddique, Mohammed. 2001. "The Masquerade Unmasked: Obasanjo and the Third Term." In Said Ademujobi (ed.) *Governance and Politics in Post-Military Nigeria*. New York: Palgrave Macmillan, pp. 173–206.

Sharma, Shalendra. 2007. "Democracy, Good Governance and Economic Development." *Taiwan Journal of Democracy* 3(1), pp. 29–62.

Sharrock, David. 2008. "Out of Africa: A Growing Threat to Europe from al Qaeda's New Allies." *The Times*. May 8. www.timesonline.co.uk/tol/news/world/africa/article3876563.ece. Accessed December 2, 2009.

Shinn, David H. 2005. *Domestic or International Terrorism? A Dysfunctional Dialogue*. Paper presented at "Africa: Vital to U.S. Security?" Symposium, Panel on Terrorism and Transnational Threats-Causes and Enablers, National Defense University, November 15–16.

Silverstein, Ken. 2000. "Private Warriors: Clinton's Trip to Nigeria." *Democracy Now!* August 25.

Spanier, John. 1962. *American Foreign Policy Since World War II*. New York: Praeger.

Stohl, Rachel. 2004. *"The Legacy of Illicit Small Arms: Devastation in West Africa."* Testimony before the U.S. Congressional Human Rights Caucus: Briefing on Small Arms in West Africa. Washington, D.C., May 20.

Stratfor Global Intelligence. 2007. *Nigeria: Opposition to AFRICOM Ends*. December 14. www.stratfor.com/analysis/nigeria_opposition_africom_ends. Accessed September 6, 2010.

——2009. *Annual Forecast 2009: War Recession, and Resurgence.* www.stratfor.com/forecast/20090128_annual_forecast_2009_war_recession_and_resurgence_introduction. Accessed September 6, 2010.

——2010. Annual Forecast 2010. www.stratfor.com/forecast/20100101_annual_forecast_2010. Accessed September 6, 2010.

Subramanian, Arvind and Sala-I-Martin, Xavier. 2004. *Tackling the Resource Curse: Illustrations from Nigeria*. Washington, D.C.: The International Monetary Fund Survey.

Tavares, Rodrigo. 2009. *Regional Security: The Capacity of International Organizations.* Abingdon: Routledge.

Templeton, Tom and Lumley, Tom. 2002. "9/11 in Numbers." *Guardian*. August 18, 2002.

Terdman, Moshe. 2007. *Factors Facilitating the Rise of Radical Islamism and Terrorism in Sub-Saharan Africa*. Project for the Research of Islamist Movements (PRISM) African Occasional Papers, 1(1), www.e-prism.org/images/PRISM_African_Papers_vol_1_no_1_Radicalism_in_Sub-Sahara_Africa_March_07.pdf. Accessed November 30, 2009.

The African Union. 2004. *Protocol to the African Union's Convention for the Prevention and Combating of Terrorism*. Addis Ababa: The AU Commission.

——2003. *The African Union's Peer Review Mechanism*. Addis Ababa: The AU Commission.

——1999. *The African Union's Convention on the Prevention and Combating of Terrorism*. Addis Ababa: The AU Commission.

The Economic Community of West African States. 2001. *The ECOWAS Protocol on Democracy and Good Governance*. Abuja: ECOWAS Secretariat.

——1978. *The Protocol on Non-Aggression*. Abuja: ECOWAS Secretariat.

The Rand Corporation. 2006. *U.S. Counter-terrorism Strategy Must Address Ideological and Political Factors at the Global and Local Levels*. Research Brief. Santa Monica, CA: Rand Corporation.

Trosper, Trygve. 2009. *West Africa's War on Terrorism: Time and Patience*. Paper #A173994. Carlisle Barracks, PA: Army War College.

Tynes, Robert. 2006. "U.S. Counter-terrorism Policies in Africa are Counter to Development." *African Security Review*, 15(3), pp. 109–13.

Tyson, Ann Scott. 2009. "Support Troops Swelling U.S. Force in Afghanistan." *The Washington Post*, October 13, 2009.

United Nations Development Program. 2008. *Human Development Report*. New York: Oxford University Press.

——2002. *Human Development Report*. New York: Oxford University Press.

——1994. *Human Development Report*. New York: Oxford University Press.

——1992. *Human Development Report.* New York: Oxford University Press.

United Nations Economic Commission for Africa. 2010. *Strategies to Promote Youth Self-Employment in West Africa.* Addis Ababa: UNECA.

United Nations Office for the Coordination of Humanitarian Affairs. 2003. *IDPs, Refugees, Returnees, West Africa.* October 16. New York: OCHA.

United Nations Office of the High Commissioner for Refugees. 2011. *Regional Operations Profile: West Africa.* Geneva: UNCHR.

United Nations. 2005. *World Economic and Social Survey: Financing for Development.* New York: United Nations Publication Section.

United States Air Force Almanac. 2009. "The Air Force in Facts and Figures, 2009." *Air Force Magazine.* May. www.airforcemagazine.com/MagazineArchive/Magazine%20Documents/2009/May%202009/0509facts_fig.pdf. Accessed November 28, 2009.

U.S. Department of Defense. 2006. *Quadrennial Defense Review Report.* Washington, D.C.: Department of Defense.

U.S. Department of State. 2006. Country Reports on Terrorism. (Washington, D.C.: Office of the Coordinator for Counterterrorism, 2007), p. 16.

U.S. Government Accountability Office. 2008. *Countering Terrorism Actions Needed to Enhance Implementation of Trans-Sahara Counterterrorism Partnership.* GAO-08-860, July. Washington, D.C.: GOA.

Uyigue, Etiosa and Agho, Matthew. 2007. *Coping with Climate Change and Environmental Degradation in the Niger Delta of Southern Nigeria.* Benin-City: Community Research and Development Center (CREDC).

Volman, Daniel. 2008. *AFRICOM: The New U.S. Military Command for Africa.* June 27. http://concernedafricascholars.org. Accessed August 20, 2010.

——2009. *Full Report on U.S. Army War Games for Future Military Intervention in Nigeria and Somalia.* August 17. http://concernedafricanscholars.org. Accessed August 20, 2010.

Westad, Odd Arne. 2006. *The Global Cold War.* Cambridge: Cambridge University Press.

Williams, Robinson. 1996. "Globalization, the World System, and 'Democracy Promotion' in U.S. Foreign Policy." *Theory and Society,* 25(5), pp. 615–65.

World Bank. 2007. *Niger at a Glance 2007.* www. devdata.worldbank.org/AAG/ner_aag.pdf. Accessed September 9, 2010.

——2008. *Accountability in Governance.* Washington, D.C.: The World Bank.

——2005. *Fragile and Conflict Afflicted Countries.* Washington, D.C.: The World Bank.

Yates, Douglas. 1996. *The Rentier State in Africa: Oil Rent, Dependency and Neo-colonialism in the Republic of Gabon.* Trenton, NJ: Africa World Press.

Zalman, Amy. 2007. "Under Secretary of Public Diplomacy, Karen Hughes, Resigns." *About.com.* November 6.

Index

Bold page numbers indicate figures and maps.